CULTURE SHOCK!

South Africa

Dee Rissik

Graphic Arts Center Publishing Company
Portland, Oregon

In the same series

Argentina	Denmark	Japan	South Africa
Australia	Ecuador	Korea	Spain
Austria	Egypt	Laos	Sri Lanka
Belgium	Finland	Malaysia	Sweden
Bolivia	France	Mauritius	Switzerland
Borneo	Germany	Mexico	Syria
Brazil	Greece	Morocco	Taiwan
Britain	Hong Kong	Myanmar	Thailand
California	Hungary	Nepal	Turkey
Canada	India	Netherlands	UAE
Chile	Indonesia	Norway	Ukraine
China	Iran	Pakistan	USA
Costa Rica	Ireland	Philippines	USA—The South
Cuba	Israel	Scotland	Venezuela
Czech Republic	Italy	Singapore	Vietnam

Barcelona At Your Door	New York At Your Door	A Traveler's Medical
Beijing At Your Door	Paris At Your Door	Guide
Chicago At Your Door	Rome At Your Door	A Wife's Guide
Havana At Your Door	San Francisco At Your	Living and Working
Jakarta At Your Door	Door	Abroad
Kuala Lumpur, Malaysia	Tokyo At Your Door	Personal Protection At
At Your Door		Home & Abroad
London At Your Door	A Globe-Trotter's Guide	Working Holidays
Moscow At Your Door	A Parent's Guide	Abroad
Munich At Your Door	A Student's Guide	

Illustrations by TRIGG
Photographs from Dee Rissik and Kamariah Rahim

© 1994 Times Editions Pte Ltd
© 2000 Times Media Private Limited
Revised 1999, 2001
Reprinted 1996, 1997, 1998, 1999, 2000, 2003

This book is published by special
arrangement with Times Media Private Limited
Times Centre, 1 New Industrial Road, Singapore 536196
International Standard Book Number 1-55868-629-0
Graphic Arts Center Publishing Company
P.O. Box 10306 • Portland, Oregon 97296-0306 • (503) 226-2402

Printed in Singapore

This book is dedicated to Nigel Folker, whose career has taken us so often to lands strange and wonderful, but who, with me, shares the lifelong ties to South Africa, that bring us home like a magnet, time and again.

CONTENTS

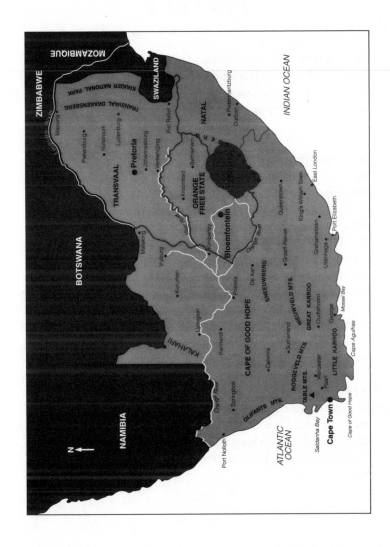

PREFACE

Moving from the cosy confines of wherever you call home to the strange and wonderful (or initially far from wonderful) ways of a new land, a new people and a new culture, is certainly no easy task. In fact, it rates very high up on the ladder of the most stressful things we do in our lives.

But one of the best ways to minimise the hassles, inconveniences and insecurities we all feel when surrounded by things strange and new is to be as well-informed as possible about each aspect of your new life.

Being a born and bred South African who has had the privilege of living in a number of foreign countries, I am only too aware of how the initial difficulties seem insurmountable: the smallest setback can seem like a major calamity in those early days. And once you are an old hand, you know that you will look back at those tetchy moments in stunned amazement.

I hope reading this book will give you a little insight into who we really are, how we live and what life is like here – I hope it will be enough of a taste of South Africa to make your stay, however long or short it may be, a positively memorable one.

Writing this book was no easy task for a full-time journalist. I had the assistance of my mother, Jan Rissik, whom I thank for all the hours of research she has done for me, for reading some of my copy and bouncing ever more ideas off me. Great appreciation and thanks is also extended to everybody who has helped me put this book together - wittingly, deliberately, or quite unintentionally by simply being South African.

—*Chapter One*—

OUR STORY

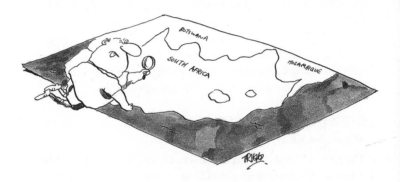

Whatever the reason for spending time in South Africa – as an immigrant, expat or long-term traveller – it's well worth understanding the high and low points of this troubled land's history. Understanding the realities of racial discrimination as it was legally applied in South Africa is a good start to unravelling the sensitivities.

Knowing what went on before will help you come to grips with the nation's hopes for its future society – a society in which the norms and values of different groups will be interwoven and interlocked, forming a web of interdependency. To achieve this, a mind-set should be created where stark differences between races, cultures and classes will blur; when each realises it has things in common with past foes. This is the dream of many for the new South Africa.

THE LAND OF MILK AND HONEY

For two million years the south African people lived off the bounty of the land as hunter-gatherers. The *Khoisan*, or Bushmen, lived in harmony with nature, wandering far across the land. They had fixed customs refined over thousands of years of nomadic life. A number of their rock paintings, more than 3 000 years old, depict scenes as diversely fascinating as their mythical, ritual behaviour. Paintings of the wild animals they hunted and the manner in which they conducted the hunt can still be found in sheltered caves across the country.

In the Kalahari desert, in neighbouring Namibia and Botswana, a few *Khoisan* still live their traditional lifestyle. Most, however, have settled on farms or reserves created for them which means that much of their tradition has given way to a western existence.

SO WHO DISTURBED THE PEACE?
First the Khoikhoi...

The *Khoisan*'s sublime existence was disturbed 2000 years ago by the *Khoikhoi* who were herders and farmers. They settled in the south and south-western part of the country and were the first indigenous people the European explorers encountered. At this time the Bantu people from the central regions of Africa had migrated southward and settled in the north and north-east of present-day South Africa.

...Then the European Explorers

Portuguese sailor Bartolomeu Dias was the first recorded European to traverse the South African coast (in 1488) in his search for a sea route from Europe to the riches of the East. A permanent settlement was soon established on the southern tip of the continent by the Dutch while many hundreds of ships – Dutch, French, British, Portuguese – called on this coastline for fresh supplies en route to the East.

In 1652 Jan van Riebeeck (a member of the Dutch East India Company who had sailed to Japan, the west coast of India and even to the Arctic circle) arrived in the Cape with over 100 men to establish a permanent base, a fort and a foothold on the southern tip of Africa. They had some clashes with the *Khoikhoi* (who they dubbed the *Hottentots*) and a few Bushmen. Who was to know that these first conflicts between European and African were to continue in varying forms to this day?

MASS MIGRATIONS FROM ALL DIRECTIONS

The population increase in southern Africa in the late 18th and early 19th centuries led to pressures that eventually gave rise to the joining of the Zulu tribes into a major fighting force under their great warrior-leader, Shaka. Warlike, he buffeted the southern African people, causing mass migrations on a far larger scale than the Great Trek (see p. 12). Violence and tremendous hardship followed.

The colonists at the Cape added to this bubbling cauldron. From the settlement now known as Cape Town, Boer frontier farmers and the French Huguenots had moved inland. The Boers were descendants of the Dutch who had come to establish the halfway station and forefathers of the present Afrikaners. The French Huguenots had left Europe to escape religious persecution at the hand of King Louis XIV.

In a quest for even more land some settlers moved up the coast towards present-day Port Elizabeth, but soon clashed with various groups of Bantu tribes who were moving from the Natal coast towards the southern Cape. Skirmishes became bitter wars as both sides tried to capture larger pastures and precious water holes for their livestock.

THAT ENGLISH TOUCH

Following the French capture of Holland during the Napoleonic Wars, Britain agreed to take over the administration of the troubled Cape Colony in 1795. This generous gesture was made to keep open the strategic sea route to Britain's vast, valuable Indian territories. It was returned to the Dutch government in 1803, but Britain recaptured it in 1806 and administered it in various geographic shapes and political forms until 'union' in 1910.

The 1820 Settlers

In 1820 nearly 5000 British immigrants landed at the Cape Colony where Port Elizabeth is today, having been promised land to farm. But they had not been told how harsh and different the conditions were, or that their farms were on the frontier, making them the buffer between the Colony and the Xhosa tribes. The battle for land between the two groups led to wars and skirmishes – and large doses of ill will.

Despite hardship, the 1820 Settlers (as they were called) made their mark as farmers, traders and craftsmen. Their cultural contributions soon became firmly embedded in the nature of South Africa. They also played a major role in the administration of the Cape as the British style of governing changed from despotic colonial power to an ever more representative system in the 1850s. British influence was strong not only in government, law and administration, but also in the broader social and cultural sense. Towns and villages had a higher concentration of English speaking people. The Afrikaners, although overall greater in number, were mostly rural. This rural-urban distribution between the two groups is fairly similar today.

End Of Slavery

The straw that broke the Boer's back was the move introduced by the British to abolish slavery in the Cape in December 1834. The Boers had expected it for years – they heard rumours of the liberal winds of change blowing in Europe – but this forewarning did nothing to reduce their ire. Although they received monetary compensation and slaves were 'apprenticed' for four years after their freedom, it was the final impetus for their departure from the colony.

THE GREAT TREK

The Great Trek, the first mass migration of immigrant South Africans, began in 1835 and only ended in 1848. The Boer frontier farmers were fiercely independent and found life under what they perceived as British misrule intolerable.

The *Voortrekkers*, as they were called, loaded their precious possessions onto ox-wagons and headed into largely unknown territory. They had no intention of ever returning south. They opposed every British encroachment on their rights and freedom with a deep and Calvinistic indignation. Staunch Christians, they considered the ancestor-worshipping African tribes in the area to be heathens, inferiors – a mentality that was to dog the Afrikaner and lead to the implementation of apartheid. The official British policy of equality in church and state was anathema to them.

Because the routes the *Voortrekkers* took into the interior crossed the paths of Bantu tribes at the time of their great upheaval, they were involved in a number of battles and bloody massacres, the most poignant being the Battle of Blood River, commemorated annually on December 16, a date carved deep into the psyche of every Boer.

Boers Trying To Break Free

At first Britain left the Boers to their own devices, but not for long. When the Boers in Natal wanted to establish the independent Republic of Natal, Britain refused but took no steps to govern them. The Boers in the Orange Free State, however, signed the Bloemfontein Convention with the British, which granted them the right to self-government, and then drew up a republican constitution in the area they called Transorangia. Although all the Boers disliked the British, they were initially not unified enough to mount a fight for independence. This disunity continued until the Boer War united them a little, but even today, the right wing is continually splintering.

THE RISE OF APARTHEID
Greed – The Root of All Evil

Before the discovery of gold and diamonds in South Africa, the country's economy was based almost entirely on agriculture. The Boers, or Afrikaners, were all farmers as were a fair number of the English. While quite a few whites had moved into the towns, almost the entire African population lived off the land under various tribal chiefdoms. Only a few Africans worked for the white farmers.

With the discovery extremely valuable diamond and gold deposits, exciting and cavalier times followed. It also led to dramatic changes in the nature of South Africa – and South Africans.

1913 Land Act

Following the discovery of minerals, especially gold and diamonds, pressure was applied to prevent Africans from making a living on their own land. This exploitative drive culminated in the 1913 Land Act which made it illegal for Africans to purchase or lease land from Europeans anywhere in South Africa, except within the designated African reserves. This law was the precursor to apartheid's policy of *bantustans* or homelands that came about many decades later.

This Act was a major tragedy for all indigenous South Africans. One of the country's most famous writers and politicians, Sol Plaatje, wrote, 'South Africa has by law ceased to be the home of any of her native children whose skins are dyed with a pigment that does not conform with the regulation hue.' Protest by the South African Native National Congress was to no avail.

During World War II, new energetic members like Nelson Mandela, Walter and Albertina Sizulu, and Oliver Tambo joined the ANC. Their names are now household words in South Africa.

Traditional Life All in a Whirl

The discovery of diamonds and gold led to huge foreign investment mostly from Europe and America. Mines grew fast and economic activity developed causing great changes to the lives of thousands, and later millions, of black South Africans. The whites owned, financed and provided the technical skills to open mines while occupying the well-paid skilled jobs. The blacks did unskilled work and were strictly controlled by the compound and migrant labour systems.

Colonial home with architecture typical of the 1920s.

These changes had a deep and lasting effect on the lifestyle and future of black South Africans. In 1867, despite the spread of Boers and British across the land, most Africans still lived under the rule of independent chiefs and worked as farmers on their own land. By 1914 the whites had defeated most of the chiefs and taken possession of 90% of the land, forcing more blacks to work as labourers in the mines, towns and on white-owned farms.

The Boers vs The British

By the end of the 19th century the Boers were again at war. The Anglo-Boer War began in 1899 and ended in Boer defeat in 1901. The reason, simply put, was that the British wanted control of the goldfields as it would ultimately give them control of the whole country.

During the war, the British uprooted almost an entire nation and place families in relief camps. These later became concentration camps. By 1902 the Boer guerrillas were worn out and agreed to the Treaty of Vereeniging, which brought them back under British domination – ironically, what they had sought to escape by trekking away from the Cape more than half a century before.

Little wonder the scars of this war are still evident in South Africa, as English and Afrikaans white South Africans count their differences, rather than their similarities. Add to this the memories of the Great Trek and the bloody battles against the Bantu tribes, especially the Battle of Blood River, and you are looking at the cornerstones of the Afrikaner psyche.

Britain Hands Back Her Dearly Won Prize

At the instigation of Generals Jan Smuts and Louis Botha, stalwarts of the Anglo-Boer war, whites from all four colonies drew up a draft Act of Union that was passed by the British Parliament in 1910. The colonies were united in a self-governing dominion, the Union of South Africa. Black South Africans realised that if they were ruled by Afrikaners their chances of a fair deal were zero, but their objections fell on deaf British ears. Their struggle for equality had begun. Black nationalism was in the making.

A split soon developed in white politics – Smuts and Botha stayed with the more liberal and English-oriented South African Party (it has mutated many times since and is currently called the Democratic Party), while J B Hertzog led the National Party of dyed-in-the-wool Afrikaners, the forerunner to the current National Party and instigators of the apartheid policy.

THE CONSOLIDATION OF APARTHEID

The 1948 election victory of the right-wing Afrikaner party, in the 'whites-only' general election, began an epoch of unbroken National Party rule. This was a turning point in South Africa's political history that ushered in more than four decades of institutionalised racial discrimination and white supremacy.

The Nationalist majority in parliament was sufficient to statutorily define, legislate and hence enforce the practice of apartheid. Hosts of laws segregating, separating and oppressing people were implemented during the more than four decades of National Party rule. Some of the more vile ones, described by the United Nations as 'crimes against humanity', include:

- Prohibition of Mixed Marriages Act (1949) which forbade marriages between whites and people of other 'colours'.
- Immorality Act (amended in 1950 and 1957) which forbade any form of sexual contact, adultery or attempted adultery between whites and people of other races.
- Population Registration Act (1950) which classified every person according to race, on a national register.
- Group Areas Act (1950) which enabled the government to implement physical separation between races, enforcing separate residential areas. Often Coloured, Indian and African communities were forcibly moved to different and usually inferior residential areas. Whites were rarely adversely affected by this.
- Separate Amenities Act (1953) which prevented people of a different 'colour' from sharing public amenities such as toilets, cinemas, restaurants, hospitals, schools and more. This aimed to prevent the different racial groups from mixing with each other. Supposedly each group had its own amenities, but in reality whites had access to all the best public facilities and the other groups, if they had any, had second-rate ones.

A major tenet of the apartheid blueprint was the Bantu Authorities Act (1951) which provided for the establishment of separate rural areas called homelands or *bantustans* where almost all Africans would be forced to live according to their tribal identity. Homelands could gain 'independence' as separate countries. Some followed that path – like Transkei, Ciskei, Venda and Bophuthatswana – but no other country in the world, except South Africa and the other so-called independent states would recognise their sovereignty.

A rural, peasant home of the modern variety in one of the homelands, Lebowa.

THE FIGHT OF THE BLACKS
The African National Congress

Black South Africans began to organise regional resistance to white rule in the late 19th century. The movement gathered strength, cutting across tribal lines, after their failure to prevent the formation of the Union of South Africa, which meant the end of liberal British control of the country. In 1912, a nationwide conference was called of all African chiefs and leaders of political organisations. They agreed to establish the South African Native National Congress, later renamed the African National Congress (ANC). In January 1913 its headquarters was opened in Johannesburg.

In 1914 the South African National Party which had tried to unite English- and Afrikaans-speaking whites, finally admitted defeat and split into two. The politically conscious black South Africans, ironically, had just established the first, and still thriving, nationwide African national movement in the country. Their first president,

Reverend John Dube, had studied in England while early members of the ANC were African men who received their early education in English-run mission schools. Many of these members were later sent abroad by the missions for further education and training in various professions.

The initial role of the ANC was to attempt to persuade the white government to recognise all people as equals.

A More Radical Approach

The Congress Youth League was formed at the 1944 annual conferences. It was a much more radical organisation than the older conservative elements that dominated the ANC leadership. It opposed the white government with growing fierceness that gained momentum when the Afrikaners took control of the government in 1948 and began to build the rigid systems of apartheid. The ANC had not been a militant organisation until this time.

In 1950 the South African Communist Party, always a close ally of the ANC, was declared unlawful by the Suppression of Communism Act. This law was used to full and brutal effect in later decades to suppress anyone or any organisation that resisted the apartheid government.

Ongoing ANC passive-resistance campaigns were organised against the exclusion of black people from the process of government. They were specifically against the laws that forced only Africans to carry identity documents at all times. In April 1960, the government banned the ANC, and it was no longer a lawful political organisation. With this act, 50 years of non-violent struggle was brought to nothing and by mid-1961 the ANC decided it would have to use violent methods of resistance to achieve its aims.

In 1961 the military wing of the ANC was formed. Called *Umkhonto we Sizwe*, it means 'Spear of the Nation'. Its tactics of sabotage were at first aimed at damaging only buildings and property, and avoiding loss of life. In 1963 the top leaders of the ANC, including

Nelson Mandela, were brought to trial and sentenced to life imprisonment. The organisation continued its work in exile. As the laws of
apartheid became more repressive, the ANC again changed its tactics
and civilians became targets of sabotage.

The ANC, with the help of many anti-apartheid organisations
worldwide, had built up a wide support network worldwide. Because
of internal and external pressure, Nelson Mandela, the figurehead and
then leader of the ANC, and other members were released from jail
in February 1990. The ban on the ANC was lifted, and it is now one
of the major negotiating forces in the establishment of the new
democratic constitution in South Africa.

Justice Through Trade Unions

The dire need for South Africa to manufacture, both during
and after World War II, launched the country on its second industrial
revolution transforming it from a solely mining community to a
manufacturing one as well. For an outsider, the trade union movement
here may not be as simple to understand as those in other countries.

During the decades that the majority black population was denied
political representation, the unions were the best, and often the only,
avenue for airing grievances – not only work-related ones. The Great
Depression, the period between the World Wars, was a desperate
economic time for a newly industrialising country. A large influx of
rural people no longer able to make a living on their farms moved into
the towns and cities. This period, which reduced many whites to dire
poverty despite their privileged status, resulted in much greater
suffering for black people who were the poorest section of the
population. Their lot was made even worse by deliberate measures to
favour white workers over them.

Little wonder the first black unions were formed at this time. Later
the African Mine Workers' Union was established with a command-
ing position in mining compounds at the end of the war. They have
held onto this position ever since. Now called the National Union of

Mine Workers, it has become the biggest, most powerful and best organised union in the country.

As the aspirations of the millions of disenfranchised people increased, so did political and union activities. The government cracked down on them and certain organisations were banned, including the ANC and the South African Congress of Trade Unions.

The new union movement of the 1970s and 1980s was more militant and politically driven. The divisions in the country were echoed in the unions. There were black and white unions, left- and right-wing ones. The upheavals led to the black unions winning the same legal rights as their white counterparts. Slowly labour laws were amended and improved, and by the late 1980s the unions enjoyed an equitable degree of power. South Africa has some 2.5 million trade unionists, more than 2 million of whom are black.

The dominant trade unions today are the Congress of South African Trade Unions (COSATU) and the National Council of Trade Unions (NACTU). There is now a realisation that South Africans of all colours are mutually dependent, especially in industry. Thus a new spirit of cooperation is encouraged with the notion that workers, capital and the state should jointly control the economy.

THE DECLINE OF APARTHEID
Sharpville Shootings – A Day to Commemorate

Under the system of apartheid all Africans were forced to carry a 'pass book', an identity document listing all their racial particulars. In 1960 the ANC called for a nationwide defiance campaign by blacks aimed particularly at the hated 'pass laws'.

On 21 March 1960 in Vereenigning, a town south-east of Johannesburg, demonstrators marched on a local police station. After calling for reinforcements, the panic-stricken police opened fire on unarmed civilians, killing 69 people and wounding 180. The tragedy at Sharpville, the neighbourhood where the incident occurred, evoked revulsion and censure from around the world. The Sharpville massacre was seen as a direct consequence of apartheid, and thus condemned vehemently.

Since then, 21 March or Sharpville Day has been a time to commemorate the horrors inflicted on the black community by the apartheid regime. This day is as important in the black psyche as the Great Trek is to the Afrikaners or 1820 Settlers' Day is to the English.

June '76, Soweto Day

For any newcomer to South Africa it is vital to understand the poignance and depth of emotions attached to the commemoration of 16 June 1976 each year. This day was not an official public holiday under the old regime, but because of its importance to the majority in the country, it has now been made an official public holiday, Youth Day.

How did this emotion-laden day come about? A new government regulation in 1976 instituted that instead of English, Afrikaans was to be the medium of instruction for some subjects in African schools. This move sparked a tinder box of discontent in the black communities and especially its youth because, while both languages are official, Afrikaans is seen as the language of the oppressor while English is seen as an international language.

(Many of the student grievances were justified. They included inferior education in overcrowded classes with poorly qualified teachers while their white counterparts received a high-quality free education. Other grievances such as poor housing and lack of electricity and running water also added fuel to the fire.)

Resistance was strongest in Soweto, the huge black and largely poor residential neighbourhood south-west of Johannesburg. On 16 June 1976 some 15 000 students marched in a demonstration, defying a police ban on marches. They were stopped by police, but stood firm despite the warning shots and tear gas. Police opened fire into the

A little girl outside her house in Soweto. Photographed by Kamariah Abdul Rahim.

crowd, killing two of the youngsters and wounding several more. A now famous photograph of two students carrying the fatally injured 13-year-old Hector Pietersen has grown to symbolise this tragic event.

First Soweto, and later almost every other township in South Africa erupted with demonstrations, riots, destructive violence and confrontations with the police. When the violence eventually subsided in October 1977, the death toll was over 700, comprising mostly youths.

23

The Final Straw – The 1984 Constitution

'Sharpville was the revolt of the parents, Soweto (June 1976) was that of the children. Now it's both,' said an experienced black press photographer in 1986.

In 1984 a new constitution gave the Indians and Coloureds some form of representation along with the whites. This tricameral parliament deeply angered the Africans whose only form of political representation was in the homeland governments, which were mostly unrecognised and termed as illegitimate, puppet regimes.

Demonstrations were held across the country, venting frustrations over issues like steep rent rises, continuing forced removals, the abysmal condition of black education and many more. Police controlling a funeral which was also a political demonstration panicked and shot dead 19 mourners. Again riots spread across the country. Confrontation became ever more violent in the black townships between demonstrators and the police, aided by the South African Defence Force. At almost every funeral cum political rally, more people were killed and the spiral of violence continued.

It was at this time that the dreadful 'necklace' method of murdering spies and informers came into being. A motorcar tyre filled with petrol was put around the neck or body of a victim and then set alight. International condemnation of both the rioting and the harsh repression of the apartheid regime did little to alleviate the violence.

In July 1985, State President P W Botha declared a state of emergency, saying the country was ungovernable – exactly the intention of the disenfranchised masses. Over 8500 people were detained, many of them children. Thousands lost their lives, thousands more were banned or jailed. Both the international and local press were severely censored.

But tragically, the violence continued. Horror at what was happening to the country caused foreign banks to withdraw capital. The value of the South African currency dropped dramatically and the country faced economic and financial disaster. By 1987 the violence had subsided a little, but almost everyone, both black and white, was more politicised and polarised than ever before. Negative world opinion, disinvestment and sanctions were forcing South Africa to consider a peaceful route to democracy.

When F W de Klerk succeeded Botha as state president in 1989 he began a process of genuine reform, lifting the state of emergency, allowing black political demonstrations and releasing a number of important political prisoners. In February 1990 he ended the 30-year ban on the ANC and legalised a host of other anti-apartheid political organisations. To world acclaim on 11 February 1990, the world's most famous political prisoner, Nelson Mandela, walked free.

And They All Came Tumbling Down Again

In a speech to the nation on 1 February 1991 President F W de Klerk finally buried the cornerstones of apartheid. The Group Areas Act, the land acts, the Population Registration Act – the laws that had caused so much grief, suffering and loss of human dignity for more than 40 years – were nullified. Through a negotiated settlement, the tricameral parliamentary system and the homeland governments was to be moulded into a new democratic political system for all.

De Klerk's release of Mandela was an act of bold and unusual trust by both men. Mandela agreed to work with his arch political enemy while balancing the expectations of those who believed in his leadership. De Klerk on the other hand had to try to fulfil his electoral promise to break down apartheid structures while working to protect the white, Asian and Coloured minorities. They had given the country a chance to take a long hard look at itself: De Klerk had to persuade his constituency they had been following a false dream for over 40 years; the ANC had to adapt from being an activist, exiled, banned organisation, committed to armed struggle, to being a political party and potential government in a democratic South Africa.

The momentum for the peace-making process of the future had been set in motion. Its continuation is in the hands of the nation.

The Beginning of the Uphill Battle

The first tottering step on the road to normality was called the Convention for a Democratic South Africa, or CODESA to the glib of tongue. Almost 400 delegates from 19 political organisations met weekly to negotiate mutually acceptable ways of moving from apartheid to something entirely different. CODESA was to draw up a declaration of intent committing the political parties to a constitution-making process. They were also to have an effective say in national policies pursued during the interim period leading to the formation of a new government.

At first things went smoothly and this nation, blighted with political turmoil for hundreds of years, was euphoric. But not for long.

The two main contenders in the negotiations process, De Klerk's government and the ANC, agreed that a constitution should be drawn up and adopted by a popularly elected national assembly. So far, so good. But then three major bones of contention arose: they could not agree on the percentage majority needed to adopt the constitution; there was conflict over the role of the Senate or upper house; and also over the time frame for creating the constitution. The upshot of it all was that the ANC suspended talks at CODESA, and the first tottering step was halted, negotiations derailed. Each side retreated to lick its wounds, rally its supporters and prepare for the next round.

The talks began again some months later at the same venue, under a slightly different guise. The notion of a negotiated settlement had not been abandoned. It was the only way forward and it led ultimately to a negotiated, peaceful solution with the framework being set for a government of national unity that took cognisance of the needs of the broad spectrum of the population through their respective political parties.

THE FALL OF APARTHEID

After years of home-grown resistance and ever increasing world censure, apartheid was finally dismantled. The culmination of that abhorrent era, and the beginning of the march to democracy, was heralded by the 'Yes for change' vote in the 1992 referendum where the vast majority of whites threw their weight behind the reform process already in motion. In the words of President de Klerk, 'Today we have closed the book of apartheid. That chapter is over. We, who started this long chapter in our history were called upon to close it.' And they did.

In probably the most historic event the country has ever faced, South Africans went to the polls for the first ever truly democratic election on 26–29 April 1994. It wasn't the smoothest-run election the world had ever witnessed, but considering it was the first, and that time was not on our side, it went off remarkably well. International observers flooded the country in their thousands to ensure it was reasonably free and fair, and later pronounced it was. We all voted – over 19 million of us stood in totally harmonious, multi-racial queues for hours, and in some areas, days, to make that all-important cross on both our national and regional ballot papers.

The result, as expected, was a resounding victory for the ANC, trailed in second place by the National Party, the rulers for the past 48 years, and then the Inkatha Freedom Party, which is predominantly Zulu and most populous in the Kwazulu/Natal area.

As leader of the ANC, Nelson Mandela is now the country's first democratically elected and first black State President, while the two deputy state president positions go to prominent ANC member Thabo Mbeki and the leader of the NP and previous state president of South Africa, F.W. de Klerk.

Within the first term of government, the law putting a liberal and high-minded constitution in place was passed in 1996.

In June 1999, the second general elections took place, with the ANC sweeping back into power.

WHO'S WHO IN POLITICS

In South Africa there is a grand plethora of political parties, quasi-political organisations and a host of fringe organisations. There are a privileged few long-standing political parties, some of them dyed-in-the-wool types while others have grown and changed to meet the challenges of the times. In case you should be in a position to vote, or are just curious to know who's who, here follows a run-down of the more prominent organisations, in alphabetical order in case I should be accused of political bias!

African National Congress (ANC)

Discussed in detail above, it suffices here to say that the ANC, once a liberation movement, now a fully fledged political party, held the majority in the first democratic elections under the leadership of Nelson Mandela. Today, it is headed by Thabo Mbeki, inaugurated as the new president after the ANC election victory on 2 June 1999.

Afrikaner Weerstandsbeweging (AWB)

Translated as the Afrikaner Resistance Movement, it is not yet a political party, yet. The AWB is a para-military organisation that has strong similarities to Hitler's Nazi movement. Its main aim is to create an independent white *volkstaat*, or nation state, which would exist 'just like any other nation in southern Africa'.

All prospective citizens must be white Afrikaners. No foreign investors would be welcome in their 'country' (should there be any that crazy), which would be run along the lines of Mussolini's corporatist state. The AWB has set up a series of vigilante groups in right-wing towns and rural areas.

Launched in 1973, its leader Eugene Ney Terre'Blanche (coincidentally, his surname means 'White Land'!) an Afrikaner farmer and former policeman, is always clad in khaki fatigues similar to those used in the Boer war in the last century. A firebrand orator, his radical right-wing rhetoric can quickly stir up his fairly small following to a frenzy. He is constantly surrounded by black-clad white bodyguards.

There are about 40 other ultra-right wing organisations in South Africa, many of which are militant. Their lack of unity, however, makes them little more than the butt of jocular media attention. There is no shortage of fanatics among their few supporters, but their fantasies, for the moment, are just that. With their racism, fantasies, and hunger strikes, they are not worth more than the mildest of curiosity.

Azanian People's Organisation (AZAPO)

Highly politicised but not a political party, the Azanian People's Organisation was established in May 1978 to fill the vacuum left when the government banned almost all black political organisations. It has its roots firmly established in the philosophy of the black consciousness movement.

Its philosophies are based on awareness among blacks that their human identity hinges on the fact that they are black (in AZAPO's case this includes Coloureds and Indians) – proud of their colour, culture and history and aware it is very different from the whites'. They do not accept being judged according to white values and norms. Steve Biko, who died in police custody and was made famous internationally by the movie *Cry Freedom*, was a major exponent of black consciousness.

AZAPO aims to create political awareness among black workers, demand education systems suited to the needs of 'Azanians', and fight for unity of the oppressed in order to distribute wealth and power among the people of Africa. It is a small organisation, but has branches nationwide.

Conservative Party (CP)

The Conservative Party, a political party, split in 1982 from the National Party under the leadership of Dr Andries Treurnicht. He is dubbed by the media as 'Dr No' for his constant and consistent opposition to any form of political reform, racial integration or power sharing.

On a world political spectrum, this core of ultra right-wingers almost falls off the extreme right end of the scale. If they were to rule the country, blacks would have no political rights in South Africa but only in their own homelands, which would all be granted 'independence'. Blacks would only be allowed in white areas if they fulfilled an economic function – which seems tantamount to a 21st century version of slavery! Separate amenities, education and residential areas would be strictly enforced. Simply put, they would return to the structures of dogmatic apartheid.

As an added extra, there would be no sport or public entertainment, movies and the like on Sundays as in the old-world Calvinist tradition. I imagine the word 'hedonism' would be erased from their dictionaries!

The CP has links with other right-wing organisations such as the AWB (described above). The Herstigte Nasionale Party is another ultra-right wing Afrikaner party with similar views to the CP, but they seem unable to form a unified front. The CP is now under the leadership of Dr Ferdie Hartzenberg.

Democratic Party (DP)

This is a mutated political party. The ancestry of the Democratic Party can surely be traced as far back as the old South African Party. Its current leader is Tony Leon.

Although small (in the last all-white election it gained some 20% of the vote), its contribution is important as it has succeeded in keeping issues related to liberal political values on the political agenda. The DP is committed to 'engagement politics', which means it is prepared to speak to everyone from the ultra-left to the far right. It is also willing to form a bridge between the parliamentary and extra-parliamentary groups, until all have the vote.

Its beliefs are the same as those of liberal democrats the world over. The more important policies include a common voters role, political and religious freedom, an independent judiciary and sovereignty of the law, an economy based on private entrepreneurship and minimum state involvement. The DP fervently believes economic growth and political democracy will ward off the threat of racial war in South Africa.

Federal Alliance

This party was formed by fertiliser king turned rugby supremo, Louis Luyt, in late 1998 and registered as a political party in January 1999 to stand in the 1999 election. Its main objective is to pose additional opposition to the ANC.

Freedom Front

The Freedom Front was formed shortly before the 1994 elections as a representative body for Afrikaner conservatism under the leadership of the South African Defence Force under the old regime.

It won the fourth largest number of votes in the first election behind the ANC, NP and IFP and had 14 representatives in the first democratically-elected parliament.

Its main objective are self-determination for Afrikaner people and the establishment of an independent homeland, or *Volkstaat.* Although at odds with the constitution, it has indicated that it sees self-determination as possible under article 235 of the South African constitution.

Inkatha Freedom Party (IFP)

A recent political convert, Inkatha was started as a Zulu cultural organisation in 1928. Since then its popularity has fluctuated until the mid-70s, when its leader Dr Mangosuthu Buthelezi injected enthusiasm and boosted its membership a decade later to a claimed 1.5 million (some dispute this figure). Its support is almost entirely Zulu-based, but not all Zulus support it. It does have a small amount of support among other groups including whites.

When, in 1990, it became evident that South Africa was en route to a democratic future, Inkatha changed into the Inkatha Freedom Party, a nationally-based political party open to all races. Placed in the centre of the political spectrum, its main thrust is for a multi-party, non-racial democracy supported by a free-market system. It believes a negotiated road will lead to this end and acknowledges the necessity for the redistribution of wealth – hopefully by creating more of it.

Although Buthelezi was a member of the ANC in his youth and supported it while it was banned, more recently the two organisations have become protagonists in the battle for political power. Tribal-type warmongering between the two has led to sporadic violence and the resulting loss of life.

The New National Party

This is the political party held ultimately responsible for apartheid, and almost anything else wrong with the country as well.

In retrospect, the coming to power of the NP in 1948 was the single most deleterious moment in the 20th century history of South Africa. The NP may have led the country to sovereign independence, and later even Republic-hood (the ultimate dream of the Afrikaner as a means of eternally shaking free of the British yoke), but they also gave it the albatross – apartheid.

After its founding in 1914 the NP championed the cause of Afrikaners who gave it almost all its support. It originally had a rural base as most Afrikaners were farmers, but as they urbanised so the NP's support base moved towards the city.

Their victory in 1948 was unexpected, but once in power, their game plan was crystal clear. The formal, or enforced relationship (or non-relationship) between whites and blacks led ultimately to extreme hardship for all people who were not deemed 'white'. It also led to these 'not-white' people attempting to redress the situation by challenging the state at every given opportunity – first peacefully and then a lot more vehemently.

Since the first general elections, the NP, now the NNP, has tried to distance itself from the apartheid era by trying to change its image. It was the official opposition to ANC government in the first democratic government.

In recent times, it has been under the leadership of a young Turk, Marthinus van Schalkwyk, but seems to have lost a lot of clout in political circles, although it still purports to wish to "play a leading role in redefining South African politics by bringing together a majority of South Africans ina dynamic political environment."

National People's Party (NPP)

This political party, formed in 1981, aimed solely at the Indian community. Their support base was small, especially because of their participation in the tricameral parliament. For this same reason the NPP took a more positive attitude to the South African government. In contrast, the long-standing Indian anti-apartheid organisations like the Natal Indian Congress and the Transvaal Indian Congress have always had a large support base.

Like the Labour Party, the NPP believed it could fight the system from within. It supports the abolition of all forms of racial, cultural and sexual discrimination and believes all groups should participate in government. The party's demise may well come with the eventual scraping of the tricameral system.

Pan Africanist Congress (PAC)

An ANC breakaway group formed the Pan Africanist Congress in 1959 because they felt the ANC was incapable of promoting black liberation – with the emphasis on 'black'. This group of Africanists believes blacks should be in control of their own liberation struggle and should not be prompted by white liberals, including communists. They feel the whites have too much to lose to be considered reliable allies.

Not a political party but a liberation movement, their early support is said to have been even greater than that of the ANC. Together they were the only 'official' South African liberation movements recognised by the United Nations and the Organisation of African Unity.

The PAC had its strongest support base in the Eastern Cape from where it launched its early resistance campaigns, anti-pass campaigns (like the ANC did), and also ran a 'status campaign' to wean the black population off its psychological subservience to whites. In 1960 the government banned the PAC, along with the ANC.

The PAC began to disband its military wing, the Azanian People's Liberation Army, in December 1998 and was integrated into the new-look South African Defence Force shortly after elections in 1994, as did the military divisions of many other freedom organisations.

One of the fundamental differences between the ANC and PAC is the question of land ownership. The ANC says the land belongs to everyone, while the PAC says the only solution to the land problem is its return to 'its rightful owners' who are the 'indigenous black nation'.

Legalised along with the ANC in 1990, the PAC has regained some of its support base, especially from the more militant ANC youth. An unofficial slogan rejected by the leadership, although used frequently by the masses at rallies and meetings is: 'one settler, one bullet'. This is a fairly crude way of stating their antithesis for whites.

Under the leadership of Clarence Makwetu, the PAC declined to be part of CODESA. Instead it threatened to increase its sabotage activity. However it has toned down its socialist views and is known to have had discussions with some of the right-wing organisations – strangely they hold similar views on some matters, albeit on opposite sides of the political spectrum.

WHERE TO NOW?

Today the mood is different. There is a quiet, and sometimes not so quiet determination among ordinary people not to go down on their knees to beg for a place in the sun, but simply to take it. Having taken such risks and reached such depths of horror to wrestle their rights from the apartheid regime, surely they will defend them vigorously for ever more.

Chapter Two

A MULTI-COLOURED TAPESTRY

'A South African by any other name is still … a South African.'

If there is one fact about South Africa that has made the country world-renowned, if infamously so, it's apartheid: the legislation that tried so desperately to drive wedges between each different group that makes up our richly coloured racial and cultural tapestry.

THE DIFFERENT RACIAL COMMUNITIES

Although it may seem to be playing into the hands of that totally discredited and recently destroyed philosophy, it is worth understand-

35

ing the cultural heritage of South Africa's different peoples. They are as different as day and night, but are now determined to forge a new life for a new country where equality pervades.

AFRICANS

The ethnic history of the many culturally diverse indigenous tribes is so complex that it has inspired hundreds of books and research documents. It is totally beyond the scope of this book to even begin to do justice to this subject, but I will attempt to give you a very potted description of the different tribes. At the very least, the differences drawn out will show that the phrase 'Oh but all blacks are the same' is derogatory and racist.

The Tribes – In Brief

The origins of the tribes lie in the sub-Saharan indigenous people who split into two groups some 6 000 years ago. The *Khoisan*, or Bushmen, inhabited the southern portion of the continent and the Negroids lived in the forests of Central Africa. Later they migrated south and population movements over the last 10 000 years have resulted in the different populations being mixed to some extent.

The following is a quick description of some random cultural traits of the African tribes who still live very much the same way as they did thousands of years ago. This information is a way of superficially letting you in on conversation where otherwise words like Xhosa or Venda may draw a complete blank. Take note, however, that some of the traditions have been changed or modified especially by the city-dwelling Africans.

Xhosa

An oral tradition traces this tribe back to a mythological founder named Xhosa, but it is also possible the word means 'angry men'. Because their traditional area falls into the Cape, they came into early contact with westerners. ANC leader, Nelson Mandela, and many other high profile political leaders come from this group.

To Xhosas leading a traditional lifestyle, social groupings and marriage are very important. Marriage is more than just the bond between man and woman, it is the joining together of two clans. Hence members of the same clan are not allowed to be married.

Bride price, or *lobola*, is paid in this culture as it is in almost all traditional African tribes. Once married, the bride moves from her family home to that of her husband's and his extended family's.

The huts in the kraal, or homestead area, are organised in a hierarchical order and the families living there are almost always related to the headman. As an outsider, a wife improves her status and secures her position in the extended family by giving birth to her husband's children.

Young children are treated with great tolerance by the older

An obviously captivating tribal-dance performance in Jo'burg. Photographed by Kamariah Abdul Rahim.

relatives and learn by imitating their elders. Once old enough they are expected to help with chores like cattle herding and bringing water from the nearest source, perhaps a river. Boys are initiated into manhood by undergoing circumcision and then their survival skills are tested by living alone in the wilderness for a few weeks or months.

The chief is the head of the tribe, and he is invariably the wealthiest man and the main religious leader to the group. Tradition requires that he rule by consensus so his power is limited by his counsellors and public opinion.

Ancestor worship forms the basis of the Xhosa's spiritual belief. Kinship relationships apply in the world hereafter with each family looking to its ancestors for guidance in times of adversity. Xhosa diviners communicate with their ancestors by seances.

Herbalists treat both people and animals through their intimate knowledge of natural medicine, rather than supernatural intervention as in some other tribes.

Zulu

In the 18th century the Zulus were a small group but rose to fame under Shaka. He usurped the Zulu throne and unified the many independent chiefdoms into one nation with the help of his mighty army. By his death in 1828, the might of the Zulus was well established.

The Zulu nation then became the semi-independent homeland of KwaZulu. It is ruled by a government under political leader Chief Mangasutu Buthelezi and King Goodwill Zwelatini. The Zulu King is the centre of political power as well as the highest judicial and military authority. It now forms part of KwaZulu Natal province.

The traditional economy is based on agriculture, cattle rearing and hunting. The Zulu material culture involves certain home industries like basket weaving; beadwork; carving from wood and, in the past, ivory too.

Traditionally curdled milk and vegetables were the staple diet and meat was only eaten on special occasions. Traditional beer is in great demand at social and ceremonial occasions.

In very traditional societies, girls and boys go through circumcision ceremonies to mark their readiness for marriage. Many other ceremonies are undertaken including marriage ceremonies similar to the Xhosa's where *lobola* is practised. However, ritual ceremonies are quite different – an example is ear piercing of children just before they reach puberty. This ceremony is accompanied by much festivity. Over the years, the holes in the earlobes are made ever bigger and often adorned with traditional earrings made of decorated wood. (You can sometimes buy them at the Mai Mai market in downtown Johannesburg.)

Traditional Zulus believe in an all-powerful being called 'Older-Than-Old' with whom ancestors act as intermediaries. For the treatment of medical problems, an *isangoma*, or diviner, is approached. In Zulu culture this term refers to a herbalist or spiritualist.

Ndebele

They have been settled in the Transvaal among the Sotho tribes for many, many years and thus their culture and language have come to resemble Sotho in many ways.

Now divided into Southern and Northern Ndebele, their traditional ceremonies come from their Zulu/Nguni origin and some are also borrowed from their Sotho neighbours. Ceremonies play a major role as they draw a whole village together in sadness or in joy.

Traditional homes are usually rectangular (but can be round too) with mud walls, thatched roofs and cow-dung floors. A distinct characteristic of the Ndebele homestead is the beautiful patterns and colours painted on the mud walls of both the homestead buildings and the wall surrounding it. These artistic skills are handed down by the women to the young girls before they reach puberty.

Very similar patterns, colours and themes to the wall paintings are used in making the beaded jewellery and garments worn during special tribal functions. The older beadwork and wall decorations tend to be more stylised and geometric in design, whereas some of the designs today incorporate modern technological symbols like aeroplanes or street lights. (Ndebele beadwork can often be bought in the Market Theatre Flea Market in downtown Johannesburg.)

Although beads are not as important to Ndebele men as they are to women, there are times when men are expected to wear them as charms. Also by being passed down from father to son, they can symbolise the continuity of generations.

Ancestor worship is part of the Ndebele culture seen in the 'throwing of the bones' for divination. The diviner has a whole assortment of materials including sea shells, stones and bones of small animals which are thrown together onto the ground. The pattern they fall in is read, interpreted and used to provide solutions to problems or events that need explanation.

The Sotho Groups

Together the Sotho groups make up about 30% of the country's African population. Because of the many generations of contact

The beautifully painted mud dwellings of the Ndebeles' traditional rural home.

between them and the other main group, the Nguni, many of the distinctions between the two groups are quite blurred. There are four main groups: North Sotho, Lobedu, South Sotho and Tswana.

North Sotho It is thought that they occupied an area the size of Transvaal from about A.D. 400. A large group of this tribe, called the Pedi, have lived in Sekhukhuneland and have been there since about the 17th century.

Their economy is based on agriculture and animal husbandry and they possess a detailed knowledge of soils and plants. Sorghum is the staple crop, but ground nuts, pumpkin, vegetables and other cereals are also grown. Land is communally owned and most of the tilling is done by the women.

Homesteads consist of one or more thatched huts with a verandah and mud walls around the circumference of each hut.

Both boys and girls have initiation rights where they receive instruction on the relative relationships between men and women, and are taught respect for their cultural values and customs. After these initiation ceremonies, they are welcomed into society as adults and allowed to marry.

The Pedi believe that the world was created by Kgobe; and that his son, Kgobeane, created the human race. The power of ancestors is important to the Pedi, who also respect the role of diviners and herbalists.

Lobedu (pronounced Lovedu) Unique to southern Africa is the fact that they have a woman ruler, Mujaji, the Rain Queen. Although she is the pivotal point and source of strength to the tribe, her powers rest not on military might, but on her ability to make rain – and on a network of political marriages. The queen is considered of divine origin and has a special affinity with nature. The role of ancestors is important in daily life and shrines of stones, earth mounds or sacred plants are made in their honour.

South Sotho Many South Sothos live in what is now the independent kingdom of Lesotho, a tiny mountainous country totally surrounded by South Africa. Homes in this mountainous area are made of stones and covered with thatched roofs.

Hunting, food gathering, herding and agriculture all contribute to their subsistence. They are well known for their Basotho ponies which are small and extremely nimble on the rocky mountain passes.

Their kinship beliefs grant more recognition to relatives on the mother's side than most other southern African tribes. Polygamy, although permitted, is reserved for the wealthy and is on the decline.

Initiation occurs for boys and girls and begins with a feast. The boys are circumcised and isolated for a while; whereas the girls receive instruction on the role of women in their society and their behaviour with men.

They believe in a supreme creator, Modimo, and ancestors play a pivotal role in their religious life.

Bone-throwing diviners and herbalists form part of a complicated system to ward off evil spirits, induce rain and protect the tribe from natural occurrences like lightning.

Tswana Tswana traditions indicate that their ancestors came in several migrations from lands north of what is now South Africa.

Due to quarrels in the distant past and also the vast amount of land in the areas they lived in, the Tswana tribe now consists of over 50 different groups. They live in very large villages of up to 20 000 people, probably for reasons of defence as they are not naturally warlike.

They run a mixed economy of cattle farming and agriculture on commonly-owned land. The Tswana make excellent crafts – the men work with skin, bone and metal while women make pots. Both are adept at making baskets.

Initiation rites take place for both boys and girls after which they are allowed to marry.

The Shangaan

Originally they lived in the Mozambique area (where many still do) and as far down the east coast as Durban, but they moved inland to the areas in the eastern and northern Transvaal.

Their homesteads are individual units that are separated from one another, instead of being grouped into villages. The buildings are usually in a circle and often surrounded by some trees, one of which is considered to be sacred. This sacred tree is specially chosen and on which they nail the skulls of the cattle slaughtered in rituals. The entire area is then enclosed by a fence which is sometimes made out of living trees.

Their economy is more varied and mixed than other southern African people's – agriculture, animal husbandry, fishing, hunting and trade are practised.

Children are taught the customs of their culture as early as possible and after completing their initiation they are allowed to begin courting.

Marriages are marked in 3 stages: a go-between calls at the chosen girl's village, the *lobola* is negotiated, then the young girl makes a show of reluctance but then joins her husband.

They worship their ancestors who reveal themselves in dreams as snakes or as a whistling sound.

Venda

The Venda, who live in the northern part of the country, have a culture and language quite different from the other southern Africans. As their oral tradition explains, they may have moved into this area from around Lake Malawi before the 17th century.

They live in relatively large villages strategically placed on hill sides, with fencing or walls for protection. Traditional huts are made of stakes or built out of stone, with thatched roofs and verandahs for protection from the sun and also for added storage space.

Their economy is largely based on agriculture. Cattle are rarely farmed. The Vendas are one of most accomplished groups of traditional potters in the whole region. Pots are made by women without a wheel, and the quality and designs are excellent. Men do metal work using ant hills as forges and animal skins as bellows to make everyday-work items like hoes.

Ancestor worship is central to their religion and they believe in a complex system of ancestral spirits. Diviners, herbalists and medicine men play a vital role in protecting people against witchcraft.

COLOUREDS

The origins of the Coloureds, or people of mixed race, go back to the Cape region around the 17th century when many of the *Khoikhoi* mixed with and married the early Dutch sailors (who were of course

Herbalists selling their organic mixtures. Photograph taken by Kamariah Abdul Rahim

all men). At the same time, Malay women were brought to the Cape as wives for Dutch sailors and settlers. Thus the Malay cultural heritage was also added to this community. Recently some of the community have looked more seriously to their Islamic roots, following the Muslim faith more closely.

In the latter part of the 1800s the Coloured people found their skills as craftsmen, artisans, fishermen and farm labourers in greater demand as the Cape Colony developed. They also had the vote because the British ran the colony on a colour-blind franchise. But this 100-year-old right was ended by the Nationalist government in one of the most despicable acts of constitutional gerrymandering. The right was removed despite a long, bitter and determined struggle in the courts by the Coloured community and the opposition whites.

Coloureds Aren't White?
One of the enduring myths of racist South Africa was that the Coloured people were a separate group like the Africans or Indians.

A Coloured family, like the one above, was forcibly removed in the 1970s and made to live in a Coloured area.

45

In reality they spoke the same languages – Afrikaans and English – practised the same mostly Protestant religions and had the same aspirations towards western cultural and intellectual values. The only thing that made them different from the whites was the status that apartheid and its racial cornerstone, the Population Registration Act, gave them – based on the darker hues of their skin.

Coloured Heritage

To experience some of the wit and exuberance of the Coloureds in Cape Town, just stop and chat with the flower sellers or fruit and vegetable hawkers in Adderly Street. You may not be able to keep up with the speed of their chatter, but their humour is unique and their laughter is totally infectious. In fact, this wit was one of the things we were often homesick for in the years we lived abroad.

Every year the community holds a carnival on *Tweede Niewejaar*, or second New Year (January 2), which is a public holiday only in the Western Cape Province. Groups of brightly clad individuals, many made up with clown faces, dance and sing traditional folk songs. A lot of drinking and merriment is made by all, participants and spectators alike.

The Coloured community has contributed some superb literature to the South African culture, with Adam Small and Sol Plaatjies being two of the best known.

CHINESE

The current Chinese community, one of the smallest minority groups in South Africa, developed from sporadic migrations from 1891 onwards. Until recently, racist laws prevented Chinese immigration except spouses of Chinese-South Africans. But in the last decade or so there has been quite keen immigration by Taiwanese. Taiwan was one of the few countries which had overt trade relations with South Africa during the dying days of apartheid. Although the divide between the old and new Chinese communities has not reached that of Canada's, there is sometimes a slight disdain for the newcomers by the established families.

Under the new government, the People's Republic of China has gained prominence and dominance over Taiwan.

The Early Arrivals

The early immigrants were mostly of Cantonese origin, traders who arrived via Madagascar and Mauritius. With the discovery of diamonds and then gold, many moved towards Kimberley and the Johannesburg area, but moved again to the sea ports and the interior with the onset of the Anglo-Boer War (1899–1902). Today there are Chinese in most major urban centres with the Witwatersrand, the Johannesburg area, having the biggest community.

In 1904 when the country needed additional labour for post-war reconstruction, many thousands of Chinese labourers were recruited for this and also to work on the gold mines. However, the present Chinese community did not originate from these labourers as they had all been repatriated by 1910.

Neither Here Nor There

Under apartheid the Chinese occupied a strange and demeaning position. Although classified as 'Asian' and hence 'non-white' with no vote, they could access white privileges by applying for permits to live in white neighbourhoods or to attend 'whites-only' schools and hospitals. This left them in a no-man's land as they were informally accepted by the white community but not officially part of it, nor were they formally part of the black community that comprised all those fighting for political rights.

Chinese Heritage

The earlier generations were mostly traders – wholesalers and retailers – and their driving ambition was their children's entry into university. One of the strongest Chinese values still existing in the community is the respect for education and career success. Today most Chinese are successful professionals or business people living in good neighbourhoods, while their children go to private schools.

Most of them retain a respect for traditional Chinese values and customs especially for major events like birth, marriage and death; but other Chinese customs are not rigidly followed. Many have lost contact with Buddhism and are now Christians. Also few of the younger generation have much more than a tenuous grasp of any of the Chinese languages.

If you take a stroll in the small Chinese area in downtown Johannesburg, you will find old traditional-Chinese folk running some of the provisions stores that stock a wonderment of culinary and other domestic Chinese delights. At Chinese New Year these few streets burst into life with cultural festivities and fireworks.

INDIANS
How They Came

In the mid-19th century the European sugar-planters needed labour skilled in this form of agriculture, so they recruited workers from the Indian sub-continent. Most of these first immigrants were Hindus, but there were also a number of Muslims, Christians and other religious groups among the arrivals. Although imported primarily to work on the sugar plantations, they had an assortment of skills and soon a number were absorbed into other businesses. Over the next five decades, some 150 000 Indians were attracted by the prospects of trade in the new colony and emigration to South Africa. Most of them came to the country under contract and were indentured to their employers for periods of at least three to five years before they could be free to work as they pleased.

Conditions on the plantations were harsh and often the Indians were seen as units of work, not human beings.

Indian Influence

Today the majority of the million-strong Indian population still lives in Durban and other areas of Natal. Some have spread throughout the country, mostly to urban areas where they are successfully involved in the professions, business and commerce, and trading.

Classified as 'Asians' under apartheid and forced to live and trade in segregated areas, the most wonderful Indian markets and bazaars have developed within these communities. There, traditional food and spices add exotic colour and aroma to a buzzing atmosphere. Garments, particularly *saris* (the traditional dress of Indian women); traditional household goods; and jewellery and trinkets were imported from the motherland despite the fairly strict trade boycotts of the past.

Civil Rights: A Burning Issue

Not all the Indian immigrants were labourers. Some of higher caste came on their own as traders and merchants. Very soon they were selling not only to the Africans and Indians, but to the white community as well.

Wealthier, more confident and ambitious, they formed an elite group that soon drew together to fight for political and civil rights.

In 1893, Mohandas Karamchand Gandhi was thrown out of a train in South Africa because he refused to move out of a 'whites-only' compartment. He had come to South Africa to defend a court case but ended up spending 20 years in the country, being a key figure in the Indian protest movement.

A crucial event in Indian political history was the formation of the Natal Indian Congress (NIC) in 1894, which was set up to fight for their rights. The NIC and the Transvaal Indian Congress have been active in the struggle against apartheid. Always supportive of the African National Congress, they were totally against the formation of the tricameral parliament – where the Indians and Coloureds each had a separate and inferior House to the whites.

WHITES

The white population of South Africa is as diverse as the others. Its heritage is mostly European, with a wide variety of cultures from the north, south and west of Europe. Nevertheless it is fair to say that although they are proud of and indulge in their Portuguese, British, Greek or whatever heritage, they are first and foremost South Africans.

Population Statistics For South Africa

The very basic figures for the last census in 1996 show that 77% of the South African population is made up of Blacks, 11% Whites, 9% Coloureds and 3% Indians.

African/Black	31,127,631
Coloured	3,600,446
Indian/Asian	1,045,596
White	4,434,697
Unspecified	375,204
Total	40,583,573

NAMES THAT DIVIDE

Because of the past, race is a tetchy subject and it's wise to steer clear of it if you can. Just refer to people as people unless you absolutely have to describe them by race. Many white South Africans still have the inbuilt 'them and us' approach to people – try to avoid it.

Since it is obviously necessary occasionally to describe people by colour or creed, it's best you know which words are acceptable.

White—Refers to anyone of European descent and is quite okay to use. However, the apartheid engendered 'non-white' which meant everyone else in the entire county is a total 'no-no'.

Black—When used as a political term as in 'black liberation movement', it applies to Africans, Indians and Coloured people – all those fighting for political rights. But quite often it is used to mean only Africans. Quite correctly it is used in terms like 'black township' although you could just name the area – Soweto or Mamelodi. There is no harm in using it to describe a person as in 'black woman', but ONLY if there is reason to distinguish colour, otherwise using just 'woman' will win you many more friends.

Coloured—Refers to people of mixed race, a group made distinct by apartheid despite their very similar heritage to the Afrikaners. Frequently referred to as the 'Bruin Afrikaners' or Brown Afrikaners.

Asian—In the apartheid race classification, 'Asian' was used to refer to almost anyone with roots in the Indian sub-continent and Asia. Many Indians and Chinese find it extremely offensive, especially as it takes no cognisance of the vast diversity of nations in that region. In fact, a Hong Kong Chinese immigrant who has lived in South Africa for over 30 years told me recently he would never put the word Asian on any government form – no matter what it meant to him.

Derogatory words—NEVER use 'Kaffir' to refer to blacks, even though you may hear a local use it. Its dictionary meaning is 'unbeliever', but in South Africa it embodies everything that is morally and racially abhorrent about the apartheid era. It is seen as totally demeaning and derogatory. You may be subjected to other similarly unacceptable words by racist whites when referring to blacks, like 'moents' or 'houts' – walk away from them literally and metaphorically. 'Coolie' is used to refer to Indians and it is also totally unacceptable, as is 'Hotnot' which refers to Coloureds.

RACISM DOESN'T DIE OVERNIGHT

Unfortunately it is a universal fact that racism still exists all over the world no matter how hard we try to eradicate it. In a land where it has been institutionalised for more than four decades, it dies even harder.

Don't be surprised if you run into it, or even if you find it directed at you. But equally, don't go about looking for racial insults as this may lead you to interpret things wrongly. There are certainly people in the country who may be insulting to you if you are less than lily white in skin hue. As always for a newcomer, the best route it to walk away from it, but remember that the vast majority of South Africans will be only too keen to jump to your defence. Don't let the small minority spoil it for you.

Racial animosity in South Africa is not just the often discussed white/black issue. The Boer War led to the English and Afrikaans South Africans hating each other. There is also not much love lost between the African National Congress and the Inkatha Freedom Party, nor between the Zulus and the Indians in Natal, and now the Afrikaners have split into groups that seem quite incompatible ... and so it goes on. But once the new South Africa is well on its way, people will realise that their differences are less important than their similarities and long common history. Those are the elements that will ultimately bind them together.

WIPE THE STEREOTYPES AWAY

An internationally stereotyped and sometimes inaccurate view of white South Africans is that the Boers or Afrikaners are the baddies, *the* racists and the perpetrators of apartheid; while the English are the goodies, liberal in their political views and keen for the best deal for all South Africans.

There are the liberal English, the Helen Suzmans of this world. She spent 36 years in Parliament, 13 of them as the sole representative of liberal democratic values, tirelessly fighting the apartheid government. But there are also the Afrikaners who have fought for human rights and a world view of democracy. Look at internationally famous author Breyten Breytenbach who spent seven years in jail for working with the ANC, and then had to live in exile until the apartheid walls came tumbling down. Karl Niehaus is another white Afrikaner who is highly regarded by the ANC and is now an ambassador to the Netherlands.

Then you will find the odd rural white Boer farmer who may even refer to his black labour in unacceptable words, but will rush them hundreds of kilometres to the nearest doctor when they are ill – and his kind is not that of the MercedesBenz-driving land baron. These are salt of the earth people, struggling to make a meagre living. Recently I heard of a woman in the Orange Free State who does the farm labourers' washing and ironing for them because, 'Ag shame (a colloquial expression of sympathy), they don't have any electricity so

The author's brother with goats – part of a rural development programme that aims to help the people forced to live in this homeland become self-sufficient.

I have to help them.' I don't know any city-slickers who would go to those lengths.

On the flip side of the coin, there are numerous stories of 'liberal white English' families treating their domestic workers like slaves, paying them peanuts for working hours that went out with the Dark Ages – and then when they couldn't cope with the situation in the country, just walked away from their staff leaving them with no pension or means of support after some 20 or 30 years of service.

COOL DUDES OF THE TOWNSHIPS

There are numerous counter-culture youth groups spread across the sprawling townships. They are young and hip, cool dudes who wouldn't be seen dressed in anything other than that dictated by their peers – it might be trousers with an immaculate crease down the legs, or two-tone black and white brogue shoes which could be the flare of the moment. They speak in jargon, fast and fun. Some revere the life and times of Sofiatown (Johannesburg's African township in the 1950s, the forerunner to Soweto): a hotbed of artistic creativity, life and love, music, music and more music. Miriam Makeaba, one of South Africa's most famous singers was discovered in Sofiatown.

IGNORANCE IS BLISS

Don't be too surprised if you meet a South African who doesn't even know that your home country exists. International and geographic isolation has led to some fairly gauche people. Not that their lack of knowledge prevents them sometimes from having a lot of strong, and strange opinions. You may still hear people expounding about 'Red China', especially less-than-liberal whites, although they wouldn't have the vaguest clue who Deng Xiaoping is! I have also had conversations with some black people who genuinely believe that life in the United States is all about having everything your heart desires and more, for very little in return. Even Hollywood would be proud of these glittering views – and is probably responsible for them too.

But with new links constantly being forged between the new South Africa and the rest of the world, South Africans should soon become part of the global community.

THAT SOUTH AFRICAN-NESS

Despite apartheid, or perhaps because of it, a South African-ness exists about all the people living here, not the least of which is a deep affection for the country, the land itself. Sometimes this is reflected in rather chauvinistic ways. You may well hear a South African telling the crowds that 'We have the best beaches/beer/rugby players/ climate in the world.' If you should be so silly as to try to discuss the virtues of say Sydney's Bondi Beach, or Munich's best Bavarian brew, the French Tricolours or southern California's blue heavens, you may well find your words falling on deaf ears. This is partly because the person making these wild and gauche statements doesn't want to know that anything better or even comparable exists, and partly because they are quite likely to have never left their home turf or perhaps never even left their home town. Bear with them. It is usually meant well.

To really get to know South Africans don't let stereotypes get in the way – you will meet a wonderful, motley crew of new found friends.

Chapter Three

LIFESTYLES

South Africa is undergoing one of the most exciting phases of political change, the very nature of which will alter the social structure that has existed for 300 years. Old laws have been thrown out and the racist beliefs they underscored are being whittled away by new-found knowledge. Consequently, South Africans are discovering that the generally deep-seated moral or ethical values that make up the backbone of almost all societies in the world, are certainly prevalent across the board in this country too. It is only the cultural or religious differences, superficial by comparison, that colour various groups differently and create exciting cultural diversity.

Generally, the deep-seated family values like parents' responsibility to their children or concern over education, are similar across all cultures, especially in urban communities. But there are differences in attitudes to matters like divorce, single-parent families, premarital sex and extramarital children; and differences in customs at weddings, funerals, and birthdays for instance. People's approach to life is also quite different in the urban and rural areas.

ASPIRATIONS

Most South Africans of all races, colours and creeds aspire to the traditional lifestyle patterns of finding a partner, getting married and raising a family. Different groups may go about it in slightly different ways, but the sentiment is the same – the desire to have a home and family life.

Circumstances in the past have made this a lot easier for whites and the other more privileged groups, but for many Africans who have homes in the countryside and work in the cities or on the mines, family life is plagued with problems. These migrant workers sometimes only go home once or twice a year and some even take city-wives, quite legitimate under tribal marriage customs.

ATTITUDES TO SEX AND BABIES

The different communities in South Africa have widely differing views on premarital sex and extramarital babies. Many Afrikaners and the more conservative English communities frown on premarital sex and actively discourage it. Babies born out of wedlock are seen as bringing shame on the families. If a young woman does become pregnant, she is often pressurised into marrying the child's father before its birth. Quite often these are not stable relationships and lead to divorce.

There are few homes for unmarried mothers, but at least, under the new government, abortion is now legal, with the introduction of the Termination of Pregnancy Act enacted in February 1997.

The law allows any woman less than 12 weeks pregnant to have an abortion. A woman up to 20 weeks pregnant can have an abortion

under certain circumstances, including the knowledge that the baby has severe abnormalities, or the woman's belief that her economic or social situation makes an abortion necessary.

In African societies, both rural and urban, there are few taboos concerning sex before marriage or premarital babies. It is not unusual for African men to say they want proof of their would-be wife's fertility ahead of their marriage as children mean additional man-power, possess income potential, and will ensure a secure old age.

The number of single-mother households is increasing all the time as rural women are deserted by their husbands who go to work in the cities or on the mines, and then never return to their tribal homes. Also a growing number of urban women have opted for single-parenthood because of the stressful chauvinistic attitude of many African men who expect their wives to feed, clothe and care for them and the children in addition to working.

Many of the young rural women, forced to seek jobs in the towns and cities, fall victim to the country's almost non-existent sex education. They send their babies back to their rural homes to be raised by their grandmothers or other members of their extended family.

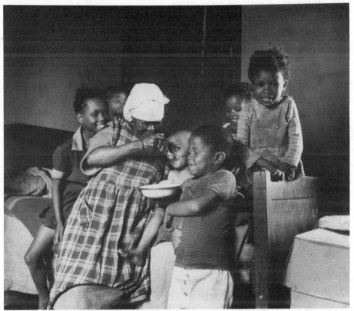

A poor rural grandmother looking after a host of grandchildren.

Although this is very much part of African lifestyle and shows a wonderful generosity of spirit, it often puts even greater strain on the poverty-wrecked rural families and communities.

DIVORCE

South Africans are certainly not proud of having one of the highest divorce rates in the world. In some parts of the country as many as one in two marriages ends in divorce. In the past women tended to get a pretty bad deal in a divorce settlement, but recent legislation has made the stakes between husbands and wives a little more even. Tribal African divorces are not conducted in court but are handled by the male-dominated tribal authorities, hence these women can get a very raw deal, often being left with nothing but the burden of looking after the children on little or no income.

In spite of the high divorce rate, strangely there are still a number of conservative people, particularly the more Calvinistic whites who see divorce as bad or wrong. Consequently they may even discriminate against a divorcee.

TRIBAL CUSTOMS

The difference between rural African tribal life and city life is even greater than in the white communities. Most of the African people in the rural areas practise tribal customs to some degree. The importance of the group is utmost and individualism is not as highly valued as in a western society. The continuity and growth of the group is of prime importance. It is impossible to do justice to the many and varied rituals in the scope of this book, but for anyone with a keen interest there are many interesting publications on the subject.

Polygamy

Of the most hotly-debated tribal issues in recent years are those of polygamy and the bride price, or *lobola*. Because of the imbalance in the ratio of men to women in tribal societies caused by many men being killed in tribal wars, polygamy had valid historical reasons for existing. Today it is felt by many, especially women, that polygamy has outlived its use and has lowered respect for women. They say that in a monogamous marriage where partnership is emphasised, women command equal respect with men. Some, however, argue that they prefer an open form of polygamy rather than a pretence at monogamy while indulging in prostitution, promiscuity and infidelity on the side.

Bride Price

Bride price, or *lobola*, is a very complex issue not easily understood by people unfamiliar with tribal ethics. Simply put, it establishes a bond and mutual responsibilities between the two families and involves the bridegroom giving cattle to the bride's family. It is a guarantee of his economic status and is compensation to the bride's family for the loss of her services. But most importantly, the *lobola* is the proof of the seriousness of the man's intentions – cattle are very valuable both economically and traditionally in a tribal culture. It is a promise that marital duties on both sides will be carried out.

However this system does not always adapt well to a western lifestyle. Quite often in an urban environment, the bride price is paid in cash and other consumer items which, of course, offer little or no protection to the wife once it is spent. In a modern urban society some women feel it is demeaning to be viewed as goods that can be bought, and that bride price has lost its relevance in cases where women work and can take care of themselves.

THE GREAT RURAL-URBAN DIVIDE

In both black and white communities there is a vast difference between the value systems of rural and urban people. The majority of

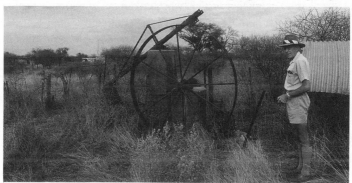

A farmer in typical khaki clothes: shorts, long socks and a wide-brimmed hat.

the whites living in the rural areas, or 'platteland', are farmers and a high percentage of them are Afrikaners. With their lives centred around the conservative Calvinist churches, their views are often very narrow and unworldly. But as a counter measure they often have very sound values, putting less emphasis on materialism and more on human decency.

In the small country towns, people make more time for social niceties. It is still customary for drivers of passing cars to give one another friendly greetings, as do pedestrians and drivers of animal drawn vehicles. Especially amongst the black people, a friendly smile is almost always returned.

If racism is taken out of the equation, rural folk are known to be friendly, hospitable people always prepared to pass the time of day with you. If, for example, you lose your way along some dusty country road, and call in at a farm house for help, it would not be unusual for them to offer you a meal, perhaps even a bed for the night, or at least drive miles out of their way to put you on the right track.

Of course their city-slicker siblings say it is merely because they have the time. But it is really because they can be bothered to make the time. Making a buck is of slightly less importance.

In the big city, however, the opposite occurs. I remember how my father's rural neighbour lost his way and ran out of petrol in an elite Johannesburg suburb late at night. He rang numerous door-bells on numerous high walled properties and not a soul would assist him. In fact many threatened to call the police if he did not leave immediately. A little, but not all, of the blame for this attitude has to do with fear of the high crime rate in the city.

City-dwellers in South Africa have developed a much harder attitude to life as they live in the fast lane. Sadly, so often their values system is based on what people own, earn and drive. Their exposure to world trends is greater than their country cousins, which means they tend to lead the country in all the fads and fashions from abroad.

CENSORSHIP
Prudity Towards Nudity

One of the guardians of South Africans' morals is the Censorship Board which is charged with the task of deciding what degree of salaciousness is permissible and to whom. In the good-old-days only some five or six years ago, the board was so conservative and Calvinistic – not surprising since it was made up almost entirely of conservative white Afrikaner men – that even a hint of sex on screen was totally forbidden. Films were cut to ribbons or not allowed to be released at all, men's girlie magazines were heavily censored and pornography was a complete 'no-no'. In fact, even now, if you forget to trash the *Playboy* or *Penthouse* before you get off the plane, you could be liable for a rough ride at customs and even a fine.

But these days, a much more enlightened attitude towards 'relevant' sex on screen is taken by the Board. Films are less often cut and more often branded with an age restriction which means that youths of a given age may not view the film. The result is that the quality and variety of films on circuit is vastly improving.

One of the more amusing ploys of the old-style Censorship Board was the insistence that white women's nipples were taboo, but not the breast. This meant that girlie pin-ups South African style were blessed with star-shaped nipples as every nipple had to be covered with a star! Today those type of magazines seem to get away with being sealed in a clear plastic bag so that inquisitive youths (and miserly adults) in bookstores are not able to flip through the magazines, but have to buy them to read in the privacy of their home.

The Written Word

In the past, the censors also had a go at the written word, more often from a political perspective. For many years one was just unable to get any literature on anything that was vaguely 'red' – that is anything that showed the 'naughty, nasty communists' in a favourable light. Criticism of the South African regime, be it in a scholarly work or a novel, could lead to the book being banned – many great works of literature are only now available.

A classic story bandied about is that when the Censorship Board first heard about the English children's book *Black Beauty* – the life story of a horse, they immediately banned it because they were convinced, without reading it, that it was salacious and disturbing to public morals. Perhaps this story is apocryphal, but it also may well have been true.

FAMILY PLANNING

Family planning is accepted more readily among whites and urbanites than among the rural communities, particularly the tribal Africans. All forms of contraceptives are available and most can be obtained free-of-charge from state clinics. There is a strong resistance from some African men to the use of contraceptives, partly because they see children as proof of their virility and manhood. Unfounded though it was, a more politically motivated resistance to contraception arose when some black communities felt the apartheid government was trying to reduce the population of Africans in an attempt to control the growing racial imbalance in the country.

Sadly the resistance to contraception extends to the using of condoms, with dire consequences for the spread of AIDS.

Family Size

In South Africa like most countries in the world, there is a definite correlation between the standard of living and the birth rate – the higher the quality of life, the smaller the family. Among the urban affluent, two- and three-child families are now the norm; but in the rural families, particularly the tribal African communities, large families of seven, eight and even more children are still common. Since it is the children's responsibility to look after their parents in their old age, they believe that the more children they have, the better care they will receive in their twilight years. Even today in many traditional African families it is the duty of the youngest child to stay home to look after the aged parents, while the other siblings contribute financially to their parents' well-being.

Before the days of easy access to contraception, many white families, especially in the rural areas, were 10 or 12 children strong; but this is fairly rare these days.

ENTERTAINING – SOUTH AFRICAN STYLE

Most people here are friendly and hospitable and invitations like 'you should come 'round for a drink' or 'pop in any time' are often meant sincerely. Casual invitations to a meal, a barbecue *(braai)*, or perhaps to have a drink with friends on your way home from work are common. So don't be a shrinking violet – take them up on their offers. But do it thoughtfully.

If you are unsure that the offer was a serious one, confirm it ahead of time. Because South Africans are very casual, it is wise to phone a day or two in advance. Nothing could be more embarrassing than to turn up on their doorstep and find that they are not expecting you, or worse, not to go then later find out that they had gone to great lengths to invite others to meet you. If the invitation is extended to you on the spur of the moment and for immediate use, just ensure it is not inconvenient and then jump at the chance to enjoy new company.

Many people will invite you to 'pop in' whenever you like. Some will even suggest you need not bother to phone first. This is often well meant, but until you know their family routine, call ahead. Arriving at the children's bath time can be a bit of a strain on your host, or just popping in when they are about to sit down to a meal could be embarrassing to both of you.

Generally, entertaining South African style revolves around a lot of chit-chat and some 'breaking of bread'. If you are invited to do something more formal like play tennis or a game of bridge, you will usually be told in advance. Since there is such a high number of private swimming pools in the country, you could just as well bring along your swimsuit and a towel, especially in the summer.

A Gesture Of Appreciation

If you are being entertained in someone's home for the first time it will certainly be appreciated if you bring a tiny gift along – a bunch of flowers, a box of chocolates, perhaps a bottle of wine. If you come from a land uncommon to your hosts, one of your local delicacies may well be appreciated. Don't go to great lengths or expense, it is not necessary and not expected. Once you are visiting your friends on a much more regular basis it is not necessary to take a gift on each occasion.

When To Leave

It is sometimes not easy to know just when you should take your leave if you are new to the land and the culture. If there are other guests, you can follow their lead, but at the same time, it is not always necessary for you to leave just because the others do. A safe guide is to remember that South Africans are early risers and 11 pm is usually considered a late night. That's not to say that they don't go carousing till the wee hours of the morning, but its not the norm on a weekday night. Over weekends – Friday and Saturday nights – people go out and stay up much later.

A strange South African habit is to walk you to your car. Now don't misconstrue this as thinking they are escorting you off the property to ensure you have really left – it is just a very courteous and friendly gesture. Accept it as that. Another strange South African habit: when you have decided to leave, you will all walk to the door for your farewells, but then stand there or at the car and become involved in yet another conversation. If you are keen to leave, just politely say as much – and indicate you can continue the conversation the next time you meet.

LIFECYCLE EVENTS

Celebrations of lifecycle events are always interesting and usually great fun too, but as an outsider you may feel a little ill at ease if you are not sure what to expect or what to do.

Birthdays

If birthdays are celebrated at all, it is usually informally – perhaps a special dinner at home or in a restaurant, or a party at home. Of course special years like turning 21 or hitting the big 40 are often celebrated with much more aplomb. A birthday gift is the norm, particularly if it is a special birthday, and my advice is, until you know the person well and know their likes and dislikes, give them something consumable – it's hard to go wrong with that.

Weddings

Most often weddings are more formal affairs. The vast majority of urban people have traditional Christian-type weddings with a church ceremony followed by a reception to celebrate the event. Some people choose to get married in a civil ceremony which is usually held in a registry office (part of the law courts) and followed with a reception similar to a church wedding. In most cases you will receive a formal printed wedding invitation which will state the time and place of both the wedding and celebration.

Men are usually expected to wear suits or, if it is a more hip affair, something casual but smart. The same rule of thumb would apply to women – dresses, skirts or suits are the norm, as are smart trousers. Bare shoulders are a 'no-no' in a church but once at the reception, especially if it is held outdoors or in a garden, you could certainly take your jacket off to reveal those lovely shoulders. For wedding etiquette, men should follow the members in the wedding party.

It is the norm to give a wedding gift, and mostly they are taken along to the reception and left for the bridal couple to open in their own time. For some of the more formal weddings, a list of what the couple would like as gifts is placed with a number of department stores and you are able to go and choose something affordable which the bridal couple want and need. It does seem a little cold and calculating, but it does mean that your gift will be appreciated.

Weddings With A Difference

The more traditional communities (particularly the Indian, Malay and tribal Africans) often have culturally specific wedding ceremonies. If you should be invited to a wedding and are not sure of the procedure, ask your host or someone else who is familiar with the ritual exactly what is expected of you. No one will be offended that you don't know, and you will enjoy the occasion so much more if you feel at ease.

Funerals

Like weddings, many funerals follow Christian traditions. Usually a notice is placed in the local newspapers stating the date, time and place of the funeral. It is up to you whether you want to attend or not. Usually relatives, personal friends, family friends, and colleagues will attend. If you are a little uncertain, ask someone for advice.

Black dress is rarely expected at a funeral today, but modest clothes in quiet colours are generally preferred. Many people are cremated, in which case a service is held in the chapel at the crematorium. If there is a burial, there will be a service in the church and then a trip following the hearse to the graveyard.

Quite often tea, drinks or even a light meal may be served after the funeral. In some cases only close friends and family are invited to the reception so watch others for your cue, or wait to be invited, if you are not sure.

Political Funerals

With the violence that has torn South Africa over the years, there have been many mass funerals for people killed in riots. They follow a Christian format, but quite often there are political speeches and acts of political solidarity such as the power salute of a clenched fist in the air and the singing of liberation songs. If ANC members have died, the coffins are often draped with the organisation's black, yellow and green flag. African funerals tend to be far less inhibited and mourners may chant and dance as they join the funeral procession.

Prior to the demise of apartheid, funerals were one of the few places where people could express political solidarity and also demonstrate acts of defiance to the harsh measures enforced during the state of emergency in the 1980s. Sadly this often led to police intervention and frequently people were killed. For a while at the height of the violence there was a cycle of mass funerals, public reactions, state interventions, deaths ... and more funerals.

Tribal Funerals

Tribal African funerals follow very special rituals, particularly as ancestors play a major role in most traditional beliefs. The whole funeral and mourning process is complex and often takes days or even weeks. Africans in the cities take leave from work and go back to the rural areas to bury a relative. If you are the employer, it is important to understand the significance of this request and thus the person's need to take time off.

Also remember that many Africans do not think of family relationships in the same way westerners do. This means that a person may refer to someone as their brother or even father but, in the strictest sense of blood relations, does not actually hold that relationship. Do not fall into the trap, as other unthinking South Africans have, of feeling the person is trying to con you. I have heard of cases where employers have become very angry when an employee has asked to attend the funeral of 'yet another sister or father' – the important thing to remember is whether or not it is a blood brother or a brother by some complex tribal link, it is important for that person to attend the funeral.

CHRISTMAS

Christmas is a major celebration especially because it falls in the middle of the school and summer holidays. Even the most irreligious tends to celebrate it by giving gifts and enjoying a special meal with family and friends. Newcomers to the country and the community are often invited to join in the family festivities of their new-found friends.

69

It may feel rather strange to many, especially anyone from the northern hemisphere, to celebrate Christmas on a hot and sunny day, but that's the way it's done here. And more strange still, is the fact that most South Africans try to approximate that special winter-Christmas feeling with cotton wool and polystyrene chips, the most common imitation of snow. Many South Africans may rarely, if ever, have seen snow! Homes and shops are decorated with Christmas trees, baubles and tinsel. And Father Christmas is a myth enjoyed by children.

Giving of gifts is certainly part of the Christmas ritual, especially to children. The type of gift depends very much on your relationship with the person you are giving it to, but generally something small is appreciated. Don't bankrupt yourself buying gifts – with a little effort and imagination you will find a number of interesting, inexpensive gifts in the shops and also in the plethora of outdoor markets that have sprung up in the last few years.

Sending Christmas greetings cards to friends, family, and business colleagues and contacts is certainly part of the festive spirit. There are many charities that sell a wide variety of cards, but buy them as soon as you see them in the kiosks or stores as the good ones tend to sell-out very quickly.

The major celebration is held during either Christmas eve dinner or Christmas day lunch. And for many, especially in the white communities, a fairly traditional British Christmas meal of roast turkey and ham with vegetables and chicken pie is served. Dessert includes the traditional Christmas pudding with brandy sauce, mince pies and other sweat meats, nuts and dried fruit. This feast is washed down with a celebratory drink like champagne, wine or anything else that takes their fancy.

Certainly a fair number of South Africans have adapted their Christmas meal to suit the summer climate and may perhaps eat a cold meal al fresco around the pool, or have a *braai*. The day after Christmas is also a public holiday, giving everyone time to recover from their over indulgence.

RELIGION

Although the tenets of government in South Africa is based on Christianity, freedom of worship is practised and upheld by the state. Restrictions, however, apply to extremely destructive cults like satanism that are deemed harmful and thus not tolerated.

All the major world religions like Christianity, Judaism, Islam, Buddhism and others are practised in South Africa. There are also some home-grown Christian churches, the two most prominent being the Dutch Reformed Church and its various branches which caters predominantly to the Afrikaner; and the Zionist type churches which are supported almost entirely by the African population.

In the days of apartheid, a number of Christian leaders took up the cudgels against the inhumanity of the system and at some levels, especially in the Christian churches, politics and religion became fairly interwoven.

The Calvinist Route

The Dutch Reformed Church, often called the DRC or the *Nederduitse Gereformeerde Kerk* in Afrikaans, is the largest predominantly white church in the country with over three million members. It is Calvinist in origins and, even today, is still fairly conservative, especially in the rural areas where the churches play an important role in the operation of the community. As an example, you are quite likely to find the dominee, the Dutch Reformed preacher, in prominent positions on school committees and the like as he is held in high esteem by the community.

There are various branches of this church, some more conservative than others. There are also two separate churches in this group, one supported mostly by members of the Coloured community and the other by African Calvinists. Part of the reason for the formation of these two separate churches is that the DRC would only allow whites to be members of its congregation.

71

African Independent Churches

The African Independent Churches (AIC) is a huge grouping of indigenous Christian churches started by Africans themselves because they did not agree with some of the teachings of the missionaries. They are controlled by Africans and have no link to other non-African Christian churches.

Most of these Zionist-type churches have a characteristic form of dress worn to all services by members – long dresses in bold, plain primary colours and capes which are usually white and often decorated with figures like crosses, stars, rings or angels. Divine healing, triple immersion and the imminence of Christ's second coming is taught within the pattern of doctrine and worship in these churches. The laying-on of hands is practised for the purposes of healing as well as for driving out the powers of witchcraft and sorcery.

Some of the AIC followers mix Christian religion with traditional African ancestor worship. Most followers honour and respect ancestors, but do not worship them. Even very westernised Africans, more often than not, will observe a few rites and customs in acts of remembrance and thanksgiving to their ancestors.

The Zionist Christian Church has, by far, the largest following of any of the AICs – estimated at some three million – and is financially self-reliant. It has always been led by the Lekganyane family. The ministering of healing and the promise of prosperity to members is seen as one of the main reasons for attracting adherents, as is its acceptance of polygamy.

Every Easter thousands of supporters flock to Moria, the church's headquarters near Pietersburg in northern Transvaal. Over this period, the roads in this area are extremely congested, particularly with buses, and best avoided unless you are in no hurry!

SOCIAL ETIQUETTE – SOUTH AFRICAN STYLE

Social mores and what is viewed as polite and by whom are very different depending on the community or the company you are in. Most people, especially in the urban and business environment, will follow international norms of polite behaviour, but there are also many little nuances from each different culture that you will surely come across and pick up once you are living and working in South Africa.

Members of one of the African Independent Churches

Although more and more Africans are adopting totally western ways, there may be an occasion when an African man will precede a woman through a door or into an elevator, for example. This should not be seen as a sign of rudeness – in traditional culture this would be totally acceptable. Even if it is not done in your culture, learn to accept that there are many very different cultures in this melting pot.

A trait from African culture that has not yet been swept aside is that of a fairly lengthy greeting before you get down to the purpose of your visit. For example, when you walk into someone's office, begin a meeting with them, or walk onto a factory floor to issue an instruction, it is courteous to first have a discussion with the person about their family or some other matter of social intercourse and only then launch into the business-of-the-day. Similarly when you greet an African – it's not just a 'Hi' or 'Hello', but rather 'Hello, how are you and how is the family?' then wait for a reply. You too will be asked a similar question.

OTHER RANDOM POINTERS:

- Always call an employee by his/her name. If you don't know their name ask for it. Many South Africans are more sensitive than you may expect on this issue because of the disrespect experienced in the past. Never just say 'Hey you'.
- Never call a black person by the name of an animal, as it is seen as very rude, even though you may mean it in a friendly way. For example, do not say, 'Oh you silly monkey, why did you not tell me there was a problem'. In western society this may be seen as a gentle rebuke, but to an African this is considered very rude.
- Quite often it is expected that when you hand something to someone, you should do it with your right hand. This is not always the case but it is worth knowing. Sometimes more traditional people will give or receive things with both hands. It is not expected that you should do the same.

—*Chapter Four*—

WOMEN

Although the status of women in each group in South Africa is different, there is one common factor: women in any group are less than equal to men. As in almost all countries men have dominated the scene, making it necessary for women not only to strive to reach the top in their fields, but to struggle against male domination as well.

ROOTED IN THE LAW

Unlike women in many modern democracies where legislation in recent decades has enforced equality, South African women are still disadvantaged to some extent by discrimination rooted in the legal system. However, more recently, and with ever growing force, women have decided not to accept this and are working through various organisations to change their situation.

Consequently, married women now have almost the same status as their husbands, are allowed separate taxation, and maternity benefits and rights. An example of success born of pressure from women's movements is the change in the divorce laws which now give women a much fairer deal. A wife's contribution to the home and family is now taken into account in the divorce settlement, she has access to her husband's pension fund even if she is divorced from him, and does not automatically gain custody of the children. This last issue makes the law more fair for both parties.

African women can elect to use either customary or western law but many, especially in the rural areas, choose tribal law as it is their cultural heritage. With the newly altered civil law, a woman's marital status is now equal to her husband's. Customary marriage laws, however, can disadvantage women as, for example, they limit their rights to own property and also allow polygamy.

BUSINESS: THE TOUGHEST BARRIERS

Although a fairly high number of white women have chosen to be home makers, (not too strenuous a task as many are able to afford full-time domestic help) the role of professional working women has become ever more important to the economy. This was first felt in the boom years of the '70s and early '80s when demand outstripped supply of skilled professionals, and also because of the emigration of large numbers of professionals due to the civil unrest. An ever-increasing number of professional working women have their foot in the door, but the battle against sexual and, in the case of black women, colour discrimination is far from over.

Attitudes to women in business are slowly changing, but South Africa still lags the rest of the industrialised world in realising women are an essential part of the work force, so important that the economy cannot operate without their contribution. Although some companies outwardly agree to equal opportunities, most have very few if any women in senior management or at board level. From discussions with the few women nearing the top of the pile in the business community, I have discovered that life is certainly not easy, with many male peers belittling and patronising them, sometimes without even being aware of it. Women say that the 'glass ceiling', an undeclared barrier to the highest ranks, does exist and they confirm that to succeed equally they have to do better than their male peers.

This is a sad state of affairs since the country's severe managerial shortage could be redressed or even overcome with the employment of women. The dice is loaded against black businesswomen even more as they have to contend with cultural discrimination from their own community and racial discrimination from other communities.

More than 40 years ago the Johannesburg Business and Professional Women's Club was founded and is still in full swing. A Business Woman of the Year award is used to encourage women achievers and give status to their achievements.

WOMEN IN THE WORKPLACE

Women comprise 40% of the workforce. Yet, it is only in the more senior positions or in companies employing more white-collar workers that conditions for women have improved. In most instances the working class woman has much less cooperation from her employer and her workplace is less woman-friendly. Less attention is paid to her needs born of all the other demands made on her by her family and home life, and especially the male chauvinism in society.

Because of this, an ever-increasing number of women are leaving their jobs and running their own businesses to afford themselves more flexibility – and their success rate is very high. For newcomers to the country who are not too keen to sit at home, this is often a good way of getting down to work while at the same time being free to attend to the matters of setting up a new home and a new way of living.

DOMESTIC WORKERS

Most working women are there because their income is essential to the well-being of their families. In the rural areas, African women find their major source of employment as farm labourers; and in the cities they are mainly employed as domestic workers, although an increasing number of women are entering the service industry and many other jobs and professions now, too.

Today there are over two million domestic workers in the country, mainly employed by affluent whites, although more and more middle-class blacks also have househelp. Many work full-time for one family and usually live with the family they work for, while others work as part-timers, or chars, working one to two days a week – in two or three different homes. In rural areas domestic workers are employed in farm homesteads too.

Although they are slowly unionising under the South African Domestic Workers' Union, they are still among the most exploited group in the country. Very long working hours, unfair dismissal, very little or no annual leave are some of their major grievances. Until the demise of apartheid, laws forbade live-in domestic workers from having their children or husbands live with them if they were working for white families. This often led to a situation where women cared for their employer's children while their own children were looked after by grandparents or other relatives in the townships or homelands. They may only have seen their children a few times a year.

The introduction of the Labour Relations Act of 1995 covered working conditions for all employees, including domestic workers and farm labourers, offering employees protection not experienced in the past. The Basic Conditions of Employment Act of 1998 further defined the relationship between employers and employees and takes precedence over all other labour legislation.

THE WOMEN'S FRONT

Today there are many women's organisations in South Africa stretching from the overtly political and politicised to the most apolitical charity fundraisers. From the ultra-left to the radical right, there are some seventy of the most important organisations united under the Women's National Coalition, with a mandate to ensure that women's rights are well respected and protected in the new South Africa, and particularly in the new constitution.

Here is a small sample of some of the women's organisations you may well like to know, but once you are in the country it will be much easier for you to link up with other organisations in your residential area.

- **Women's League of the ANC** Re-established in 1991 after being banned for some 30 years, it has a more political or socio-political bent. It now aims to formulate the ANC's on-going policy of women's liberation and the promotion of women's development, among many other issues.

  It is the ANC's stated policy to ensure the future state of South Africa is based on non-sexism and non-racism. Gender sensitivity is a frequently used expression in ANC corridors and the incorporation of gender equality into the future Bill of Rights is definitely on their agenda. The ANC's Emancipation Commission, consisting of women and men, has been set up to look at women's rights and gender equality within the organisation, as well as to monitor its policy and employment practices regarding women. It also takes a broader look at women's issues within the country and works hand-in-hand with the Women's Charter campaign.

- **Women For Peace** This group was formed in the mid-1970s for women of all races who felt they could not sit around and watch their country in crisis after the student uprisings. The organisation is committed to peace through communication across the cultural divides.

- **Black Sash** The courageous women of this group draw public attention to issues with silent, non-violent public demonstrations. They also run advice offices throughout the country to help people still suffering from the consequences of apartheid. Fundraising is also part of their agenda.

SOME NON-POLITICAL GROUPS ARE:
- **South African National Consumer Union**
- **South African Co-ordinating Consumer Council's Women's Bureau** This group concentrates on women's and consumer issues.
- *Suid Afrikaanse Vroue Federasie*
- *Federale Vroueraad Volksbeleging*

The above two groups are organised along more cultural lines. Both aimed at Afrikaner women and their needs, but are certainly not mutually exclusive to Afrikaners. The *Vroue Federasie* has a very good reputation for organising support for poor and under-privileged people, particularly children.

MALE CHAUVINISTS – NOT A DYING BREED
Male chauvinism is alive and well in South Africa – in all communities. So if you come from a society where MCPs are scarce, you are in for a bit of a shock. On one level most men are overtly polite and courteous to women, and as with chauvinism, the courtesy comes in different forms depending on the person's cultural heritage. My advice is to accept gracefully the fact that men may open the car door for you, stand up to greet you when you enter a room, or let you proceed them through a door.

But there are other acts of a more overtly belittling manner – such as referring to businesswomen as 'girls' or addressing a member of staff, even a senior one, as 'my dear girl', or 'my young girl'. In a meeting, men will often expect the woman who might be their equal if not their senior, to serve them tea.

Of a more serious nature, a number of women in companies and corporations report often being deliberately excluded from discussions where their input is essential, or where the decisions being made will directly affect the division they are responsible for. One very senior woman in a major computer company related a very amusing, if irritating experience. She, the only woman, and a number of male colleagues were having a major strategy planning meeting. When they adjourned for a tea break, the men continued the discussion in the toilet while they were relieving themselves. When they reconvened the meeting, she was generally confused and felt that she had been left behind in the discussion!

WHO HOLDS THE REINS?

In all fields in South Africa – business, politics, home life – the proportion of male decision-makers in relation to female decision-makers is very high. This is partly because women are so accustomed to taking a back seat that they don't push to be in the front line. This certainly applies more to white women than black women as there have been many black women involved in the liberation struggle.

Even at the negotiating forum for the new democratic constitution for South Africa, there are far too few women making inputs and far too few women's issues being heard. It is not fair to lay all the blame at the feet of South African men. Despite the man-made hurdles, it is up to our women in all societies to stand up and be counted.

MEN IN THE HOME

Most South African men are totally unwilling to do domestic chores, household shopping and the like. Some of this is because they have wives who do not work and hence they feel it is the 'wife's job'. But more often the resistance goes deeper as men feel it is 'women's work' and therefore beneath them to get involved in it. It's a perception that is changing – but very, very slowly.

A rather humorous example of this happened to a single businesswomen friend recently. The man she has been seeing for some months (who is divorced) ran out of toothpaste. Instead of going to the nearest emergency pharmacy (since it was after working hours), he drove right across town to borrow some from her. He did this two nights in

Women, particularly white women, have to empower themselves in their fight for equality and ensure a greater role in the decision-making process of the new South Africa.

succession! In the past, no doubt, his wife was responsible for all domestic matters including seeing that the toothpaste did not run out. Imagine his surprise when my friend did not rush out to buy him more toothpaste.

A DEEP-ROOTED VIEW

Among many South Africans, particularly men, there is a deep-rooted belief that women only work 'if they have to'. It often comes as quite a shock to them when they learn that many women, just like the men, work for personal fulfilment; to support or help support their families; to make their own decisions, and be in control of their own lives.

If you are from countries that have long-since closed these type of debates, you may find that having to re-invent the wheel, so to speak, is rather trying. For the good of all, don't hold your tongue – educate the ignorant!

Women crocheting a table cloth for sale to the public – an example of a small business. Hence, traditional female skills are turned into income earners that help to sustain the family.

Chapter Five

COMMUNICATION

English is certainly the lingua franca in South Africa. But don't for one minute think that means that everyone can understand English, or that you will understand their English – well, not easily, anyway. There is a host of other languages spoken by various groups in the country – African languages, Indian languages, various European languages and Afrikaans (home-made by the early Boer settlers).

There are dialects within languages and lingoes of many sub-cultures, like *tsotsi taal* or 'jive talk'. Colour, expressiveness and vivacity are co-partners in South Africa's verbal communication, probably because people are often talking across a language and cultural barrier.

It will be almost impossible for you to master all or even most of South Africa's vast array of languages, but you can certainly have fun trying – and you will so often endear yourself to so many people if you make the effort to learn at least something of their language.

A TOWER OF BABEL

South Africa is certainly a land of linguistic diversity with 14 main groups of languages and 24 sizeable 'home languages' or languages spoken solely or predominantly in the home. The majority of these languages are African and thus, as a newcomer to this country, you are unlikely to have learned or even heard many of them. Don't feel alone because many white South Africans haven't either, thanks in most part to the stringency of apartheid, and the fact that African languages have only been taught in some of the 'white' schools, mostly in the last decade or less.

Besides English, Afrikaans and some African languages, most South Africans have not learned languages from anywhere else in the world, except a privileged few who may have studied traditional Western European languages at school or university.

THE OFFICIAL LANGUAGES

South Africa has 11 official languages, although English is accepted as the common medium for business and, to a large degree, education as well. This means that should you choose to, you can receive communication from government and other official sources in whichever of the 11 languages you prefer, but, in practice, English and three or four of the main languages seem the most commonly used.

It also means that most South Africans can speak more than one of the official languages and many speak English, but not always perfectly, so be patient, especially when it is obvious that it is not the speaker's native tongue.

More than 57% of all South Africans can speak English, not necessarily perfectly, nor as a first or home language, but still well enough for you to communicate with them in English. Of course accents and even colloquial words may vary but they certainly add flavour, flair and no doubt a good dose of confusion and humour to your interaction with locals.

An equivalent amount of South Africans speak Afrikaans, but it is likely that the percentage could drop as ever more political refugees return home – most have learned English while living abroad. As the country re-enters the international community after years of being shunned, there is a growing realisation among South Africans that English is the language of international communication, especially in the business world.

HOME LANGUAGES

Home languages are those spoken most often and by choice in homes. The users of the country's 10 major African languages jointly make up at least 67% of the population. Of this group, over six million people speak Zulu as a first home language which accounts for 24.5% of the population! About 20% of the population speak Afrikaans at home which translates into nearly five million people. Contrary to many foreigners' beliefs, a large number of Afrikaans speakers are not white. Instead, a very high percentage of the Coloured population speaks Afrikaans as a first language.

Xhosa is the next most popular home language with some 11.6% of the population using it. English clocks in at just over 11%, having a much lower concentration throughout the rural areas compared to the metropolitan areas. These include Cape Town, the Durban-Pinetown area and the vast metropolitan area of greater Johannesburg (which is also called the PWV area as it encompassed the geographic triangle of Pretoria, Johannesburg and Witwatersrand, and Vereeniging).

Asian languages (which includes Tamil, Hindi, Telugu, Gujarati, Urdu and Chinese) are spoken by only 0.4% of the population. Slightly more than 0.5% of the locals speak a European language other than English as a first language. These languages include Dutch, French, German Greek, Italian and Portuguese.

ENGLISH

English became the official language in 1910, making the Boers unhappy so by 1925 they had seen to it that Afrikaans had become the second and equal official language. Strange that no one seemed to consider the vast bulk of the population who did not see either of those languages as their own. But such was the colonial era.

Today, however, vast numbers of the population use either or both English and Afrikaans as a means of cross-cultural communication. English has also become the medium of instruction in most schools, universities and other tertiary institutions. If schools choose another language as a medium of instruction, English is almost always learned as a second language.

Early British Origins

With major depression and unemployment in England after the end of the Napoleonic Wars, and the reduction of the armed forces which put thousands out of work, it seemed an easy choice for some 5 000 immigrants to sail towards the African sunset, in 1820.

They arrived in what is now called Port Elizabeth, on the eastern seaboard. At that time, these newcomers made up over 10% of the English-speaking population, and as they slowly spread into the interior of the country during the 19th century, they took the language with them. Hence, English became a major communicating force across the country, particularly after the establishment of Port Natal (now the sprawling city of Durban) in 1825, the British annexation of Transvaal in 1877, and the gold rush in 1886.

With the establishment of the Union of South Africa in 1910, English and Dutch were made the official languages, with Afrikaans superseding Dutch only in 1925. English is spoken across the cultural and racial spectrum in South Africa. Even as a first home language, it is spoken by Asians, blacks, Coloureds, and a fair portion of the white community.

With the British occupation of the Cape in 1795, the roots for an English-speaking community were put down and certainly hit fertile soil. Cape Town today still has a strong English, albeit South African English, flavour.

South African English: A Language of its Own

No language is static, and those in new and developing countries are often the most creative. South African English is no exception, being influenced by the many other languages being spoken in the country, especially Cape Dutch. Many words were assimilated, especially for all new things that the English had certainly not encountered in their own land.

Today the compilers and publishers of the world famous Oxford Dictionaries have collated a special *South African English Dictionary*. Even in the traditional *Oxford Dictionary* there are a number of South African English words that have become common usage by all English speakers. Examples are: 'kraal' (pronounced 'krahl'), a noun meaning 'South African village of huts enclosed by fence, or enclosure for cattle and sheep'; and 'trek' which is a verb of distinctly South African origin meaning to 'pull a load, travel by ox-wagon, migrate, proceed slowly' and it originates from the early settlers who 'trekked' into the interior, ironically, to escape the English!

As the use of English spread in the sub-continent, words of even more diverse origins were assimilated from Arabic, French, German, Malay, Portuguese and Persian. The distance in time and culture between South Africa and the United Kingdom isolated African English from its source. South African English soon developed very regionalised characteristics especially in vocabulary, pronunciation and idiom. The grammatical construction of the language, however, is still the same as traditional British English.

The Queen's English? Not

Although written English in South Africa is the same as most other English-speaking countries, pronunciations and accents are quite a different matter. As a newcomer you could well be forgiven for not even knowing it was the Queen's tongue you were hearing.

In large measure, the South African English accent is hard and fairly flat. A lot of its tone may well come from living in such close proximity to Afrikaans, but the different accent is also because the language has grown up in its own time and space – and at great distance from the motherland.

Accents: A symbol of class to some, but a pain to others.

The Colonialist Wanna-Be

There are a few remaining wanna-be colonialists, quite often found in Natal Province, who try so hard to speak English 'like their great and glorious Queen' that they tend to outdo even the most 'hot potato in the mouth' British. In fact, a recent British visitor told me she had never heard such exaggerated pronunciations anywhere in her home-land as those encountered on her trip to Durban!

AFRIKAANS

The ground for the beginnings of the a new language, Afrikaans, were set in 1652 when the Dutch East India Company established a halfway

89

house at the Cape. Those first Dutch settlers came into contact with the languages spoken by the indigenous Khoi people and those of the later settlers – Malay, English, French and Portuguese. Linguistics boffins here think that by 1800 or at latest 1850, Afrikaans had developed, in most part, into the language it is today.

The majority of the Afrikaans vocabulary is derived from Dutch, but changed quite substantially, especially in pronunciation. Although there are strong grammatical similarities between Afrikaans and Dutch, it has a far less complex structure, making it a fairly easy language to learn.

Also, a great number of words were coined, especially for local plants and animals. Because of the mixed racial origins of the Afrikaner, the language has borrowed words from almost all the cultures which make up South Africa's diversity. There are words from African languages like '*mampara*' which means 'an untrained or stupid person' and most often is used as a form of gentle rebuke; or '*babelas*' from the Nguni language which means 'hangover'.

Words of English, French, German, Malay and Portuguese origin are also liberally sprinkled throughout Afrikaans. Because of their mixed backgrounds, the Coloured population had considerable influence in shaping the Afrikaans vocabulary as it is used today.

Afrikaans: Not Only The Language Of The Boers

In the early years of jockeying for power in South Africa, Afrikaans struggled against English and Dutch, the early colonial powers, for recognition as a medium of cultural expression. But by the beginning of the 20th century it was generally recognised as a cultural language and vernacular. In 1933 the Bible was translated into Afrikaans, which did a lot not only to standardise the language but enhance its credibility among the many Boers, Coloureds and others who spoke it. Of course with the coming to power of the apartheid regime it received extensive, and in the views of many, undue support from the state.

Afrikaans is now used extensively on radio and TV and has become the language of religion, education, economics and science. There are Afrikaans language newspapers across a broad political spectrum, as well as many famous Afrikaans authors of all races. The most world renowned being Andre Brink who started writing solely in Afrikaans, but who now writes in English as well.

Enforced Afrikaans: A Spark In Dry Tinder

Although racially discriminating policies were the underlying cause of the Soweto riots in 1976, the actual tinder that drove the students to rebellion was the insistence by the government that African students should study subjects such as maths or geography in Afrikaans rather than English or their native tongue, which they used in the past.

Surrounded By Afrikaans

In some of the western and south-western areas of the Cape Province as many as 80% of the people speak Afrikaans as a home language. Apart from the white Afrikaners, this region has a large number of Coloured communities, known often as the 'Brown Afrikaners', who speak the language fluently.

In other parts of the country the density of Afrikaans speakers is only some 20% or less, particularly in the urban areas. Of course a very large number of the rural white farmers speak Afrikaans especially in the two ex-Boer republics, Orange Free State and Transvaal.

Language Rivalry

In the early days, Afrikaans was looked down upon by both Dutch and English speakers as it was seen as merely a dialect and language of the poor whites. Hence, the Afrikaners' feelings of inferiority and persecution in the early days of their culture and language development was sharply contrasted by the arrogance of the Calvinistic and conservative British whose views on life isolated them from world opinion and change.

Today as barriers on all fronts come tumbling down, the language rivalry is dwindling, except among the few staunch conservatives.

AFRICAN LANGUAGES – THE GREAT DIVIDE

The subject of African languages is enormously complicated, especially in terms of the complexity of the different language groups, the relationships between some languages and the intermixing of the groups and languages. So here I will give a very simplified and potted account to begin your understanding of the African languages.

The four major African language groups in South Africa are: the Nguni (made up of Northern Ndebele, Southern Ndebele, Siswati, Xhosa and Zulu), the Sotho (Northern Sotho, Southern Sotho and Tswana), the Tsonga and the Venda.

The linguistic differences between the four language groups are so great that they are mutually unintelligible from group to group, while the languages within a group are closely related for a speaker of one language to understand the other.

There are some 90 different dialects of these 10 major languages, and then add the cross-cultural developments like 'Townie Sotho', an urban-mixed lingua franca, no doubt, developed because people have been thrown together in the sprawling urban townships like Soweto.

But don't let this linguistic stuff fool you – the vast majority of African South Africans can communicate in many, if not all, of the prevalent African languages there!

An Overview of the African Languages:
Nguni:

Ndebele The Northern Ndebele probably originated in Zimbabwe, mingled a bit with the Swazi's from Swaziland, and then settled north of Pretoria. Some of their dialect is influenced by Sotho, Afrikaans and English. The Southern Ndebele lived in the Pretoria area as early as 1650 and probably came from Natal originally. The strong sense of Southern Ndebele identity is reinforced by their distinctive mural art and beadwork. As a written language it is still quite new with only a few published books.

Siswati Not dissimilar to Zulu, it is mostly spoken in the areas near Swaziland where the tribe is predominant. The first Siswati catechism and then the Bible appeared in 1846.

Xhosa From the regions along the east coast, before the 16th century, they moved down the coast towards Cape Town. Along the way they met the Khoi people and adopted some of the words and the click sound, made famous by singer Miriam Makeba. Some Khoi words in Xhosa are *igusha* (sheep) and *iiqgira* (diviner) and a word with a click sound – *gei-xa* (magic). It was also influenced by Dutch and English – *ijoni*, meaning 'soldier', is from the British word 'Johnny'. Most written Xhosa originates from 1857 and is somewhat different from the spoken word.

Zulus Like the Xhosa, they have inhabited regions of the east coast of South Africa since the 16th century. Now a very high percentage live in the Durban and other outlying Natal areas. Zulu, which has signs of Afrikaans influence and even greater English influence in vocabulary, is a fairly uniform language with few regional differences. It became a written language in the 1850s. It is more than a regional language as it is the most widely spoken African language in the land, and is used as the African lingua franca from Natal to Zimbabwe.

Sotho (Northern and Southern): About 300 years ago the Pedi empire, later called Northern Sotho, was founded. By the mid-1800s their language appeared in the written form. It is sometimes also called Sepedi and is spoken most in Lebowa, a homeland in northern Transvaal. Southern Sotho, spoken mostly in the areas of the Orange Free State and the Qwaqwa homeland, became a written language with the assistance of the French missionaries in the mid-1800s. As a result, there are a few French words on loan in Southern Sotho, as well as a host more from English and Afrikaans.

Tswana: Not only is Tswana spoken in South Africa, but it is also the official language of its northern neighbour, Botswana. The history of the Tswanas, from as early as the 17th century, has been one of fragmentation and amalgamation, of war and peace, of losing and regaining independence. The New Testament, translated in 1840, seems to be one of the earlier records of the written language.

Tsonga: Spoken in Mozambique and parts of Zimbabwe, present-day Tsonga is a blend of Zulu and the original Tsonga dialects.

Venda: These people crossed the Limpopo River from Zimbabwe into South Africa in about 1730, and have lived in the northern Transvaal ever since. It is a homogenous language with only slight dialect variations.

THE OTHER GROUPS

Apart from the Dutch and the English, a number of other immigrants from Europe and the East impacted on South Africa's languages, cultures and creeds.

The most prolific early immigrants after the Dutch and English were the French Huguenots. They were Protestant refugees who landed at the Cape in 1688, adding their touch to the local languages, especially Afrikaans. Other European immigrants were the Germans, Greeks, Italians and Portuguese.

In 1860 the first Indians arrived in South Africa to work on the sugar plantations, importing a variety of indigenous languages which are still spoken by many at home. The Indian community has a near perfect command of the English language, which in many instances can be called a first language as well. Among the younger generations, quite often it is their first home language.

The first Chinese arrived in South Africa after the Anglo-Boer War, and by 1906 some 50 000 were working here. Later they were all repatriated. A second small group arrived in the 1920s and settled down. Their native tongue is most often Hakka or Cantonese, but almost all South African-born Chinese speak excellent English. Sadly, among the younger generation, this has often been to the neglect of their mother tongue.

LITERACY: A SADLY LACKING SKILL

Literacy in South Africa is in a sad state of affairs! Estimates of between 33% and 55% of the adult black population is illiterate. Thanks in great measure to apartheid's privileges, the adult white population is fully literate. Both the Indian and Coloured populations have high literacy levels of 80% and 69% respectively. Because of traditional cultural beliefs, the Indian community shows a significant, but decreasing, number of illiterate women. In the Coloured community there is a striking difference between the high literacy rate in urban areas and a very low literacy level in the rural areas.

And It Gets Worse

Only a decade ago, slightly fewer than 12 million people in South Africa over 15 years old were literate in ANY language! And it is felt that this has not changed much today. The highest percentage of literate people live in the four major metropolitan areas: the PWV, the Durban-Pietermaritzburg region, Port Elizabeth-Uitenhage area and the greater Cape Town region.

INTER-PERSONAL COMMUNICATION
Greetings

There are ever so many different ways of greeting people in South Africa and much of it depends on the culture and language of the person concerned. But as a general rule, do greet people whenever and wherever possible – 99 times out of a 100, it is worth the effort.

Any traditionally western person is quite accustomed to the quick 'good morning' or 'good afternoon' as you rush by. In the more traditional African societies much more importance is placed on greeting someone and exchanging a few pleasantries, so it may well be necessary to say a bit more than a rushed 'good day' by adding a few questions like 'Is all well today?' or 'Is your family well?' or anything else that crosses your mind – and do remember to await the reply and to answer the questions that are put to you. It costs very little time, yet builds strong bridges and working relationships.

The Handshake And Beyond

When meeting a person for the first time, men are almost always expected to shake hands – just grasp right hand to right hand and shake. More often women meeting men follow this ritual too, while women meeting women may shake hands or may just nod an acknowledgement.

In a social situation, once you are more familiar with people, you may find that men will greet women friends with a kiss on the cheek, while they will greet each other with a handshake, and the more avant garde will give each other a hug. In a business environment it is appropriate for women to greet male colleagues with either a nod or a handshake. A kiss would be a little too familiar for the business community.

The African Handshake

This is used cross-racially, and especially when greeting blacks, to indicate solidarity and affiliation with the non-racial politics of the country. For example, I use it when I meet members of the ANC hierarchy, or even when greeting my black postman. First you shake in the western way, then without letting go slip your hand around each other's thumbs, then back again into the traditional grasp.

Swearing Is A 'No-No' But ...

Generally swearing is not acceptable in South African society, but as the country opens up more and more to the international world, a lot of the strict Calvinistic mores are being pushed aside.

Swearing in front of women and children is certainly frowned on, while in all-male company swear words are more frequently sprinkled over a conversation. But circumstances and situations vary according to the group you are with, the age, your familiarity with each other and a host of other factors. A safe rule is not to swear at all until you know the people you are with well enough, then you will be able to gauge for yourself.

On the odd occasion you may be shocked to hear someone using quite foul language in a situation where it is certainly inappropriate. Your best route is to ignore it, as very often people are not speaking their mother tongue, and may thus use swear words they have heard but have very little grasp of the real meaning, implication or offensiveness.

Words like 'damn' or 'blasted', 'Oh god', and 'Jesus' which is often pronounced 'jeez' do not usually cause major offence; but left out of your conversation will certainly make integration easier. The F-word is certainly a 'no-no' until you are very familiar with your crowd, and even then it is best avoided. That's not to say you won't see and hear it used both in company and in the movies, so if it offends you be prepared to shut your ears a little.

KALEIDOSCOPE OF COLOUR

Because of the cultural melting pot that is South Africa, there are a multitude of words that have grown up with this fairly young country. Sometimes they are bastardisations of words from other languages, and as such may mean something quite different from their original meaning in their original land. A classic example is the phrase 'Just now' which in South Africa means at some stage in the not-too-distant future. 'I'll see you just now' means they will meet you in a short while. It does NOT mean what is says, which is 'immediately'!

There are also many words that are typically South African, and although used in English conversation, it may be words a native English speaker may never have heard before. There are a few books and dictionaries to help you get a handle on the local lingo, but if in doubt, just ask the speaker to explain – there will be 'no hard feelings' which means they will not be offended at all by your asking the meaning of a word or phrase.

COMMON SOUTH AFRICAN WORDS USED CROSS-CULTURALLY:

A frostie A beer.

A shebeen This is a township pub, and a 'shebeen queen', most often, is the mama who owns and runs it. Some shebeens are quite informal arrangements in the backroom of someone's home, but more recently many have gained liquor licences and are members of the Taverners Association.

A skollie Refers to someone who is untrustworthy, a scoundrel.

Babelas This means hangover and, although of Nguni origin, it is used and understood by all.

Black Sash This is a women's organisation that has stood up to the inequities of apartheid for many decades. In the past when members held passive demonstrations they wore a black sash across their torso, hence the organisation adopted the name.

Biltong A speciality snack of spiced and sun-dried meat, quite often venison. An acquired taste according to many immigrants!

Bobbejaan spanner It is a direct translation into Afrikaans from the words 'monkey wrench', a tool.

Bobotie This is thought to be of Malay and/or Dutch origin and is a traditional Afrikaans dish made of minced meat, curry and other spices.

Bundu Used in English to mean 'grassland', it is derived from a Shona word of the same meaning.

Camp 'Kamp' in Afrikaans, meaning an enclosed portion of a farm, a field or paddock for animals.

Chicken run This is a local version of a chicken coop, but is also a colloquial and fairly new term for the action of emigrating because of the political instability.

Cocopan This is a fairly squat-shaped tipcart on rails used in the mining industry. It is a word of Nguni origin, perhaps coming from the word *'ghoekoe'* which means 'hedgehog' whose shape is similar to this specialised rail truck.

Fanagalo It means 'do it like this' and it comes from over simplifying a string of words made up of English, Afrikaans and various African words. It is used to communicate across many cultural divides, especially on the mines.

Fundi Used in English to mean well-informed, or an expert on a particular subject. It comes from an abbreviation of the Zulu word *'umfundisi'*, which means teacher or minister.

Ghoen Apparently derived from Malay or Hottentot, it is schoolboy slang for a big and heavy steel marble, used in certain games of marbles.

Green mamba Colloquially this means a peppermint liqueur and has been adopted from the Nguni word. Literally 'mamba' is the name of a type of deadly snake.

Mampara Of bantu origins it is used colloquially to mean an untrained or stupid person. Mostly it is used as a form of gentle rebuke or even fondness, as in 'You silly mampara'.

Mebos Probably of Arabic origins, mebos is minced, dried apricot formed into little cakes. It is a Boer delicacy or sweet/candy.

Pampoen A word of Dutch origin used in Afrikaans literally to mean 'pumpkin', but also used colloquially and humorously to mean 'blockhead' or 'bumpkin'.

Putu Of Nguni and possibly Dutch origins, it means a fairly stiff porridge made from maize meal, which is also called 'mealie meal'.

Queen In this instance it does not refer to royalty, but is a colloquialism for barren female animals and is derived from the Dutch word 'kween' of the same meaning.

Rondawel A circular, thatched room or cottage. Of Dutch origin, this word is used in both South African English and in Afrikaans.

Smous A colloquial Afrikaans word for 'hawker', but it is quite often used in English, and at times is used metaphorically meaning 'touting something around'.

Spoor The track of a person, animal or vehicle. This word is Afrikaans, but used in English too.

Twak This a contraction of the Dutch and Afrikaans word *'tabak'* which means tobacco. It is also used colloquially in a dismissive manner to mean that you think something is nonsense.

Witblitz A potent, local and usually home-made brew. Rather like European schnapps, drink it at your peril! Literally it means 'white lightning', and much more than a thimble-full could well strike you down without warning. The word has Dutch and Afrikaans origins, but is used colloquially by anyone who knows the drink.

SOUTH AFRICAN EXPRESSIONS:

A bakkie A small truck or van, the farmers' most favoured form of transport.

A couple of As in 'Give me a couple of minutes' meaning wait a few minutes for me. Generally it is used to mean 'a few' not 'two'. Even when buying fruit a South African would say 'I'll have a couple of bananas, please.'

A flick A very colloquial word for film show or the movies.

Ag shame An expression of sympathy for someone or something as in 'Ag shame, you have been ill.'

Girl/Boy. When not used in their normal sense, these words often refer to a black maid/domestic worker/gardener/office messenger. They are seen as derogative and certainly politically incorrect. It is highly advisable not to use them at all, even if you hear other South Africans doing so.

Ja Afrikaans for 'yes', but it is used by all to mean 'yes'.

Ja nee Although these are two Afrikaans words meaning 'yes' and 'no' respectively, as a phrase it is used in English to show ambiguity, and it can be used to begin a reply. If you ask someone how they enjoyed the rugby match, they could reply 'Ja nee it was good' which means 'It was good but...'

Ja well, no fine This is an opener or even a conversation closer. It doesn't really mean much but is seen as chatty.

My China Meaning 'my friend' or 'good buddy' As does 'okes' (pronounced 'oaks'), like the tree, and usually meaning 'the guys' (not women).

Offload This means to unload.

Or whatever This is often used when someone has run out of words, ideas or even arguments. When making arrangements for the evening, someone may say 'We can go to the flicks (the movies), the pub, have a meal, or whatever...'; then it is your chance to add any suggestions if you wish.

Sis An expression of disgust and not to be used in very polite company. For example: 'Sis, look at the dirt on the floor'. It can be used to express dislike of food, but that is rude.

So long A colloquial way of saying 'goodbye' or 'cheers' and does have the connotation of 'we will see you again soon'. Also the phrase means 'in the mean time' and can be used in 'I'm going home so long' indicating that the person is going home while you, in the mean time, will do something else.

Tackies Sneakers or tennis shoes.

Voetsak An impolite word and should only be used on animals, and even then not within earshot of very polite company. It is a means of telling dogs, especially, to 'go away'. Strangely, dogs everywhere in the world seem to understand this. The word is derived from an old Afrikaans/Dutch expression *'Voort se ek'* which literally means 'I say go ahead/away'.

Wiff Used as a replacement for 'with'. Some South Africans, especially Afrikaans speakers tend to have a problem pronouncing 'th' in English – hence 'with' becomes 'wiff', or 'the' becomes 'va'.

There is also quite a common phrase, 'Can I come with' which means that they would like to or are going to join you in wherever you're going.

ACRONYMS:

South Africa is not a particularly acronym-loaded land. But there are a few, and so often they are taken for granted by the locals that they can leave a newcomer totally confused. The most common ones are:

ANC The African National Congress.

COSATU It stands for Congress of South African Trades Unions and is the umbrella body for most of the trade unions.

GPO More often in writing than in the spoken word, this means 'post office'.

ANGLO More often than not it refers, not to anything of English origin, but to the country's largest corporation, Anglo American Corporation.

Chapter Six

SETTLING DOWN?

This chapter gives you an overview of what it's like being a migrant or expat. The broad outlines of immigration and residency will be discussed, as will the best ways to settle down and become 'one of them'. But once you have decided to take the 'great leap' it is essential you contact the correct authorities for detailed guidance and information. Policies, laws and customs duties change continuously. The South African Embassy or Consulate in your country is the best place to start. If there isn't one, you can write to the Secretary for Immigration, Department of Home Affairs, P O Box 2072, Pretoria 0001, South Africa.

APARTHEID: EFFECTS ON IMMIGRATION

With the onset of apartheid many people did not wish to come to South Africa, many more deemed 'not white' by the authorities were not welcome. At various stages during the 40-odd years of apartheid rule, Indians, Chinese and other Asians were unwelcome.

Bizarre as it may seem, the Japanese were deemed 'honorary whites'! No doubt their economic might and the vast amount of trade they were doing with South Africa at that time had some role to play in their 'honorary' title. But in the 1980s, when practically the whole world united against apartheid, the Japanese joined in and cut their links too. Now, of course, almost all diplomatic links with the 'new' South Africa have been re-established.

Africans were also not looked on kindly, except as migrant workers for the mines. But this was certainly not immigration. Mine workers were recruited in neighbouring countries like Lesotho, Swaziland, Mozambique and Malawi. They worked under contract and were sent home once their contracts were over. Their families were never allowed to join them and a portion of their salary was paid directly to their government.

A NEW VIEW

Obviously with the sweeping away of apartheid laws, immigrants are now being judged on the contributions they can make to the future of the new South Africa, rather than the colour of their skin.

The South African government wants to broaden the country's economic base and therefore any would-be immigrant is judged by his possible contribution to the economy. South Africa does have certain skills shortages and immigrants in those categories are obviously given preference. Like Australia, the categories change continuously so it is essential you find out which ones are in demand at the time you are considering moving to South Africa.

In the turmoil of the student uprisings in the 1970s and the anti-apartheid violence of the 1980s, many South Africans emigrated, leaving the country with a dearth of skilled manpower and management personnel. There have been times, and I am sure there will be times again, when South Africa will make moves to encourage skilled immigrants to settle and impart their knowledge to the many who have not had the privilege of a good education. Currently with the long recession and hence the large-scale unemployment, active moves to encourage immigration have been curbed. This does not, however, mean that immigration itself has been curbed.

ALIEN – THAT'S YOU
If you are faced with the words 'Aliens Act 1 of 1937', don't think you are headed for the Dark Ages in the Dark Continent. It is merely the Act of Parliament that prescribes what requirements you have to meet to be allowed onto our sunny shores.

Things like being of 'good character', able to 'assimilate with the local population' and being 'a desirable inhabitant' are important, but one of the more crucial aspects of the law is to ensure that new immigrants do 'not follow an occupation in which there is already a sufficient number of persons engaged' or if there are sufficient locals who can do the same job that you can. These requirements are quite fair to have, especially in a country struggling with major unemployment particularly amongst the semi- and unskilled sectors of the population.

WHO ARE MOST WELCOME?
The immigration policy is selective. Like many developing countries we wish to move upward and onward, so immigrants who will be the most welcome are those who can offer knowledge or skills that are in short supply, or loads of money (so that the government is sure you and your family are financially independent). Industrialists and entrepreneurs are in great demand as they are seen as prime producers of jobs, a scarce commodity in our land.

In other words, anyone who will genuinely benefit the economy and the country will be hailed heartily. And remember, the policy does change with the country's changing needs.

THE WORK PERMIT WAY

To work in South Africa, foreigners who have not immigrated must either get a temporary work permit or a residence permit. Because of the shortage of skills, obtaining a work permit rarely proves difficult. It may require tenacity and bucketfuls of patience when dealing with all the red tape and bureaucracy, but then show me a country where it does not!

Temporary work permits are valid for six months, but can be renewed almost indefinitely. However, if you are planning to be here for some time, the hassle of dealing with bureaucracy and red tape twice a year should be enough to encourage you to apply for a permanent residence permit.

Also a temporary resident, that is a holder of a temporary work permit, will be required to pay a deposit equivalent to the customs duty of all your personal effects. This deposit will only be repaid when you take all your goods and chattels out of the country again, or when you become a permanent resident.

Permanent residents are treated in much the same way as immigrants and do not have to pay customs deposits on their personal goods and household effects. Although it may sound like a contradiction in terms, the status of a permanent resident is a relatively temporary affair because when you decide to leave South Africa the permit is withdrawn and that's the end of it. Thus it does not affect your status in your country of origin, but makes things easier for you while you are in South Africa. If you do develop an overwhelming love of the land, its people and its climate – and you may well do so – you can convert from being a permanent resident to immigrant.

Matters relating to work and residence permits, and the like are administered by the Department of Home Affairs whose headquarters is in Pretoria, but they have offices in the major South African cities.

NEED SKILLED PEOPLE FOR BUSINESS?

If you, an employer, cannot fill crucial positions in your business with local people, you may certainly look further afield. Just approach the Department of Home Affairs. Once they have consulted the Department of Manpower (to ensure there is a shortage of the type of employee you are looking for), they will assist you to recruit and 'process' your new staff. South African Embassies and Consulates will also offer you assistance.

PRE-IMMIGRATION ADVICE
Visit It First

In the words of Hong Kong Chinese immigrant, Kelly Lai, who has made South Africa his home for over 20 years, 'I caution anyone I can, to come and look first before you make that big leap. Not everyone is suited to the complex socio-politics of South Africa.' He is quite right!

You would almost certainly have seen television newscasts or read newspaper reports of the violence in South Africa, especially in the 1980s when the bid to unseat apartheid was at its strongest. The government of the time tried hard to play this down, and there were times when some reports may not have been a reflection of the entire picture, but violence was part of the struggle. Although apartheid is firmly on its way out, the albatross of its legacy will be around our necks for decades to come.

But remember socio-politics is not the only side to this complex country. There are so many issues, cultures, creeds, landscapes and seaboards that it really is wise, if finances permit, to plan a visit to South Africa to see for yourself the lie of the land. Unless you know you are destined for a particular city or town, try to see as many different areas of the country as you can, or at least the following major cities:

- **Johannesburg** – The hub of the business community. A hard, fast and exciting city. Not always pretty, but stimulating. Most business emanates from Jo'burg, or Egoli, as it is often nicknamed.

- **Durban** – Sub-tropical, balmy and by the sea. Fast growing, exciting and always abuzz, both socially and now also from a business point of view. It is South Africa's major port city too.
- **Cape Town** – Also called the Mother City, it is the most refined of South African cities or so it likes to think. A harbour city, it is certainly the most beautiful city as it hugs the sides of Table Mountain. It is a little sleepy, but some corporates do have their headquarters here.

Read All About It

If you don't manage a trip, get as much reading material as you can from as many sources to try and get a balanced view. All the promotion blurbs from your closest South African Embassy or Consulate will give you the rosy hues – factual but rosy. Also try to get information from other sources like your local library and news-papers.

Johannesburg's city skyline, showing the modern metropolis.

If at all possible, read as many of the broad spectrum of newspapers and local literature South Africa has to offer. Each major city has its own papers, while some of the Sunday papers are national.

The Star is a large, Johannesburg-based daily, which prides itself on fair, middle of the road reporting and is centred on middle-class values. It has sister papers in the other major centres too. *The Sowetan*, also based in Johannesburg, aimed more at the African reader, will give you a good perspective of the issues affecting many an urban black. *The Weekly Mail*, fairly radical, is published on Fridays and carries a good deal of socio-political information and investigative journalism – good when you want to know who has been up to no good, especially in political and government circles. It also has a wide-ranging arts and entertainment section – ideal for familiarising yourself with the different ways people spend their leisure time.

A wide range of novels based on South Africa and factual accounts of the country's history, politics and socio-economic situation are published locally and also by most of the major international publishers. They will add to your overall understanding of the country and its people – and in the long-term it will make your settling in easier.

INFLATION AIN'T LICKED YET

It can be hard to get a handle on the cost of living (COL) in South Africa. Don't be wooed by the fact that the Rand is fairly weak against major developed world currencies. Although it is expected to stay this way for some time to come, this has positive and negative effects.

Any imported goods are dramatically expensive, and as a newcomer you may occasionally hanker after a bit of 'home'. Just remember, such little luxuries are almost certain to cost an arm and a leg. On the positive side, if you are spending any first-world hard currency (e.g. US, West European or even Singapore), life will be fairly inexpensive.

If you consider the COL in relation to earning a local, Rand-based salary, a quality lifestyle in South Africa's major cities is probably as expensive as in England, Singapore or Sydney.

South Africans have been battling inflation for well over a decade now, and until very recently, with very little success. Due to a host of reasons including politics, sanctions, droughts and economic bungling on the part of the government, inflation has been in the high double digits which has created a Catch 22 type havoc on the economy. Since the early 1990s, however, new economic policies have had a positive effect and inflation is dropping steadily – but has certainly not reached developed-world levels and is unlikely to for many years.

CURRENCY EXCHANGE CONTROL

There are still currency exchange controls in South Africa, but in recent years, they have become more lenient and are expected to be phased out slowly in the next few years. Like many developing and

WHEN WE...
WHEN WE...

often politically unstable countries, South Africa needed to stop huge outflows of capital at times of intense turmoil. It is also felt that currency exchange control would ensure a measure of stability in the currency markets.

It has been successful on both counts, but there is now much debate on the inhibiting effects it has on foreign investment. Although no date has been set, the scrapping of exchange controls is on the agenda of the emerging new government.

The laws governing currency exchange control are complex in the extreme and should be carefully discussed with the Reserve Bank of South Africa, responsible for all such controls; an accountancy and auditing firm which is up-to-date on the latest laws and changes; or even a local bank that you have decided to be a client at. It is worth making a careful study of exchange controls as it alters depending on your status – i.e. of a temporary work permit holder, permanent resident, immigrant or an expat on a fixed-term contract.

The most stringent controls apply to South African citizens – they have the least legal chance of moving their money out of South Africa. Income/earnings are more or less locked in the country. Citizens can only take a certain amount out per annum to spend on holiday or business. Even if citizens emigrate, they are limited by a quota – so put this in your pipe and smoke it if you are considering citizenship.

Some of the biggest, best and multi-national firms of auditors and accountants include Price Waterhouse, Ernest & Young, KPMG Aiken & Peat, Deloitte Pim Goldby and Arthur Andersen & Co.

MAKING FRIENDS

South Africans are a very mixed bag. Not only do we have a very wide variety of African/indigenous people, but add to the melting pot the new and not-so-new immigrants from almost every country in the world and you are almost reaching United Nations' levels. To really know and enjoy the country it makes a lot of sense to try to meet, mix and socialise with as wide a section of society as you can. This is not always as easy as it should be as the remnants of apartheid still separate people residentially and socially. It is well worth the effort of transcending these crumbling boundaries.

Put shyness, preconceived ideas, fears and prejudices aside. Try to communicate with anyone and everyone you meet – in the street, in shops, at work, everywhere. Mostly you will be pleasantly surprised at the easy rapport you will establish with the most unlikely of people. If you have a moment, ask them about their lives, their homes, their families. Explain that you are a new-comer to the country and want to learn to love it, all of it! Always be a ready listener as you can learn so much that way which may be invaluable later in a work or social context.

Remember, too, that South Africans have taken one hell of a beating from the rest of the world, particularly about apartheid, and hence are rather twitchy about criticism. Until you really know your friends, don't go knocking the country and its people. Almost all South Africans are fully aware of their major shortcomings – as a people and as a nation. But right now as we try to build a new and hopefully beautiful future, it is positive reinforcement that everyone is seeking.

The When-We (Were Back Home) Saga

One of the easiest ways to lose new-found friends and alienate yourself from your new community is to harp on, too loud and too long, about all the good things you left behind. Keep comparisons or complaints about what you don't have, can't get or have left behind, to yourself. Such feelings are natural to newcomers, but your hosts won't necessarily understand that, and are unlikely to be too sympathetic. Focusing on what is new, beneficial and positive in South Africa will be of far more use to you and will ingratiate you with your hosts.

Remember many South Africans will be much worse off than you are, especially financially and materially. Their options, choices and quality of life may be far more limited than yours. Many may never have had the opportunity to leave South Africa, some may not even have left their home town, even for a holiday.

South Africa is geographically fairly remote from many parts of the world and so most people will be naturally curious about your origins. By all means discuss your country, your home and your culture to bring about understanding, but not to put South Africa in an unfavourable light.

The 'When we ...' comparisons do not carry a very positive connotation and have been used quite extensively to refer to a certain sector of white Zimbabwean immigrants, who moved to South Africa during and after the Zimbabwe war of independence in the 1970s and early 1980s. Despite their choice to leave their newly independent homeland and move to a then racist South Africa, they frequently whined about the marvels of the lifestyle they had left behind '...When we were in Rhodesia (the pre-independence name of the country) ..." – It won them very few friends among the South Africans.

THE SPOUSE: TO WORK OR NOT TO WORK?

Each person applies for a work permit in their own right, thus there is no reason why as a spouse you should not work in South Africa if you choose to. If you are a dual-career family you may well wish to pursue your career. Finding a job, for most professionals, will not pose much of a problem.

If you find the casual lifestyle too appealing and don't want to commit yourself to full-time work, there are numerous charities, self-help schemes and fundraising organisations that will welcome any help you can offer. They include organisations like Operation Hunger which in the long-term tries to help the impoverished back onto their feet, while in the short-term feeds millions of starving people, especially during the droughts that so often ravage our land. Others include Child Welfare, SPCA, various religious organisations and the political and cultural organisations discussed in the chapter, 'Women'.

THE SCHOOL SYSTEM

With the decline of apartheid, the school system is in the process of changing. Under the apartheid system, all schools and other educational institutions, except in special cases, were racially segregated. The vast majority of schools were, and still are, state schools.

There are a fair number of private schools, generally considered to offer a far superior education. Most are based on the British public school system of education and fees are dramatically more expensive than state schools, which were free until recently. There are also private schools like the Japanese, American, German or Greek schools, which are funded by specific immigrant groups. These schools are obliged to teach a syllabus similar to the South African schools, but have added subjects on their curricula such as their mother-tongue and their country's history.

Education for whites has been the best by far since the state spends the most money per student, on whites. By comparison, African education was very poor with some teachers not having much more education than their students. One of the most serious results of the discriminatory education is that a very large percentage of the black population is very poorly educated and as a workforce, lags far behind their counterparts in other parts of the world.

Asian and Coloured education were better than that given to Africans, but not nearly as much money was spent by the state on either of these groups as on whites. Most of the good facilities found in these schools were provided by the communities themselves.

Education is divided into three blocks: primary school (7 years); secondary school (5 years); and tertiary education which includes universities, technical colleges and the like. It is compulsory for all children to attend school until they are 16 years old or have attained a 'school leavers' certificate which means they have passed 10 of the 12 grades that make up the primary and secondary school education.

Your Child In School

Today children of either immigrant or expatriate families are allowed to attend any state school alongside South African children. Of course they may also attend private schools as long as they pass the entrance qualifications.

With the dissolution of apartheid laws, the white state schools had to find ways of becoming integrated. To try and satisfy various political groupings, some of which were not happy with multi-racial education, the state introduced various different models of integration and funding. Some schools have more parental participation in the running and funding of schools. Others receive varying levels of state funding. The different models are complicated and are still in their trial phases, so it is wise to enquire about the different systems when you get to South Africa as options may change until the most suitable ones are hit upon.

Although all universities do receive state aid, fees are still relatively high and climbing continually. University education in general is of a high standard and in many fields – especially medicine, dentistry and some of the sciences – compares favourably with the developed world. A certain level of high-school education has to be passed before a student is eligible to apply for university entrance. The university then applies its own screening process to the applicants, based on merit.

HOW YOUR KIDS WILL FIT IN

It is certainly not easy for any newcomer to settle down in a new environment, so expect your children to be a little unsure of themselves at first. One of the best places for them to make new friends is at school, so if possible try to move at a time that will coincide with the beginning of a the school year or, at least, a new term. South African academic institutions start their year with the calendar year.

What many parents have told me is that once settled, children tend to adapt to their new home far quicker and more easily than their parents. Often they tend to take on the social values of their peers to be 'part of the crowd', rejecting their own and probably quite different cultural values. Although this may be a little disturbing to parents, especially if you are finding it difficult to adjust to a culture quite different from your own, there is not much you can do about it. Frankly, it is better to let your children feel part of their new environment and more often than not, as they grow older they will take a renewed interest in their roots.

SHIPPING IT

The best way to get your goods to South Africa is obviously by sea – unless you are bringing very little with you. If you are bringing an entire household of goods, try and fill a container. It makes it much easier for shipment and certainly helps prevent loss or theft of your possessions. Also be sure goods are shipped door-to-door, especially if you will be living inland in South Africa. Distances are vast and you may find yourself living many hundreds of kilometres from the port of entry. It could become a major undertaking to 'just pop down to the port' to fetch your cargo. Also, it is unlikely to save you any money by trying to do it yourself.

The shipping companies strongly recommend you insure your goods under a 'marine all-risks policy' that covers goods from the door of your old home to the door of your new one. When you choose a removal company, check who their counterpart is in South Africa to be sure the handling at your destination is as good as on your departure. If you are not using a door-to-door removal service, then you will find it well worth the cost of using a clearing agent to help you through the maze of import and customs procedures.

Customs Regulations

Generally, immigrants and people applying for permanent residency do not have to pay import duties on bona fide 'household effects and removable articles' as long as the customs officials have no reason to doubt the goods belong to you and that you have no plan to sell them. 'Household effects' includes anything that is normally necessary to equip a self-contained home – such as furniture, curtains, linen, crockery, electric appliances like fridges and stoves as well as TV, video and hi-fi. 'Removable articles' refers to large items like boats, trailers and caravans. Before you pack up your home, it would be wise to contact a South African Embassy or Consulate to check the up-to-the-minute customs duties and regulations as they are often changed and updated.

There are certain goods you are not to bring into the country, like unnumbered firearms, automatic rifles and pistols, any honey bee product, drugs, and 'indecent, obscene or objectionable goods including books and publications' – simply put, pornography. The list is long and worth enquiring about as its contents are not always obvious, and are frequently changed.

There are other items that you need to get a special import permit for, in advance of your arrival here. These include firearms, plants and seeds, unwrought or semi-processed gold, live animals and more.

117

Again, check the list and the address of the department you need to contact for the relevant permit. And do it well in advance, as speed does not seem to be of the essence in many of these government departments.

Your Own Wheels

Unless you can't bear to part with your car, or are sure you will be staying in South Africa for a fairly long sojourn, it is rarely worth the hassle and cost of bringing the vehicle with you. The high cost of shipping it, the insurance and the customs duties make it an expensive move, while the import procedures make it a complex one. And although new South African vehicles are becoming costly, you can usually get a good second-hand car at an affordable price. If you do wish to bring your car you must contact the Department of Customs and Excise, Private Bag X47, Pretoria 0001, South Africa, a good few months before you leave to find out the duties you will need to pay and the procedures to follow.

That Four-Legged Love Of Your Life

The four-legged love of your life – that faithful mutt that is always so pleased to see you when you get home from work, or that aloof and self-contained pussy who needs tender loving care as well as her steamed chicken bits – Can't bear to hand them to the neighbour? Well, you don't have to! You certainly can bring your pets with you to South Africa, but whether it is worth it is a very debatable question.

The facts are thus: Pets can be imported free of duty, but they are subject to a number of quarantine restrictions depending on the country they are coming from. They will need to stay in quarantine for a number of weeks so you must obtain details of the procedure for importing them months in advance of your and their departure either from the nearest South African Embassy or Consulate; or from the Director of Veterinary Services, Private Bag X138, Pretoria, 0001, South Africa. The reason for the very early start is that, depending on the country you live in, there are any number of health certificates, a list of vaccinations and checks need to be compiled before you can get an import permit from South Africa. Also, getting the necessary Veterinary Import Permit (from the address above) also takes a long time.

Probably the greatest advantage of bringing your furry friends to your new home is that they are one tiny link with home and the past that will be of great comfort to you in those early days when you feel, which you will at times, that you are totally alone in a strange world! I have friends who have immigrated with small children, and the family dog provided that all-important continuity link until the children had re-established a lifestyle and circle of friends like they had back home.

Their are several disadvantages, though. The costs of flying an animal are very high and the experience, especially on older pets can be traumatic enough to shorten their lifespan dramatically. The head of one of the quarantine stations told me that some of the older dogs died of things like kidney failure soon after arrival – they were just not able to deal with the shock adequately. There are also a number of fairly virulent pets diseases in South Africa and newly imported animals will obviously be susceptible to them, from not having a natural immunity. This means that you have to take special care until they have developed an immunity. You can vaccinate against some of the diseases, but not all of them. If your pets are out of quarantine before you have found a permanent place to live, they can hamper your movements and may even become upset by the unsettled lifestyle, or even get lost.

GETTING A PET IN SOUTH AFRICA

If you decide to leave your pet behind to minimise its trauma, you could always get a new one in South Africa. The Society for the Prevention of Cruelty to Animals, the SPCA, is a wonderful place to find yourself a pet if you don't have a breed preference.

If you prefer a pedigree dog, the best route is to phone the Kennel Union of South Africa, KUSA, who can put you in touch with the relevant pedigree breed societies. Since almost all breeds of dogs are available in South Africa, you can have your pick from champion bloodlines which are brought in from overseas.

Working dogs are very popular as guard dogs, for example German Shepherds, Rottweillers or Dobermans. Gun dogs, like Labradors or Pointers are also very popular for hunting and for pets. There are a number of clubs, especially in the urban areas, where you can take your pooch for obedience training – a worthwhile effort especially if you have a big dog in a city garden.

From The Wilds
There are strict laws regarding the keeping of wild animals in captivity. If you are considering doing this, I would strongly advise you to get in touch with the Department of Nature Conservation

MUMMY, MUMMY CAN I KEEP IT?

headquartered in Pretoria. You may well find a regional office in the city you live in too. It is totally forbidden to keep certain wild animals in captivity. For others, there are strict regulations concerning cage size and the like. Many do not thrive once taken from their natural habitat and it can be a costly and futile exercise if the animal dies. You are not allowed to 'take' a wild animal from the wilds unless you are in possession of a permit. And remember to NEVER touch a wild animal in a game reserve as the penalties are huge.

MAKE YOUR OWN SAFETY NET

South Africa is not a welfare state. There is no dole queue and very little other social security. Old age and disability pensions are paid to people who have no other means of support, but the amounts are not large. Many people who can afford it, organise their own pension schemes or retirement annuities either through the company they work for or privately – or both. It is a wise move.

Most companies offer subsidised medical insurance schemes to their employees. If this is not part of your package, it may be wise to look into private medical insurance. At present South African private medical care is expensive, but not as high as in Europe or the United States. However costs are rising fast. There are a number of state hospitals, many of which are very good but are not necessarily free. A 'means test' determines how much you pay for their services. For more complicated procedures, many people prefer the private health care route as the hospitals tend to have some of the most up-to-date technology – but you pay for the privilege!

Most political parties have stated that they would like to improve on the country's social security, but with a flagging economy and increasing demands being made on government coffers, it is felt that it will be many years before South Africa can afford a Western European style social security system.

Chapter Seven

SURVIVAL TIPS

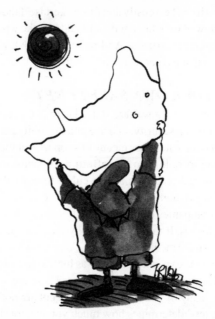

It may appear that life in South Africa, at least urban life, is quite similar to almost any western lifestyle you may know or have become accustomed to. You may even speak one of the many languages many South Africans speak. Probably English. But look further, and dig deeper. It's not always that simple to settle in and the littlest things can cause you enormous amounts of unnecessary aggravation until you remember it's done just that tiny bit differently here.

The people who find it hardest to adapt to their new environment are those whose lifestyle in the past has been quite similar to life in South Africa. You expect things to work like they do back home and when they don't, you're thrown quite off-balance. Sometimes people coming from dramatically different cultures are better geared for the differences.

Whatever your position on the 'sameness' scale, take heed of the little 'smoothers' below and your adjustment will become easier.

WORKING HOURS

Most people begin work fairly early in South Africa, so if you're not an early riser, beware! Actually, early morning, especially in summer, is often the most pleasant part of the day, and many people take advantage of it to enjoy outdoor exercise like jogging, swimming or cycling. Golfers also tee-off very early on occasions.

It is not uncommon for businessmen to be up, showering and having breakfast not long after 6 a.m., ready to leave for work by about 7 a.m. Their work day usually begins at 8 a.m. or 8.30 a.m. Most office workers stay until 5 p.m., and with the early start you may often find that 4.55 p.m. is not the most appropriate time to begin a long-winded business discussion. Of course there are exceptions.

A few businesses do start and end later, say 9 a.m. and you may still catch them at work at 6 p.m., but only if you have a direct line. To the best of my knowledge, there is not a switchboard open one second after 5 p.m.!

Factories and labourers in many industries like the building industry also begin work very early, quite often at 7 a.m. and finish by 4 p.m. at the latest.

Government Departments

The civil service and anything government-related officially begins work as early as 7.15 a.m. or 7.30 a.m., but remember this means they may close anytime from 3.30 p.m. to 4.30 p.m. This also includes the ex-parastatals, many of which have been semi-privatised recently like Telkom (the telephone department), Spoornet (the railways), Portnet (the harbours) and a number of others.

So when you are trying to organise your life on first arriving in the country and may need to return to government or local authority departments to collect documents, or even if you need to telephone them, just check the time they close.

City and town councils also operate on civil service type hours and remember, especially in the smaller towns and villages, almost everything including banks and the post office closes for lunch between 1 p.m. and 2 p.m.

A Five-Day Week

Monday to Friday is considered the working week, thus as a rule, businesses do not operate on a Saturday. Almost all shops are open, although their opening hours vary. Many South Africans are reluctant to work on Saturdays, partly due to their rather well-developed leisure culture, and partly due to the rather inconvenient shopping hours during the rest of the week.

Leave Periods

With South Africa being in the southern hemisphere, our summers run from about November to the end of March. This means that the long summer holidays fall over the Christmas/New Year period. And be warned, almost everyone goes on leave at this time, especially as it coincides with the long summer holiday that schools and universities have. From about the second week in December to the middle of January it appears as if the entire country has shut down! Most inlanders migrate to the coastal resorts for the summer hols which also means that the roads, as well as the resorts, can be very congested.

Other peak holiday periods are over Easter and, to a lesser extent, during the winter school holidays that come around in the middle of the year.

Generally people in senior positions have four weeks or 20 working days of leave a year, while others range from two to three weeks.

SHOPPING FOR THE BARE ESSENTIALS
When To Shop

In the past, South Africa's Calvinist tradition gave rise to rigidly controlled shopping hours. Governed by law, shops were only allowed to trade at very specific hours – usually between the hours of 8 a.m. and 5 p.m. This shopping period is not a whole lot of use to anyone who has to be at their place of work during those hours.

This gave rise to the manic drive for many people to 'shop till they drop' on Saturday mornings, as closing time was 1 p.m. Fortunately, sense and public pressure has prevailed and the trading hour laws have been eased dramatically, as has the enforcement of the laws.

Today most residential shops operate between 8.30 a.m. to 5 p.m. Closer to the inner cities, shops tend to open earlier but still close at 5 p.m. Of course opening times can vary from city to city and neighbourhood to neighbourhood.

Major supermarkets have extended shopping hours, often opening earlier towards the end of the week, remaining open on Saturday afternoons and are even open for a period of time on Sunday mornings. The do-it-yourself shops also keep these extended hours as do hardware shops, gardening shops, nurseries and some pharmacies.

Remember, that the above opening times apply in the cities and larger towns. In the smaller towns the shopping hours seem to have remained more strictly 8 a.m. to 5 p.m., often with the 1 p.m. to 2 p.m. lunch-time closure and they close on the dot of 1 p.m. on Saturdays as well.

The Great South African Cafe

There is a strange and wonderful entity in South Africa called the cafe, or corner cafe. Not to be confused with a coffee bar a la the French! In South Africa, a cafe is more like a general provisions store carrying small amounts of almost anything, except booze, that you are likely to run out of when the shops are shut. Mostly consumables likes eggs, bread, milk, some vegetables and fruit, tinned foods, a wide range of sweets, cool drinks, cigarettes, newspapers and magazines are sold … and much, much more! Some also sell a range of fast foods, like fried chips, pies or sandwiches. Some cafes in the smaller towns, and especially those on the main arterial roads, have tables and chairs and offer a sit-down tea, coffee, snacks and light-meals service.

Cafes are open seven-days-a-week, usually on public holidays too, and keep very long hours from around 7 a.m. to 10 p.m. at night. Prices for provisions are higher generally than in supermarkets – but you are paying for the privilege of your forgetfulness and their long opening hours.

Sale Of Alcohol

The outlets for the sale of alcohol in South Africa are limited. Mostly you buy it in 'bottle stores' which sell only booze. You can now also buy beer and wine in most of the major supermarkets which have special liquor-trading licences.

Trading laws pertaining to the sale of alcohol have not been eased along with the others, so remember to buy what you need between 9 a.m. and 5 p.m. during the week and before 1 p.m. on Saturday. Never on a Sunday!

Even the wine and beer sold in the supermarkets has to be closed off 'after hours' to prevent you purchasing it with your other shopping! This can be extremely irritating and sometimes even embarrassing, because often when impromptu dinner invitations are made, you could be asked to 'bring along some wine or beer', so it's wise to keep a little in stock.

The laws for selling liquor to children under the age of 18 have been tightened and fines for bottle-store owners who transgress this are R 20 000 or six months in jail. Of late, monitoring and enforcement of this law has been stepped up.

Where You Least Expect It

Speaking from my personal experience of moving from Africa to Europe and then to South East Asia, I've learned that some household items are sold in different types of stores, in different countries. An example is a purple liquid called methylated spirits in South Africa which is used for cleaning windows or getting greasy marks off surfaces. It is freely available in all supermarkets and virtually every grocery store across the land. In England, you can only get it in a pharmacy, and then you may be asked exactly what you want it for! So if there is some household application or even cooking ingredient you just can't seem to find, ask around – and don't be shy to ask in the most unlikely places. You may win, and you are sure to establish a rapport with the shop owner who will want to know more about you, the newcomer to the land. Making acquaintances at every turn is one of the quickest ways to integrate.

TRANSPORTATION WOES

Many people who live in the satellite cities (like Soweto is to Johannesburg, or kwaMashu is to Durban) and work in the major centres, leave home in the wee hours of the morning – some at early as 4 a.m. to catch the slow, erratic and very crowded public transport. It can take them many hours of commuting to reach their places of work, and on occasion, no matter how good their intentions, they may not get to work on time.

If such a situation arises with one of your employees, give them the benefit of the doubt, at least, at first. Don't just chastise them as you would someone late for work in, say, Singapore or Germany where public transport is rarely the cause of a late arrival. You will soon find out the truth for their delay.

Long, Expensive Journeys For The Blacks

Because the system of apartheid forced many black people to live in the homelands, hundreds of kilometres from the urban centres and the largest job pools, there are people who are forced to commute by bus for as long as three hours each way! Very often they have jobs as unskilled workers, who are not well paid. Thus these journeys to work dig deep into their shallow pockets. Their plight has been highlighted by the media, both locally and internationally, but until the economy picks up and many more jobs can be created in outlying areas, their plight is not likely to ease much.

GETTING AROUND IN THE CITIES AND TOWNS

Public transport in South African towns and cities leaves a lot to be desired! Although the pros and cons of metros or mass rapid transport systems reach heightened debate now and again, at local authority and even government levels, there is still not a single system in the entire country. The reasons usually boil down to one factor – that it is too costly to be viable.

Driving

For an easy, happy lifestyle a driver's licence and a car are essentials. Cars are rather expensive and the price of petrol is ever on the increase, especially as the government frequently raises much needed funds by slapping yet another tariff or tax on petrol. But it is still the best route if you can afford it.

A foreign driver's licence is valid in South Africa for a period of six months, provided the licence is written in English and has a picture of the driver on it. You can exchange it for a South African licence within those six months, but if you let this slip beyond six months you will have to take the South African driver's test.

Another way around this, if you are sure of the length of your sojourn, is to get an international driver's licence in your home country as this will be valid for 12 months and can usually be renewed, but in your country of origin. You should check this up with your home authorities.

Using Public Transport

If a car is out of your reach, it is possible to get around by public transport, at least in the major centres like Johannesburg, Cape Town, Durban and Pretoria. It just requires a lot of tenacity to get used to the various types of transport available.

The combi-taxi The newest public transport industry and one of the largest growth areas in the economy is that of the combi-taxi. It began in the mid-1970s in the predominantly black communities where the lack of public transport was, and to a large extent still is, chronic.

Initially, the apartheid government tried to put a stop to it, probably because it owned the inadequate black bus services. But the need was so great that the industry took off like a bush fire, informally at first but now in a more ordered fashion, with a number of mostly black-owned organisations controlling it. Now, public opinion is that there should be assistance from both public and private sectors to help more taxi operators become the transport businesses of the future.

A combi-taxi stand.

A combi-taxi, or mini bus, as they are sometimes called, seats between 8 to 15 people – and in extreme and rather unsafe illegal conditions, closer to 20!

In the early days the combi-taxis were sometimes called 'Zola Budds', referring to the world-record-holding South African runner. The implication therefore is that combi-taxis drive too fast!

There is quite a complex culture to catching and using a combi-taxi, especially since they run specific routes although they may deviate a little depending on the will of the majority of the passengers. Using them can be great fun, but get a local to explain the hand and finger signals as well as the method of payment before you try. They are remarkably inexpensive, especially when compared to their relatives, the 'sedan taxis'.

Sedan taxis These have operated in South Africa since the 1930s, but are extremely expensive and have had their hands tied by restrictive legislation forbidding them from cruising. You often have to catch them at a taxi rank, if you can find one, or you can order one by telephone.

They should all operate strictly by meters, but check this before you board one. On the other hand, you may wish to try bargaining for a good deal if you know where you are going. This, of course, is not playing the game by the rules, but it's up to you.

The Bus The quality and availability of municipal or city buses vary considerably from city to city and even from suburb to suburb. Relatively inexpensive, they run infrequently except during peak hours and have few routes. Remember South African towns and cities are fairly spread-out so a paucity of routes may mean quite a long walk from the bus-stop to your destination.

Commuter train Both Cape Town and Soweto have this service and in neither areas is it very extensive.

GETTING AROUND BETWEEN CITIES

South Africa's intra-city transport is generally very good, but certainly not cheap. All major centres are linked by fairly frequent flights, trains and luxury buses.

By Air

Until recently the national airline, South African Airways or SAA, has been the only operator of significance for all internal flights. It had a total monopoly and could get away with not offering good service for the steep prices of internal airfares.

Only a few years ago the entire government-controlled transport industry was semi-privatised, leading to far better service. Also the introduction of a number of other locally-based operators, often in conjunction with international airlines, has created healthy competition which led to an improvement in SAA's service as well as a drop in fares on certain routes. But internal airfares, in terms of one's earning power in South Africa, are still quite high compared to other countries.

There are a few smaller air services, flying small planes on specific routes. They operate between major cities and developing industrial areas, for example from Johannesburg to Nelspruit, or Durban to Richards Bay (up the coast).

By Train

Inter-city trains run on an almost daily basis, but remember the distances are so great that even an express trip from Johannesburg to Cape Town takes over 24 hours, while a trip to Durban is an overnight affair. Train fares are divided into various classes offering degrees of comfort and privacy. They range from Third Class rides which are not much more than a seat, to a First Class fare which offers comfortable sleepers with attached dining cars. Right at the top end of the luxury market is the Blue Train which travels from Cape Town to Johannesburg and back, much in the fashion of the Orient Express.

By Bus

Much like the airlines, the long distance bus transport system was for many years controlled almost entirely by the state. But more recently, competition has crept in and a number of bus services are available from city to city, varying quality at differing prices.

By Car

And then there is always the option to drive from city to city. The main arterial roads in South Africa are generally good and, other than at peak holiday periods, the traffic on the roads is not very heavy. But beware. The distances in South Africa are great so it may well take you longer to get to your destination than you ever expected.

A trip from Johannesburg to Durban takes some six hours provided you stick to the speed limit of 120 km per hour. Cape Town is 1 600 km from the Johannesburg area and it is wise to break the journey overnight unless you have someone to share the driving with.

THE PRESS

Probably because of the British influences on the country in the last century, the news industry in South Africa has been intent on maintaining responsible press freedom. Make no mistake, this has not been easy. The earliest newspapers in the 1800s were often at loggerheads with the government of the time, and in the politically turbulent times of the 1980s the government implemented a barrage of harsh press restrictions on both local and foreign press to curb reporting on the horrors of those violent times.

The media gave a bold fight, challenging the government in the law courts on every turn. With the scrapping of apartheid laws, so many of the laws restricting the press were also lifted.

There is a wide range of newspapers in South Africa, ranging from the most conservative to the fairly liberal. There are both morning and afternoon dailies, Sunday papers and weekly newspapers. They are aimed at various sectors of the population and often the debate can be quite lively, be it on politics or sport – probably the two most discussed subjects! On an international news level, even the best are rather thin.

Foreign newspapers are available in the major centres, but they are very expensive. You can also subscribe to almost any overseas publication you wish to.

A fairly large magazine market exists, topped by a few good business magazines. Women's magazines are in the majority and, although not world-class calibre, are good if you want to learn more about the new environment. A relative newcomer to the magazine

market is *Tribute*, a general interest magazine aimed at the multi-racial New South Africa. Certainly a good read. There are a number of sport and car magazines, and industry specific publications on computers, engineering, shipping and the like.

Television And Radio

The semi-government South African Broadcasting Corporation (SABC), controls most of the television and radio stations across the land, although in recent years competitors have fought tooth and nail for a share – and won.

M-Net is a pay TV station offering a wide variety of predomi-nantly entertainment programmes, good films and sport. Radio 702 is the most successful independent station with excellent on-the-spot local and international news coverage, and a selection of phone-in and discussion programmes. It operates only in the greater Johannesburg-Pretoria region at present, but intends to expand to all major metro-politan areas in the future.

SABC TV runs three television channels. The content varies from serials and soaps (local and imported) to documentaries, news features and, of course, newscasts. Local productions are improving, but we still lag far behind the developed world in the quality of our programmes. One of the reasons for this is that TV only became part of our lifestyle in 1976!

For technical buffs, or anyone who wants to bring their telly with them and needs to know if it can be converted, the system used in South Africa is based on the C.C.I.R. 625-line system 1 standard, and is PAL.

Under the new government, opportunities have been given for the establishment of many more independent radio stations, many of which broadcast in small, localised environments, some more successfully than others. One new independent free to air TV station has also begun broadcasting.

Books

The bad news is that books are expensive in South Africa. Some of the blame is foisted on the fact that many are imported and our exchange rate is not good. But even locally produced books are expensive by American, British or Singaporean standards. Foreign magazines also fall into this category, but at least there is a fairly good selection of European and American publications to choose from.

The good news is that there are some excellent bookstores which carry a wide variety of both fiction and non-fiction. Books by South Africans and about South Africa – our past, present and our hoped-for future – are currently in great abundance. This is good news for anyone who needs to get to know the country and its foibles. Library services are also generally good, even in the smaller towns.

HOUSE HELP

Help in the home is very much a part of the lifestyle in South Africa, for anyone who can afford it. Because of the high rate of poverty and unemployment, and the huge unskilled labour pool, there are many people willing to work as domestic workers, nannies or child minders, and gardeners. Make use of their availability: service staff will enhance your lifestyle by giving you more free time, and you can enhance theirs by creating jobs and helping them learn skills.

But don't expect to exploit them. Fair wages for fair work will inevitably lead to good results and a good working relationship. It is wise to set out your terms of employment before someone begins work for you, explaining carefully what you expect of them, the hours they are expected to work, their time off and, of course, the salary. Don't forget that many people in this land are only semi-literate so be clear, precise and, above all, polite and patient. The rewards are immeasurable. And remember their employment is now governed by the new labour laws.

Depending on your needs you can employ full-time live-in domestic help, or you can have a *char* who helps you a few days a week. Full-time staff are usually paid by the month. *Chars* can also be paid monthly, or by the day or week.

Many homes in South Africa are geared to having live-in maids or nannies, but sometimes the quarters are not fit for human habitation, so if you are going to have live-in help, and are buying or renting a home, check these quarters yourself – don't just take the word of the owner or estate agent.

African nannies are most often exceptionally good with children, patient and understanding and usually err on the side of spoiling them. So you must set the parameters of what your children may and may not do, and also insist on their respect for their nanny.

Depending on the size of your garden, you may need a gardener a few times a week, or perhaps only once every week or two. There are many gardeners who work for a different family every day of the working week, and the best way to find someone is to ask around in your neighbourhood. Often you will find someone who has a day or two free per week and can be recommended by another employer.

Because of the high unemployment rate, many people may knock on your door seeking some form of work or even food. Be cautious.

The crime rate, especially in the bigger cities, is high and it is advisable to get some form of reference before you employ someone. However do not fall into the trap of paranoia common to many South Africans, of thinking every person who knocks on your door is a criminal-in-waiting.

SWIMMING POOLS

As you fly into Jan Smuts Airport in Johannesburg, or over any other major South African town, you will see thousands of tiny turquoise patches alongside the rows of homes. They are private swimming pools and almost every home in nearly all medium to affluent suburb has one.

A lot of summer-time socialising takes place around the pool, including the *braaivleis* or barbeque. And there is no doubting the amount of pleasure the entire family, but especially the children, will get from a pool.

But don't be totally seduced by this cool, turquoise beauty. Pools require a fair amount of time-consuming maintenance and fairly costly chemicals to keep them looking cool, sparkling and turquoise. If maintenance is not kept up, the pool quickly turns a murky green from algae, and begins to resemble your suburban lawn!

In the past, you also had to scrub the walls and floor, and clean the leaves out. But now, thanks to a great South African invention, the 'Kreeply Krauly', with a flip of a switch this magical creature made up of weights and counter-weights wiggles its way around your pool, sucking up leaves and dirt and spewing them into the filter system. It's worth its weight in gold!

A pool can also be dangerous. If you do have small children, you cannot be too safety-conscious and a good fence or pool net is essential. It is also essential to ensure your children learn to swim, especially if you come from a country where swimming is not so much a part of life as it is here.

CLIMATE

The weather is very volatile in South Africa, with droughts, high or low pressure systems, hail storms and the like. You may well experience the occasional totally unseasonal weather conditions. In November 1992 it snowed in parts of the Cape Province when normally at that time of year temperatures there are in the high 20s or even 30s.

Other than some amount of unpredictability, the South Africa climate is renowned for its warm to hot summers and mild winters. Even when a cold spell hits the country, it rarely lasts more than a week or so at a time. Snow seldom falls, except on the mountain tops, but when it does fall, every decade or so, it is cause for great excitement. Then you will quite likely see besuited businessmen building snowmen or throwing snow balls in the streets of downtown Johannesburg.

Winters are not long, between June and August, but homes are not geared for the cold weather and you may find yourself a lot more uncomfortable than expected. Central heating is not common, nor is double glazing or well fitted doors and windows, especially in older homes.

Because we are in the southern hemisphere, the sun is almost directly above us in summer, while in winter it is north of us and its angle is more oblique. This means that north-facing houses are best for light and warmth in winter. So get your bearings when house hunting.

Summers are generally pleasantly warm, but can become quite hot, especially in the northern parts of the country and in and around Durban, where the sub-tropical climate adds a good dose of humidity to the high temperatures. Although most office complexes are air-conditioned, other than in Durban, few homes are. So if you do feel the heat, try to find a home that has good ventilation, a big verandah (also called a 'stoep' here) or a shady tree!

DRESSING FOR THE SEASON

Dressing for the weather is a big part of enjoying the climate here. In summer, light cotton or linen clothes, formal and informal, are the order of the day. Businessmen usually are expected to wear suits, so be sure to have a few light-weight ones. In the evenings, temperatures usually drop a few degrees, and a light jacket or wrap may be necessary, especially if you are outdoors.

In spring and autumn, you can usually get away with wearing your summer wardrobe and adding a light wool jacket or cardigan. Both seasons are very short and hardly worth a wardrobe of their own.

In winter, especially in the central part of the country (the Johannesburg area) and also the southern Cape, you will certainly need winter wear. Woollen suits, sweaters, jackets, and even boots are quite appropriate attire. A coat will certainly come in handy, especially at night.

Dressing For The Occasion

Not only is the dress code quite different across the different cultures in South Africa, but it also varies quite a bit from one region to another. Your easiest option is to imitate your work colleagues and friends until you have a grasp of it. You are seldom likely to cause major offence to your hosts by inappropriate dress as they are sure to take into account your recent arrival in the country, but you may well feel ill at ease standing out like a sore thumb in your jeans at a function where everyone else is smart and fairly formal.

In big cities, like Johannesburg and Cape Town, people from all cultures dress formally for work. Businessmen are expected to wear suits or at least a jacket and tie. Evening wear is sometimes less formal, but still smart, unless your hosts insist that it's very casual – which can mean jeans and open-neck shirts or T-shirts. In some of the seaside or resort towns and cities, dress is less formal as the beach culture permeates the business one.

In rural communities, the Boer or white farmers often wear khaki

139

shirts, short knee-length socks and boots or shoes. However, being the conservative element of the population, their formal dress that is worn mostly to church is quite old-world. Therefore wearing off-shoulder dresses may be seen as quite risque .

Traditional or tribal Africans mostly wear western-style dress today, but for certain celebrations they may don their ethnic attire. This varies from group to group and often includes clothes and other adornments made from animal skins, while they may carry spears, shields and fighting sticks which are referred to as 'traditional weapons'. There has been a controversy over these weapons as they have been used in some of the faction fights, with severe consequences. In most cultures it is quite normal for traditional African women to go bare-breasted.

SUCCESS BREEDS RESPECT

The most highly regarded areas of achievement are business and sport and, even today, men are expected to be the achievers. Making good money and splashing it about a bit, is certainly well-regarded by most. Successful entrepreneurs, like Sol Kerzner, the self-made multi-millionaire and master-mind behind the Sun City and Lost City casino and entertainment resorts, may not be much liked, but he is certainly admired and emulated.

Chapter Eight

CULINARY CROSSROADS

Eating, whether at home or eating out, is most often a sociable and shared occasion. Among the western and westernised communities, who are mostly city dwellers, sharing a meal is done often in friendship and in the interests of a good business relationship. But in the more traditional, rural, or tribal communities, the sharing of food characterises the spirit of the people and is a cultural tradition to be shared even with a stranger and an enemy.

Because South African society developed with the arrival of various European and Asian immigrant communities over the centuries, the cuisine has grown out of a healthy and varied mixture of cultural ideas and flavours, tempered by what was locally available. This era of the 'global village' has also enabled an ever-widening array of food to grace the tables of restaurants and the fast food joints across the country, making our cuisine as open to change and experimentation as is the new and developing society.

Sometimes dishes or ingredients are not what they seem, not what you are accustomed to, but on many occasions they are simply hiding behind a different guise. You just have to dig a little deeper, or become accustomed to finding them with a different label or a different name. Some things will certainly be a totally new experience so try them with an open mind, or unbiased taste buds. You will certainly love some and no doubt you will loathe some too. It's all part of the excitement of being a newcomer.

TRADITIONAL FOODS

Traditional South African foods are becoming so popular that a Farm Food Route has been developed in the scenic areas inland from Cape Town. Here, locals and tourists alike can enjoy a wide array of traditional cuisine, savoured from a number of little taverns and restaurants, as they drive through some of the country's most idyllic rural scenery. Besides the Cape, speciality restaurants in all the major centres also offer a wide choice of traditional local cuisine.

Cape Malay Cuisine

Some of South Africa's greatest traditional dishes come from the Cape Malay cuisine. The Dutch had brought some Malays to work for them at the Cape during their many voyages to the East in their quest for control of the Spice Trade. The Malay women, who were excellent cooks, brought a vast knowledge of both oriental and Indian spices with them, then developed a culinary tradition based on the ingredients available at the Cape at that time. Refined over the centuries, these dishes are now considered a great delicacy and are served in traditional homes and restaurants.

There are some excellent and unusual Cape Malay dishes to look out for. Try one of the 'bredies' for example. They resemble a vegetable and meat stew, but it's the unusual additions that give them a mouthwatering edge. Some have a strong tomato base, others have quince, pumpkin or cabbage in them. And one of the most famous is called 'Waterblommetjie', a bredie made with the addition of a special water flower that grows wild in the ponds in rural areas in the Cape.

'Bobotie' is another hot favourite. Originally made from leftovers, it is a baked minced-meat dish that is deliciously spiced and sometimes has some dried fruit added to it. Before being served, curled fresh bay or lemon leaves are poked into the top of the pie and then an unsweetened custard is poured into the holes made by the leaves, as well as over the rest of the surface.

Or you could try some of the more traditionally Malay fare – 'Pinangkerrie', a meat curry to which tamarind and fresh green leaves from an orange tree are added; or 'Denningvleis', meat flavoured with bay leaves and tamarind. Each dish has special accompaniments like sliced onion sprinkled with powdered chilli, fresh grated quince fruit mixed with chilli powder, a mixture of mint leaves, and powdered chilli moistened with vinegar. Sometimes a drink made of soured milk with a slice of orange is served with the curries. A variety of preserved fruits and other sweets are also served.

Don't be at all surprised to find many of the traditional Cape Malay dishes served with bright yellow rice. This is a local speciality, coloured and delicately flavoured with saffron or tumeric and often has saltanas added for that tiny touch of sweetness quite common in this style of cooking.

Sauces/Chutneys/Atchars

The Malays also gave South Africa the heritage of wonderfully pungent and well-spiced sauces, chutneys and atchars (pickles). The chutneys and atchars have vegetables and fruits that are boiled and preserved in strong and spicy chilli, vinegar and sugar mixtures. Tangerine peel and pickled peaches are other delicacies. These are frequently served as condiments or side dishes.

From The West

Much of the rest of the cuisine in South Africa is based on an amalgam of European – French, British, Flemish, German, Italian, Portuguese, Greek and others – influences. Pasta dishes are a firm favourite in many homes. A large Portuguese immigrant population has meant that the likes of a 'prego roll' (similar to a steak sandwich, but encased in a crispy Portuguese-style bread roll) is quite common fare, especially as a pub snack.

From The East

Indian and Chinese food, although it has not become as mixed into the local cuisine as European food has, is eaten with relish by all communities, especially in restaurants and in the homes in those communities.

Many South Africans do prepare curry dishes in their homes, with the assistance of some excellent local Indian cookbooks like *Indian Delights* edited by Zuleikha Mayat, and Romola Parbhoo's *Indian Cookery for South Africa*. In the Indian markets – in Durban they are by far the best – there is an abundance of exotic spices and curries. One of the most notable, at least by name is 'Mother-in-law Exterminator' which gives an indication of the potency of much of the Indian food in South Africa. Nearly all the exotic spices and herbs are also available in speciality shops in the main centres. Quite a few are even found on supermarket shelves now.

Chinese food is more often eaten in restaurants as South Africans are only now becoming acquainted with the complexities of this style of cooking. Although the Chinese population is fairly small, its heart is in Johannesburg. In the city centre, there is an enclave of a supermarket and a few shops that carry a wonderful array of dried or canned imported Chinese delicacies: from dried shrimps to water chestnuts, umpteen varieties of soy sauce … and much, much more are available. An endless array of noodles is also stocked. The more commonly used Chinese ingredients can also be found in some supermarkets, especially in the residential areas favoured by the many new Taiwanese immigrants.

WHERE TO GET THAT BIT OF HOME

In the main cities, the bigger and better supermarkets as well as the delicatessens and speciality food stores carry a fairly good array of foreign food. But you will have to curb your desires a little as anything imported carries an unrealistically high price-tag. This is partly because of the novelty value but mainly because South Africa still imposes massive protective import tariffs on anything considered a luxury item. So be warned.

But be consoled with the fact that because this is a culturally diverse community and has been for many years, there are a number of things made in South Africa, but modelled on foreign foods. If you are hooked on the Australian spread 'Vegemite', you will find a South African substitute called 'Marmite' (vegetarian) and 'Bovril' (meat extract) both of which are just like their namesakes in England. A lot of the international food conglomerates manufacture in South Africa and you will probably be surprised at how many western-style and western brand-named ingredients are available here. For anyone coming from lands that have had minimal links with South Africa over the years, like Thailand or Indonesia, you may find your home treats few and far between.

Many of the health food shops stock the unusual goodies you may just need for your own special brand of home cooking – pine nuts (at great cost!), carob powder (cocoa substitute for chocolate flavouring), buckwheat, tofu, tahini paste and a wide variety of vegetarian foods are available. They may also stock unusual cheeses, goats milk and natural yoghurts, as will some of the speciality food stores.

SEAFOOD

There has always been an abundance of seafood in South Africa's coastal waters. Because of the icy coastal seas and the markedly warmer Mozambican current on the east coast, the variety of seafood is extensive. Hence due to the hot and sunny climate, preservation has always been of prime importance. In the good old days pickling was popular, with pepper, chillies, ginger, coriander seeds, caraway, aniseed and cumin being favourite pickling spices. Today the tradition is carefully followed to gourmet delight! In fact, it is one of Nigel's most favourite treats – and, as a dead giveaway to my culinary abilities, I have to admit that some excellent canned varieties are found in most supermarkets!

Snoek, a type of cod found in the Cape seas, is very popular today and often sold smoked. They are ready to eat cold on sandwiches and are often served at picnics, or as an excellent side-dish at lunch or on a buffet spread.

Crayfish, mussels, oysters and clams are seafood favourites and the French Mauritians, owners of some of the sugar cane plantations on the Natal coast, have added their creole touch to these dishes.

Landlubbers Have Their Share

Although many of the major cities are not coastal, this does not prevent landlubbers from getting very high quality fresh and frozen fish. Demand is so high, especially in the Johannesburg region, that some of the coastal dwellers complain that inlanders probably get some of their best catches, popped on a plane and rushed to the restaurant tables and supermarket shelves, almost quicker than they do.

MEAT – THE REGULAR AND EXOTIC KIND

Most South Africans like to eat meat and the country certainly does have a reputation for producing good quality beef. In fact, many people just do not consider a meal complete without a meat dish.

Chicken, mutton, fish (more recently) and pork (to a much lesser extent), follow hot on the heals of beef on most shopping lists. Unfortunately, the once very reasonable cost of meat has skyrocketed along with the cost of all food.

Venison, that is game meat from antelope and warthogs, (similar to wild boar) is a winter favourite, probably because this is the hunting season. More recently, a number of commercial farmers have started farming these animals as well as game birds to supply the city markets throughout the year, so you certainly will be able to get venison out

of season, but not quite as readily. Certain restaurants specialise in wild cuisine and have some of the more exotic ones on offer most of the time – try a steak of crocodile, a slice of ostrich, or an elephant stew if traditional venison is not exotic enough for you.

BILTONG AND OTHER SPECIALITIES

Biltong, this strange local delicacy, originated when the Trekboers decided to explore the interior of the country and needed to preserve any extra meat, from the game they shot, for the pot. It is made from strips of meat, very often game, but now also frequently beef, which has been marinated in spices and salt and then dried in the wind and sun. It is often served as a snack with drinks, but more and more restaurants serving traditional fare are using it in salads and as a topping for some of their dishes. Try it – you may be surprised how easily you take to it.

Other specialities, born of necessity by the explorers, are rough breads and meat dishes which are baked in an outside clay oven, fairly similar to those used in some of the Arabic countries to bake bread.

Cooked green maize, a local version of corn-on-the-cob, is still a favourite even among city-slickers. If in the mid- to late summer you hear a high-pitched shriek as you quietly go about your business in your residential neighbourhood, don't be alarmed. It quite often is, what seems to me, the unintelligible call of the green mealie sellers. Their wares are worth investigating as they are usually freshly picked in the rural areas and make a delicious easy addition to a meal. Just boil until tender and serve with butter, salt and pepper. A microwave oven short-cuts this process to a matter of three or four minutes! Maize is called 'mealie' in South Africa: maize meal is mealie meal. Mealie refers to the cob and its pips or to the plant actually growing in the fields.

AFRICAN DISHES

Some of the very indigenous dishes may well be a touch out of your ambit, as they are for many westernised South Africans. But the adventurous could do a trial run on 'morog', a local version of spinach and not totally unlike its European cousin; or 'sorghum porridge' which is quite delicious with milk and sugar, in place of cereal, for breakfast. For the very adventurous, you could try 'mopani worms' which are dried and eaten as snacks (like biltong), or added to rural African type stews. But along with flying ants, they are not obligatory and very unlikely to crop up in your food circuit unless you purpose-fully seek them out!

Quite a delicious snack found at the end of the summer and in early winter is a fairly dry mealie on the cob, which is roasted over an open brazier. Fairly dry, chewy and crispy, this is one of my favourite snacks and is usually sold in the downtown city areas, near the bus and train stations and the taxi ranks.

FRUIT AND VEGETABLES

Good quality fruit and vegetables are grown in South Africa and a large variety is available in the supermarkets and green grocers, but prices can be quite high, especially when something is not in season. Also, an increasing quantity of fresh produce is exported to earn that much needed hard currency, leaving those of us who live here with second best, at times.

Some of the more exotic Eastern fruits like star fruit, rambutans or papayas are quite new to these shores, but entrepreneurs are starting to grow them as certain areas in the country are well suited to sub-tropical fruit production. Guavas, paw-paws (similar to a papaya), avocados and bananas are long traditional to these shores, as are pineapples and a wide variety of citrus fruits. Deciduous fruits are mostly grown in the Cape with apples, peaches, nectarines, plums, apricots and the like being easily available and of high quality, when in season. Watermelons, lychees and Cape gooseberries are other more unusual favourites.

A large, fresh fruit-juice industry has grown up in South Africa with many au natural juices (with no added sugar, colour or preserva-tives) competing for your attention on the supermarket shelf.

THE SMALL TIMER

In recent times, the small fruit and vegetable producers have become disenchanted with the monopolistic approach of many of the large chain stores and supermarkets. Consequently, a host of vegetable and fruit stalls and farmers' cooperatives have sprung up on the outskirts of the cities and bigger towns, as well as along some of the trunk roads. Although not quite as convenient as the store just down the road, prices are often much more reasonable as the middleman has been cut out and freshness is usually assured.

There are also a number of small farmers on the perimeters of the cities who are now growing fresh herbs of excellent quality – quite novel in South Africa.

LOCAL DESSERTS

'Marula jelly', made from the fruit of an indigenous tree, it is a sweet accompaniment for venison and, sometimes, game birds too.

'Koeksisters', very traditional Afrikaans fare, are made from plaited dough which is deep fried and immediately dropped into icy-cold sweet syrup. The dough immediately absorbs vast amounts of the syrup and the result is a crunchy, very sticky dessert – ideal for the very sweet-toothed!

PRICES GO UP, UP, UP...

Don't expect inexpensive food in South Africa just because of our sunny skies, an abundance of agricultural land and a strong farming tradition. Sadly, the cost of food – even the staples like bread, maize meal, meat, fruit and vegetables – increases constantly and, most of the time, by a few percentage points higher than the average rate of inflation! Public pressure groups seem powerless in curtailing this, and no one can give a clear-cut reason for it either. Each group blames the other – the farmers say they are not responsible for it, the supermarkets say they are cutting prices to the bone – and the consumer pays and pays and pays!

Some of the blame has been laid at the feet of the government's control and marketing boards, like the Maize Board or the Banana Board, which had monopolistic rights over all products sold. However, recently many of these boards have been scrapped giving the producers the right to sell their products as they choose. Let's hope the application of market forces will have some affect on curbing the increasing price of food.

ALCOHOL
Where And When To Get It

South Africa has some of the most antiquated and strange drinking laws still on any statute books! For example: you are not allowed to order a drink in a hotel or at a bar on a Sunday, unless you consume it with food! Many big city hotels ignore this with gay abandon, so it would seem that it is not often enforced by the keepers of the law; but when you are in a small town in the 'platteland', the rural and more Calvinistic areas, you are much more likely to find it strictly enforced.

For the most part, alcohol is sold in 'bottle stores' which are separate shops designated for the sole sale of alcoholic beverages. They have specific opening and closing times, which are much shorter than other shops; so don't set off too late on a Saturday, expecting to buy your booze when you do the rest of your chores. Liquor selling hours between Monday and Friday are from 9 a.m. to 8 p.m. On Saturdays they open from 9 a.m. to 5 p.m. only.

Beer and wine are also sold in big supermarkets, but subject to the liquor-selling hours, which are much shorter than the regular supermarket hours. So don't be surprised if you see a whole lot of wine and beer in the supermarket firmly locked behind bars – it just means that you've hit the supermarket after hours for the booze. This inconvenience will no doubt result in you having a very abstemious weekend unless, like many locals, you have learned to keep a few stock at home.

Generally, you can get almost any regular alcoholic drink in a

South African bottle store. There is a big range of brandy, many of which are locally made and very good. Nearly all whiskies are imported; while the other usual 'hard tack' like gins, vodkas, rums and such are both imported and locally produced.

Local And Potent

There is also a local speciality called 'cane' – the name is derived from the fact that it is a sugar cane distillate – and frankly, it has very little taste. It is not the most sophisticated of drinks, but adds an alcoholic kick to any mixer. You'll hear people yell, 'Gime a glass of cane an' coke' which means 'May I have a glass of cane spirits and Coca Cola'.

There are a number of other weird and wonderful local concoctions which are based on a simple alcohol like cane and flavours like the marula tree berry, or pineapple, perhaps, or even strawberry or mango. These drinks are definitely for less sophisticated palates, but

quite good fun. Beware of the morning-after headaches, though!

Talking of headaches and hangovers, beware if you are offered 'mampoer' or 'witblitz', the latter meaning 'white lightning'! These are home brews, similar to European schnapps, and are famed in some of the rural farming areas. Illegally brewed, they contain very high levels of alcohol, and need to be drunk with caution by the uninitiated. Locals seem to be able to quaff them with great abandon and love nothing better than for you to join them at it. You will fall over long before they do. You have been warned!

Beer – The National Drink

Indigenous African beer, made from sorghum and called 'maheu' (pronounced 'ma-he-oo') is a fairly thick drink, sometimes even like very runny porridge, quite sour, and very much an acquired taste.

Farm labourers enjoying some traditional beer, maheu, after a hard day's work.

However if you do learn to like it, it has a fairly high nutritional value and a low alcohol content.

The real home-brewed thing is most often found in the African rural areas and drunk in great quantities at special feasts and traditional ceremonies. Beer consumption often forms part of the ritual at a ceremony like a tribal marriage, a courtship or a funeral.

'Sorghum beer' is also made commercially for consumption in the urban areas. They are packaged in glazed cardboard cartons, rather like milk cartons, and are sold almost solely in the townships. In the 1976 riots that flared across South Africa's black urban areas, angry students burned the state-owned beer halls in protest, not against the beer, but against the fact that so many people spent so much money there and it was all for the state's coffers.

Drinking clear beer is a national pastime among almost all South Africans. No social function – *braaivleis*, sports match (live or on the TV), party – is thought complete without the consumption of vast quantities of beer – both local brews and, at a far higher price, imported beers, too.

However, with the advent of yuppies and the quest for a little more individualism, a fair number of small breweries have sprung up around the country, sometimes only selling their beer in the locality. Many of these beers are of excellent quality and often worth the extra cost. But do a taste test yourself across the board. If nothing else, you will have a lot of fun and endear yourself to local drinkers with your superficial knowledge of the brews which can be shared during those endless discussions in the pub.

Wines And Vineyards

The French Huguenots brought viticulture to the southern shores of South Africa, and an extensive and internationally acclaimed wine industry developed, and flourished over the years. Some stalwart brand-names that will help you negotiate the copious racks in the bottle stores until you have a handle on the whole subject are:

Boschendal, L'Ormarins, Nederberg, Backsberg, Thelema, Hamilton Russel, Meerlust and Bellingham. Of course there are many more, but these will be a good guide to begin with.

In the wine-growing area of the south-western Cape, not far into the hinterland from Cape Town, you can visit a number of the country's best wine estates on what is called 'the Wine Route'. You can drive from one to another tasting the wares and, when you find what you like, you can buy it directly from the estate. Although you won't effect a huge price saving compared to some of the larger bottle stores, you certainly will have a wonderful time. You may even discover a small hidden-away estate that suites your taste buds and your pocket, and does not sell its products through the retail outlets.

Many of the estates are hundreds of years old and the traditional Cape Dutch architecture is idyllically, set against mountainous backdrops. Some estates offer wonderful lunchtime spreads which gives you a chance to sample the local cuisine with the fruits of the vine. For the more popular ones, like Boschendal, it is advisable to book ahead of time. As the day wears on – beware – the wallet gets progressively lighter along with your head, while the crates of wine weigh heavily on the axles of your car.

The Cape Publicity Association will give you information on the Wine Route – which estates are open to the public, the opening times, what is on offer, etc.

There are also some excellent pocket books written by wine buffs to help guide your choice without you having to make too many costly mistakes. John Platter's *South African Wine Guide* is the best known and is updated each year to include the new vintages. There is also a book called *The Plonk Drinkers Guide* which rates the cheaper wines by price as well as quality. These books will also explain the meaning of the blue, red and/or green bands around the neck of the bottle.

Drinking In Restaurants

To add to the alcohol complexities, some restaurants have a full liquor licence which means they can sell any alcohol, while others only have

Some South African wine labels, showing the diversity available.

a wine and malt licence which means you are restricted to beer, wine and the odd liqueur only. Then there are restaurants that do not have a licence at all, so you bring your own drinks. This lack of licence does not necessarily denote a lack of quality in a restaurant, it just means they have not been able to get a licence or have not wished to have one. For the customer, as long as you are familiar with this quirk, it means you can drink exactly what you choose because you bring it along, and at half the price! As with restaurants the world over, drinks, especially wine, have a huge mark-up.

Although many licensed restaurants will frown rather long and hard at you, you are allowed to take your own alcohol into any restaurant you like. They are, however, allowed to charge you a corkage fee, for letting you drink it there. It is not an unforgivable thing to do, but it honestly doesn't win the friendship of the proprietor.

I think that the most appropriate time to bring your own wine to a licensed restaurant is when you have been there before and have found the wine list inadéquate or of bad quality.

ENTERTAINING AT HOME

A lot of entertaining is done at home and most of it is pretty casual – in fact South Africans are not very formal people in general. It is quite common to have people round for dinner or even a casual supper during the week, but it is most often done over the weekends. It is also fairly standard to offer to bring something: either a dish of food, or a salad, or (less complicated for a newcomer) some beer and/or wine. Often your host will tell you not to worry about bringing anything. It is then up to you to gauge the situation, to see if it is really meant or not. Except in the most pretentious homes, a bottle of wine or a box of chocolates is always welcome.

Dress for home entertaining is usually casual too. Men will be fine in jeans or slacks and an open-neck shirt. Much the same goes for women. There is no harm at all in asking your host how you should dress, rather than arrive in a dress suit and find everyone else around the pool in swimsuits!

Don't be too casual in manner, however. Slouching on someone's lounge suite (unless you are really good friends) or prying into the private rooms will not be welcomed, unless you are invited to view a new possession or to have a look around the house. And don't take your pets to visit your friends! Most people have pets and animals which rarely get on with their friends' four-legged friends.

The Braaivleis Or Barbecue

The Braaivleis, literally meaning 'roasted meat', is a barbecue – a distinct cultural occurrence, especially among white South Africans. Usually shortened to the word 'braai', it is one of the most favoured ways of outdoor entertaining, and is also one of the easiest and most relaxed. And it's very much a family affair – kids are always welcome.

If you are invited for a *braai* here's the ritual: it's always outdoors, and around the pool if your host has one. It could be for lunch which means you arrive at about noon and expect to eat an hour or so later. Then the afternoon is usually spent chatting. If it is a dinner *braai,* you arrive in the early evening for a night-time affair. Of course when a *braai* is going well, a lunch-time one can stretch right through to suppertime and beyond. Vast quantities of beer are consumed, wine too.

The spread includes a variety of meat, fish (on occasion), a range of salads, bread rolls and special sauces. 'Sosaties', a traditional favourite, consists of little blocks of marinated meat sometimes interspersed with pieces of onion, green peppers (capsicum) and other vegetables. Another favourite is 'boerewors', or 'farmers' sausage', which is a South African-style sausage, not too refined and often spiced with many 'secret' ingredients. Sometimes home-made 'boerewors' is served, but often they are bought from good butcheries.

If it's a very traditional *braai* you will have 'mieliepap' or 'stywepap' which is a type of stiff, dryish porridge made out of maize (a little like Italian polentta). 'Mieliepap' is often an acquired taste for newcomers. Often, guests chip in by bringing a salad or a dessert, or perhaps some beer or wine. When you are invited, ask your host what you should bring along.

Early on at a *braai* you may find all the men in a huddle and the women forming their own social group. It's the men's role to cook the meat to perfection – probably the only time most South African men can be persuaded to do anything remotely domestic, so leave them to stand around the fire, always with a can of beer in their hand, discussing both the merits of cooking methods and the day's sporting events.

Once the meat is ready everyone tucks in and a grand time is had by all.

—*Chapter Nine*—

LAND AND FUN

South Africa's geography certainly has determined the nation's approach to life and leisure. It has engendered a general love of the outdoor climate, sport and the country's wide open spaces. Leisure time is very important to almost all South Africans and many of the national pastimes take full advantage of the warm and sunny climate.

GEOGRAPHY

The country has an extensive range of geographical diversity. A warm and chilly ocean, each separately enveloping the two coasts which are lined by extensive sandy and, sometimes, rocky beaches. Dramatic mountains scale the land and areas of vastly differing rainfall give rise to scrubby deserts, rolling plains and delicate indigenous forests. But it's not all beauty and wonderment. A fast-growing population means the need for ever more industrial and infrastructure development, and the exploitation of natural and mineral resources.

Being at the southern-most tip of the African continent gives the country its geographical diversity; but it also means it is a very long way, even by air, from Europe, Asia, North America and even North Africa.

Where is it?

South Africa's land area is 1 184 825 square km compared to the continent of Africa which measures some 30 million square km. From west to east, it stretches from longitude 16°E of Greenwich to 33°E. The northernmost tip of South Africa is at latitude 22°S, just north of the Tropic of Capricorn; while the southernmost point, Cape Agulhas is at latitude 35°S.

There are three major land masses in the southern hemisphere and South Africa is part of one of them. It does not stretch quite as far south as Australia or even Tierra del Fuego in South America, however. Summer is from December to February which means no white Christmases. Winter is from June to August, so it will be a bit of a battle to get those strawberries (and cream) to eat over Wimbledon.

A World in one Country

The tourist board's most favourite slogan is 'South Africa – a world in one country' because of its enormous geographic diversity. In the east, there are the rolling grasslands (Natal midlands), lowveld bush (eastern Transvaal), forests and sugarcane plantations (sub-tropical coastal belt of Natal). In the north-eastern corner, near the border of Mozambique, there are lakes and swamps. However in the west, the earth is baked-dry by furnace-like skies, fanned by desert winds, and sometimes threaded with rivers that are frequently dried by the droughts.

The Central Plateau

Perched atop a dramatic mountain range, the Drakensberg, the central plateau was mostly a treeless savannah at the time of the African migrations and the early settlers. Today the geography is much the same, save for massive urbanisation and extensive industrialisation. Major cities like Johannesburg, Pretoria and Bloemfontein rise high into the radiant blue African sky where once only grass swayed in the wind and thousands of antelope grazed peacefully.

Outdoor fun – diving into a crystal-clear mountain pool in the Magaliesberg, only an hour or two's drive from the harsh hustle of Johannesburg.

The Eastern Seaboard

From Kosi Bay in the north to Cape Agulhas in the south, the eastern seaboard is washed by the warm, balmy Indian Ocean. The Mozambique current brings the Natal coast mild weather and a warm sea, so holiday makers can 'do Durban' in mid-winter and still enjoy the surf. The eastern Cape coastal areas are much drier than Durban and are cold in the winter, however they have also developed into plumb holiday areas. Because of their long sandy beaches, interspersed with rocky outcrops, inlanders flock there over the Christmas/New Year holiday period.

The Western Seaboard

Washed by the icy Atlantic Ocean, there are long, deserted, wind swept beaches along this coast, which until recently saw nary a soul bar a few local fishermen. Today the region is becoming more popular – ironically because of its isolation and semi-desert beauty. Just inland from this coast, if the rain comes in the early spring, the desert bursts into a magical carpet of brightly coloured flowers. It is called Namaqualand and the most populous flower is the Namaqualand daisy. In the centre of the southern Cape is the Karroo, a sparse and scrubby landscape, quite beautiful in its vastness under a domed sky.

Taking in the solitude and beauty of the semi-desert areas in the northern Cape Province. Colours are delicate and subtle, and temperatures are extremely high in the day.

It is well worth a trip to the Cape Point Nature Reserve to observe the exact point where the warm water of the Indian Ocean merges with the cold water of the Atlantic.

GAME RESERVES: A WALK ON THE WILD SIDE

South Africa is renowned for its game parks and well it should be. Most are state-owned and controlled by the National Parks Board which generally does a sterling job in running the parks for the benefit of the public and the game alike.

The most famous is the Kruger National Park which stretches down the full length of South Africa's border with Mozambique.

Zebras in a game park.

It is home to the country's big game like the lion, elephant, leopard, cheetah, rhino, giraffe, buffalo and thousands of other species of African wildlife and birds. It is very well stocked so it is highly unlikely that a trip to this game reserve (as they are usually called) will go unrewarded.

The Natal Parks Board also has some superb parks and wilderness areas worth visiting, both in the lowlands and in the Drakensberg.

Private game lodges are mushrooming across the country. They range from the ultimate in luxury worth hundreds of US dollars a night, like Mala Mala in the eastern Transvaal, to those that offer very rustic accommodation. Many are now equipped to cater for business conferences too.

Lions at a kill – not a common sight, but fascinating to see the food chain in operation if you get the chance.

A privately-funded organisation, the Endangered Wildlife Trust, commonly called EWT, specialises both in the protection of endangered species and in running special-education programmes for youths at the game reserves. Membership is not expensive and the benefits are tremendous.

Because of the extreme popularity of the game reserves, bookings may need to be months in advance, particularly during the school holidays.

SURVIVAL SENSE

To enjoy the wild side of South Africa's great outdoors, you must be well prepared. There are few things that are seriously dangerous in the bush, and you should be all right as long as you play the game by the rules. There are a few tips that will certainly go a long way to making your experience a pleasant one. Since many South Africans have grown up with the wilds being part of their experience, they may forget to prepare you sufficiently regarding the clothes wear, or what to take along with you. Remember, in the wilderness areas there are no shops just down the road!

Organisations like the Endangered Wildlife Trust, the National Parks Board, the Natal Parks Board and others run courses and outdoor programmes like hikes and trails for enthusiasts, which are a combination of education and pleasure. They focus strongly on educating the youth to environmental matters, as many schools do.

Some Practical Tips
Snakes

South Africa has a great variety of snakes, many of which are poisonous. There are anti-venom preparations for most species, but there are one or two that are deadly and have no antidote. Don't be alarmed by this as very few people get bitten by snakes. Take precautions and you should be fine.

DO NOT pick up or provoke any snake you may see, unless you are with an expert! And even then let them deal with it. The chances of doing this are slim as almost all snakes slither away instantly upon feeling the vibrations of your approach.

If you are bitten, which is highly unlikely, do not do the trick you probably have seen in the movies of tying a tourniquet between the bite and your heart – this does more damage than the snake bite. Act quickly. Apply firm pressure with a crepe bandage, a piece of shirt or nylon stocking wound extensively around the bitten area. This limits the blood supply but does not cut it off. Keep as calm as possible. Get to a doctor or hospital as soon as possible. You can take snake bite serum with you; but many people react very violently to the serum, so it is far wiser to have a doctor administer it if it is necessary.

If you do disturb a snake unwittingly, this will give it a huge fright and may cause it to be aggressive – the closest thing to it will most often be your feet, so when you are out in the bush always wear closed shoes or hiking boots.

Ticks

Ticks are common in most rural areas in South Africa. They are parasites that latch onto a host animal – wild or domestic, or you – and feed on the blood. They carry a wide variety of animal diseases especially something commonly called 'Biliary' which is found in dogs and can be deadly. So if you do take your dog to a farm (which in not really recommended) be sure to watch it, once you're home, for any signs of lethargy or being off its food. Go straight to a vet if that happens.

There are two types of human illnesses caused by ticks. You can get tick-bite fever. But that is not to say that every tick bite gives you the illness. Symptoms include a severe headache, fever, and hot and cold sweats. It is not a dangerous disease, but you can feel really bad for quite a while. If you are feeling ill and have been in the bush, tell your doctor.

It is even possible you may walk into a nest of ticks in the bush. Often they are so tiny at first that you may not even see them. People have landed up with hundreds of tick bites on their body and the collective poison from many of them can make you ill. One or two bites are unlikely to do much damage other than itch and be a nuisance.

Wearing long trousers when in the bush will help keep them off you, as will any of the anti-mosquito preparations like Peaceful Sleep or Tabbard. If you do find a tick on your body DO NOT pull it off. Often the head remains in your flesh and can cause a septic sore. The easiest way to kill it is to cover it with oil, after which it will just drop off your skin. Something simple like bath oil or even cooking oil is fine.

Getting Lost

If you are out walking in a wilderness area, remember that it is very easy to get lost. Land marks may be unfamiliar to you and your sense of direction may get a little confused. If you are adept with a compass, it is useful; otherwise, just don't wander too far from your camp site at first and familiarise yourself with the terrain slowly.

Fire

Bush or veld fires are one of the greatest hazards in rural and wilderness South Africa, especially in the dry months of the year: winter, for most of the country; but in the southern Cape, it is summer.

If you do make a fire to cook over, be sure that every last spark is dead before you leave it or go to bed. Also, if you are a smoker, DO NOT drop your match or cigarette butt. The veld can be so dry that it ignites better than tinder and a fire could break out in seconds. If you do notice a veld fire, alert the nearest authority you can. If it is caught early, it can be curtailed and eventually put out; but once it has become a run-away blaze, it can do enormous amounts of damage.

If you do stumble upon a veld fire, move away as fast as possible. These fires burn very quickly and are often fanned by the wind. If the wind changes, the fire can change direction which might put you in danger. With the very dry grass and scrub veld, fires sometimes burn very quickly and, fanned by even a small wind, can run a great deal faster than you can!

Some Dos and Don'ts

- If you are going on a walk for an hour or two, be sure to take a flask or bottle of water. Summers are hot and you may easily get dehydrated. You may even get lost or take a little longer getting home than intended. Be prepared, rather than thirsty. Many people like to take along cool drinks, but when you are really parched the most effective thirst quencher is water!

- Try not to wear very brightly coloured clothes when in the bush. It makes you very conspicuous and far less likely to blend in with nature. Also keep your voice down, so as not to disturb or scare away any wild animals like antelope or birds that you may come upon.

- Do not litter at all. And if possible, take all your rubbish home with you. If this is not possible, at least bury it deep in the earth so that wild animals cannot easily dig it up. It will eventually decompose. To save you the trouble of disposing the rubbish yourself, many of the wilderness areas have good rubbish cans that are cleared frequently

- Almost all property is private in South Africa, so don't just wander into any bush area you may come across. Most often it is farmland and the farmer could become exceedingly angry and may even prosecute you for trespassing.

There are other dos and don'ts which may be relevant in a specific situation. The best way to find out is to ask a local who may be with you. It is far easier to take your cue from them than to do something that is a little silly or dangerous because you are unfamiliar with the situation. But most of all, enjoy one of the great privileges of Africa – wide open spaces!

CONSERVATION VS DEVELOPMENT

As in most developing countries, the South African wilderness areas have been threatened by urban development, but the concerned public has fought back. Long, hard and bitter battles have finally stopped the state from allowing mining in the Kruger National Park accompanied by national slogans like, 'We dig our park. Don't you!'.

Less successful, have been attempts to stave off mining a part of

Cape Town's Table Mountain area and also the St. Lucia estuary on Natal's north coast. But battles must rage on for a long time before the balance between development and conservation materialises.

Conservation versus development is an emotive issue, but it is important for South Africans to realise that this is a developing country, so the balance must be determined relative to our level of development. For too long, white-dominated South Africa thought of itself as a developed country aligned with the United Kingdom, the rest of Western Europe, and the United States. With the spotlight now on reality, it is important to consider the country's needs as a developing nation.

WILDLIFE AND ENVIRONMENTAL MANAGEMENT
The early settlers in South Africa shot for the pot and hunted for pleasure too, until vast herds of wildlife had all but been wiped out. Because of violent reaction to this, hunters today have become conservationists. Forced to sustain the wildlife available, the national policy focused on wildlife management rather than care of the whole environment – admittedly a thought process new to most parts of the world. For this reason, South Africa does boast some of the best wildlife management in the world with up-to-date theories based on good research.

Now the broader issue of environmental management, as opposed to wildlife conservation, is being addressed. In the past, the vast majority of the population had no vested interest in the country; but with the new political dispensation, everyone will have a stake in the bounty. The United Nations believe that increasing people's standard of living is the best, and probably the only, way of increasing their care of the world around them. This holistic approach has been adopted by the ANC, since the greatest environmental problem in the country is poverty.

The world trend in environmental management is to work with business in a more open fashion. However, in South Africa a great shift of mind-set is sorely needed as the apartheid era encouraged secrecy.

LEISURE – IT'S A WORLD OUT-OF-DOORS

South Africans love being outdoors. Whether it is socialising, relaxing, watching or playing a game – if they are out-of-doors, they tend to be happy.

Weekends are a particularly special time for outdoor living which is why so many South Africans are reluctant to work on Saturdays. This is not good for the work ethic, nor the country's productivity, but certainly good for the soul, or so they feel. What people do depends a lot on the city they are living in.

In Johannesburg, especially in the more affluent areas, a great deal of entertaining is done at home, in the garden. Otherwise, a Sunday drive out into the Magaliesberg mountains north-west of the city, or a picnic at one of the parks, or the zoo, is quite common.

In Durban, with its mellow climate, even in the winter, people flock to the beach to soak up the sun and enjoy the sea. For a longer outing, Natalians drive to the southern end of the Drakensberg mountains in not much more than an hour.

Cape Town also has a beach culture especially during the summer months. In winter, it is far too cold to swim and beaches are best for long walks in this season. An added bonus for the outdoors-enthusiasts is Table Mountain which offers some of the most beautiful, if sometimes strenuous, hikes. It is also possible to walk a short distance up one of its slopes and then settle down with a bottle of wine as you watch the sun set over the sea. A drive around the peninsula is a firm favourite, as is a wine-tasting trip into the hinterland.

On weekend nights, the city centres tend not to be the bustling metropolises they are during the workday week. Part of the reason is that South African's don't like to live in city centres, and partly it is because there tends to be very little, if any, residential space there. Durban has tried to integrate its lively after-hours life into its city centre and to some extent it has succeeded.

DRESS CODES

Leisure time dress code is fairly casual, but it's as well to know just how casual to be. For starters there are still a few places, mostly elegant bars and some restaurants, that may deny you entry if you are wearing blue jeans – no matter how prominent the designer label is! To be truthful, I recently tested this rule in a top hotel bar that had a well displayed sign saying: 'No jeans Allowed'. Donned with a smart silk shirt, formal jacket and a pair of designer blue jeans, accented with a touch of jewellery, I marched right in. Not a word was said. Knowing the management well, I later asked why the sign was up if I had been admitted. The answer was obvious: Being a top-rate hotel, they insist on a degree of formality in their formal bar. Dressed in jeans or shorts and a T-shirt, I would have been asked politely to use the casual pubs that are aplenty in the sea-side resort.

For casual outdoor functions, and especially sports matches, jeans or shorts and T-shirts, sweatshirts or open-neck shirts are perfect for both sexes. Sundresses and cotton skirts too are ideal for women in the hot-summer sun. South Africans are quite accustomed to women baring their arms and backs, so sleeveless tops and dresses or halter-neck tops are just fine even in a more formal situation, except in a church. Men, on the other hand, may need to wear a jacket and, sometimes, even a tie for more formal functions.

In summer, most people wear sandals or sneakers to any casual event. Going barefoot in your own home or in a friends', if they suggest it, is fine; but in public places, it is not the done thing. Of course if you are being entertained around a pool, then bare feet is the norm. Mostly children can get away with bending any of these norms.

Generally, Johannesburg is a tad more formal in its casualness. In Durban, a much more laid back seaside city, flip-flops (rubber thong sandals), shorts and a T-shirt is quite often the dress of the holiday makers. Cape Town is a strange mixture of the two. More formal and proper in manner, it also has a great beachwear culture. However, in the city centre, people are more formally dressed.

171

THE SUN FACTOR

Remember that, in South Africa, the sun shines almost every day of the year. Sounds great in theory, but it takes its toll of your skin. The fairer your skin and the less accustomed you are to harsh sunshine, the greater the toll. So be weary and make use of the umpteen different sunscreens and suntan lotions available on the market. They certainly are quite costly, but worth every cent you spend as the incidence of skin cancer in this country is very high. Children are often out-of-doors for much longer hours than you are, so try to ensure they are smothered in lotion, at least during the summer months. It is so easy to forget the time or the intensity of the sun when you are sitting absorbed in a game of cricket. Your scarlet face, neck, shoulders and ankles will remind you of your folly for days thereafter! In Africa, sunstroke can be a reality – spending too long in the sun when you are not accustomed to it can make you feel really ill. It's not worth it.

NIGHTLIFE
Pub Culture

Like so many things in South Africa, the pub culture is divided into western-style pubs and 'shebeens', or African pubs. But, of course, today with the ever growing integration, there is a move towards a mixture of both.

Most western-style pubs are attached to hotels (all pubs have to be licensed by the government), but there are certainly many independent bars too. Pub culture is generally similar to pubs anywhere – often, rounds of drinks are bought by one person for the group. This can get a bit tricky if you don't want to spend all night there, but have to wait your turn to buy a round! If you want to leave early, try to buy an early round, so that when you leave, no one will call you miserly for not having paid your share.

Do remember that not all pubs admit women. There are still 'men only' bars, often attached to what is euphemistically called a 'ladies bar' which is one that admits women as well. On the advice of men friends and my own cursory observations, I would say that no self-respecting woman or man would really want to spend too much time in a single-sex bar.

Because, in the past, the state would not grant pub licences to Africans in the townships, the small backyard shebeens developed. Usually a room in a home was set aside where home-brewed beer could be bought and consumed in a rather congenial, if spartan, atmosphere. Most often they were owned and run by women and as the trade was quite lucrative, the more successful women became known as the Shebeen Queens.

As time passed, more and more 'white' alcohol was served in shebeens, especially beer. Many shebeen queens (and kings) began to openly flout the law with big successful, music-filled establishments. Today the laws have been relaxed, shebeens are legal and have become big, serious, lucrative businesses which are part of the South African Taverners' Association.

The Night's Bright City Lights

Night life in South Africa is limited almost entirely to the cities where, with a bit of help from friends and the *Weekly Mail* newspaper guide, you will find the kind of entertainment that suits your fancy. Clubs, pubs, discos, jazz bars (one of the most famous being Kippies in the downtown Johannesburg Market Theatre precinct where some of the world's greats like Hugh Masekela or Dollar Brand, otherwise known as Abdullah Ibrahim, are likely to appear) and a wide variety of traditional and local theatre are available. There are also many movie complexes with ten and more cinemas screening much of the mainstream movie fare and even some of the more alternative and artistic international films.

Remember one thing about nightlife in South Africa, and this applies to restaurants too – it begins and ends earlier than, say, in Europe. There are not many restaurants that will seat you much after 10 p.m. so be sure to check when the kitchen closes if you are planning a meal after a show!

Where Can You Have a Flutter?

Gambling in South Africa is no longer illegal, but is still controlled by the Lotteries and Gaming Board.

Since the dissolution of the homelands, the only places in the old South Africa where gambling was allowed, the board has been responsible for issuing gambling licences throughout the country. The more lax attitude to gambling resulted in a number of "back street" joints springing up across the country, illegal, but initially not often severely policed. Today, they are frowned on and many have been forced to close.

At the beginning of 1997, the process of awarding gambling licences was started and each of the nine provinces was allocated a certain number of the 40 casino licences made available in the country.

The National Gambling Board controls casinos, horse racing and national lotteries and imposes tough penalties on illegal gambling. Dog racing is banned.

Horse-racing is quite legal and there is a lot of it in all the major centres. Most races are run on Saturdays, but there are also weekday races. The most famous, moulded on the British Derby, is the Durban July. Always run on the first Saturday in July in Durban, it attracts huge crowds and attention is always focused on celebrities and outrageous dress sense. The Cape Met, Cape Town's equivalent, is not quite as famous but a lot more stylish.

SPORT

Most South Africans are sports mad. If they are not playing it, they are watching it – either live or on the TV. You may even find sports-mad colleagues taking a day off work to watch cricket or some international competition on the television that is not scheduled over a weekend. If they are not watching the games, they are talking about it. Almost every major international sport is played in South Africa and many of the major international sports competitions are screened on local television. Strangely, there seems to be very few home-grown games though.

The Sexes and Sport

A lot of outdoor activity and socialising has always revolved around non-competitive sport like cycling, jogging, swimming, sailing and generally being active in the sun. So when the health-and-fitness wave swept the world at the beginning of the 1980s, South Africans were ready and waiting.

Generally South African women have been less participative in sport than their men. Often their men rush off to play soccer, rugby, squash and more; while the women either stay at home, sit on the sidelines watching, or perhaps organise the social activities of the event. However, over the last decade or more, this has been changing and now a number of women do play almost every form of sport. Only recently, a young woman soccer player, who had played in a women's soccer team for a number of years, was incorporated in a regular men's club competition and she proved her salt immediately.

At competition level, women have held their own in some sports more than others – tennis and athletics being notables. But still, the dominant national sports are the male preserves of rugby, soccer and cricket.

The Bicycle Buzz

Like the trend in other parts of the world in recent years, cycling – particularly social cycling – has increased in popularity by leaps and bounds. Over weekends, and especially on Sundays, people jump on their bikes and either pedal down the sweeping trunk roads in the city suburbs (never cycle on a freeway or motorway as it is against the law!) or they go mountain biking on any rugged terrain around.

The most famous and the most fun bicycle race in Africa is the Argus Cycle Tour which takes a 105 km tour around the Peninsula and back to Cape Town. It's a very hilly course, so you do need a modicum of fitness to enjoy it. Racing rules and etiquette apply as it is a serious race for the serious racers, but it can be a day of great fun. If you have any energy left, there are beautiful scenic views to admire. South Africa's own version of the Tour de France, the Rapport Cycle Tour, attracts a fairly large number of international teams.

If you are a cyclist or would like to start cycling, contact the Western Province Pedal Power Association in Cape Town at (021) 689-8420 during office hours. They will give you information about cycling organisations throughout the country, or you could buy a copy of the organisation's magazine *LifeCycle* in which you will find a list of all the regional Pedal Power organisations.

Joining any form of sports club is a great way to meet a wide variety of new friends, people that you would perhaps not meet while going about your day-to-day life.

Pavement Pounders

Jogging has always been a favourite way of exercising for many South Africans. At first light on a summer's morning, or in the evenings after work, you will see people of all shapes and sizes pounding the pavements, running round tracks; or if you are in the rural areas, you may see someone taking off down a dusty track. On the mines, running has become somewhat of a cult and many of those who started running for pleasure have become some of South Africa's top marathoners.

A lot of joggers draw their inspiration from the competitors of the ultra-distance Comrades Marathon, an event which is run uphill and down dale for some 87 km each year between Durban and Pietermaritzburg. Over 14 000 people enter in this race each year which has some of the greatest spectator support of any road race in the world, according to international athletes who have recently begun competing in it.

The camaraderie it engenders is quite special. Of course, you will have the country's best marathoners out to prove they are the best; but even among them, the spirit of friendship is always of first importance. In the field, you will find every shape and size of person imaginable. There are blind runners helped every step of the way (and every step of the year-long training sessions leading up to the race) by fellow runners; veterans, some well into their seventies; and a number of women, whose membership is rapidly increasing. Recently, a woman who suffered from multiple sclerosis completed the gruelling course to huge applause from the crowd that usually lines the entire route from start to finish. Each year, the route alternates between Durban-Pietermaritzburg and Pietermaritzburg-Durban.

To get in touch with a running club, you can telephone Athletics South Africa in Pretoria at (011) 402-4973. They will be able to give you a list of the running clubs in the area you live in.

Golfers' Paradise

Because space is not really at a premium in South Africa, there are a number of golf clubs scattered across all the major cities, and there is hardly a small town that doesn't have at least a 'nine hole'. By western and Japanese standards, club memberships are not too expensive and playing the game does not usually cost an arm and a leg either. Many of the golf courses are owned by clubs and admittance of casual members is allowed by some.

The Million Dollar Bash

The locally grown hotel and leisure conglomerate, Sun International, hosts the Million Dollar Golf Tournament each year at their flagship resort, Sun City. It is by invitation only and all the big name players are keen to test their prowess for this mega prize. It also has a huge spectator following. For the rest of the year, the course is open to guests in any of the hotels in the complex. A second international golf course has recently been completed at The Lost City, part of the Sun City complex.

Anyone for Tennis?

Tennis has certainly been the preserve of the more affluent in South Africa. Saturday afternoons and Sundays see almost every tennis court in the urban areas in full use. Most tennis courts belong to clubs, but there are some that are owned by the city or town municipalities where anybody is allowed to play. For competitive players, all the local tennis clubs take part in the various levels of league tennis. Sometimes, this becomes very serious stuff as inter-club rivalry is intense.

There are also a number of tennis tournaments and competitions held across the country. With South Africa back in the world circuit again, the South African Open and the Standard Bank World Doubles Championship attracts international players of high standard now. Both these tournaments are for men only.

Because properties tend to be quite large in the affluent residential suburbs, there are quite a number of private tennis courts. Consequently, tennis parties are quite a common feature of weekend social life. You may well be invited to play a few games on a Saturday afternoon and then stay on for a casual dinner.

Most clubs insist tennis players dress in traditional white (or nearly white) and even on private courts, most people wear standard tennis gear.

Soccer

Soccer is one of the most widely followed and played games in the country, especially among the African population. The overall controlling body is the South African Football Association (SAFA), an amateur body representing all soccer organisations in the county. It also runs the amateur league wing. The National Soccer League (NSL) is the body responsible for all professional soccer teams.

If you are a keen amateur player, there are a host of clubs you can join. Soccer has been the most multi-racial game in the country for many years. If you are a player, joining a club is an ideal way to meet

anything else about South African soccer, call SAFA in Johannesburg at (011) 494-3522/3.

Local amateur soccer players enjoying a neighbourhood game.

The Price You Pay

Most sports equipment is imported, which means you pay over the top with the added import tax. Some clothing is locally made and not as prohibitive in price, but it is also not always of the best quality. So, especially if you are coming to South Africa from the US or the Far East, buy your sporting goods at home. I recently needed new running shoes and when I commented on the astronomical price of a good pair of shoes, the sales assistant quipped, 'Well, take a second mortgage on your house. That should do it.'

The General Sporting Helplines

Whether you have a competitive bent or just want to play sport for fun, the Confederation for South African Sport, contactable in Pretoria at (012) 343-2470, can supply you with the contact numbers

The General Sporting Helplines

Whether you have a competitive bent or just want to play sport for fun, the Southern African Federation for Movement and Leisure Sciences in Pretoria has a research department and a sports information centre that will help you with any sporting enquiries. It can be reached at (012) 663-3290/1/2/3.

The Politics of Sports

One of the most effective weapons used by the international community against the apartheid society was the sports boycott. Very little hurts a truly South African male as much as not being part of the world rugby community; this means not being able to pit their favourite scrum against the equivalent Lion or All Black or even being able to view many of the international matches on television.

But that is all in the past now. The first major step back into the great sporting world was South Africa's participation in the Barcelona Olympic Games after being excluded since the early 1960s. The effects of international isolation had certainly taken their toll. As in most sports, South African athletes were far outclassed. But the nation's joy of being back with the rest of the world was encapsulated in the touching gesture of African solidarity when South African Elana Meyer, silver medallist in the women's athletics 10 000m, embraced fellow African and gold medal winner, Darartu Tulu, from Ethiopia, and ran with her as she was doing her lap of honour.

The Green and Gold

When a sports person is referred to as a 'Springbok' it means they have represented South Africa for their sport and have received their national sporting colours. These colours are depicted on a bottle-green blazer with a pocket badge bearing the gold-coloured head of a Springbuck, an antelope. Although the 'Springboks' can refer to any South African sports team, it is most often used to describe the rugby team.

GLOSSARY OF SPORTING EVENTS

- **Bankfin Currie Cup** is an annual inter-provincial rugby-league championship played during the winter months.
- **Comrades Marathon**, the ultra-distance run between Durban and Pietermaritzburg attracts over 14 000 competitors.
- **Duzi Canoe Marathon** is a three-day race down the Umsinduzi River, from Pietermaritzburg to Durban.
- **Gunston 500** is part of the top five international professional surfing championships always held in Durban.
- **J&B Metropolitan Stakes** is a horse race.
- **Rothmans July Handicap** is a horse-race that is always run on the first Saturday in July.
- **South African Athletics Championships** comprise four meetings which make up this annual event.
- **The Castle Currie Cup** is a premiere league inter-provincial cricket competition played during summer over four days.
- **The Castle League** is the professional soccer league which is played from March to November each year. One-off internationals are great drawcards these days since South Africa is back in the international sporting arena. There is also an annual professional knock-out competition.
- **The Sunshine Circuit** is a series of 12 golf tournaments over the summer which attract international players.

With all these inter-provincial competitions it is necessary for you to know the meaning of four words: 'Vaalies' (pronounced vaahlies) refers to supporters from the Transvaal province, 'Banana Boys' come from Natal, 'Capies' are from the Cape Province and 'Vrystater' (pronounced 'fraystaters') are from the Orange Free State.

PROFILE OF SPORTS PERSONALITIES

- **Barry Richards** – a stylish opening right-hand batsman. Retired.
- **Brian Mitchell** – a junior heavy-weight world-champion boxer. He has now retired from boxing and is a businessman.
- **Bruce Fordyce** – an ultra distance marathoner of world fame. He has won the gruelling Comrades Marathon nine times and, since the lifting of sports boycotts, is now competing on the world ultra distance circuit. Having a social conscience, he is contemplating entering politics. Blond, blue eyes and very slightly built.
- **David Frost** – one of the world's top ten golfers. Now living in the United States and plays the United States' circuit.
- **Elana Meyer** – a diminutive middle-distance athlete, particularly good at 10 000m and 5 000m. She won a silver medal at the 1992 Barcelona Olympics for 10 000m, while also holding a number of records in Africa. Small, dark and vivacious.
- **Gary Player** – South Africa's most famous and world-class golfer. He has won many international competitions and played the world circuit for decades. Player is also making a name for himself internationally by building world-class tournament golf courses.
- **Graeme Pollock** – a Springbok cricketer and a left-hand batsman. At 16 years old, he was the youngest player ever to make a first class century. He is retired and is now a cricket selector.
- **Johann Kriek** – he played the world tennis circuit and was ranked in the top ten at one time. Now married, he lives in the United States.
- **Jomo Sono** – one of the country's best ever soccer stars. He played in the United States and alongside world great, Pele. Retired from soccer, he is now a wealthy businessman who owns the Jomo Cosmos football team.
- **Kaizer Motaung** – also a retired soccer great who now owns the Kaizer Chiefs, one of the top teams in the country.
- **Karen Muir** – as a 12-year-old, she was South Africa's greatest

swimmer. By the time she was 16 years old, she held 15 world records. Today she is a medical doctor.

- **Mathews Temane** – a middle-distance and long-distance runner, one of the few South Africans to wear Springbok colours for track and road running.
- **Naas Botha** – a Springbok rugby player with great kicking skill. Captained the Springbok side at times. Not the world's greatest diplomat. Retired now. Blond, blue eyes. Married.
- **Shaun Thomson** – a world-class surfer, world champion at times. Now retired and in the clothing business.
- **Willie Mtolo** – An international name, international fame. A world-class marathon runner who has won the New York City Marathon and has a host of other trophies under his belt. He takes an active role in helping the poor rural community he came from when he is not on the world circuit.
- **Zola Budd** – A barefoot-wonder child who broke a host of South African middle-distance records and, for a while, held a world record too. After all the fuss of getting a rushed British citizenship to be able to overcome the sports boycott and compete in the Los Angeles Olympics, she collided with Mary Decker in the race which put her out of the running.

Chapter Ten

LANDOWNERSHIP

Although landownership is one of the great South African dreams, it has also been one of the most controversial issues around, at least since the arrival of the white settlers. And it is going to remain so for many years to come. The Land Act of 1913, which basically stripped Africans of the right to own land where they chose, and the enforcement of apartheid led to a great discrepancy in landownership between the different racial groups. Access limited by race is now a thing of the past and redistribution of land is one of the most thorny issues the new South Africa will have to grapple with in the years to come. In fact, the question of who really owns which piece of land is seen as the Sword of Damocles for the political party that runs the country in the future.

Almost everyone aspires to own land in some shape or form. Some may want a home in the city, some prefer the rural areas. Others may wish to be part of a tribal community with communal landownership rights, and yet others may want a second home – a seaside cottage, for example. There is a lot of land in South Africa, still enough to go round.

One of the biggest purchases you are ever likely to make in South Africa is your own home. So a good grasp of the nitty-gritty of home buying and renting is a valuable starting point in the long search for a new home.

CORRECT THE PERCEPTIONS

A mistaken belief among many white South Africans, and possibly foreigners too, is that black farmers moved to the southern parts of the country at the same time the European immigrants moved north. By implication then, their stake to the land was equal as allegedly neither group got there first. But recent research shows that this idea is fallacious as black pastoral farmers were farming at Table Bay (which is now Cape Town) some 2 000 years ago and that the first crop farmers had entered what is now South Africa, from the north, by about A.D. 200 – a wee while before the European immigrants arrived!

VERY DIFFERENT APPROACHES

Precolonial African farmers had a markedly different approach to land ownership compared to the Europeans who arrived from the 16th century onwards. Firstly, land belonged to the community and access to it was linked to membership of the group. The tribal chief, as head of the community, allocated the land to individuals as long as they used it. Land was not measured and no record of access rights were kept, but boundaries were pointed out so people knew who had rights of access to which particular piece of land. Right to use the land could

185

be inherited, but its size could be changed as the needs of the family or another family developed or changed.

IMMIGRANT INTERFERENCE

The first European immigrants altered these African concepts vastly. They believed land was privately owned or rented and owners were individuals. Land could be bought and sold with total security of tenure. Farmers were allowed to mortgage their land to raise money to pay their debts. They also believed that land could be inherited as it was, or the owner could divide it into pieces for the heirs. And contrary to the African practice, land was measured with written records of transactions and ownership.

This meant that over the years, land ownership tended to be concentrated in fewer and fewer hands and many people became tenants or wage earners on land which belonged to someone else – invariably it was black tenants and labourers on white-owned farms, which is still very much the case today.

These dramatically different concepts of land access and land-ownership sometimes caused a great deal of misunderstanding, bitterness and conflicts between the two groups in those early days. For example: chiefs willingly shared land with whites in their area, but the whites then settled on it and behaved as if they owned it. Neither party properly understood the others' approach to landown-ership thus leading to conflicts. Certainly these early problems hint at the complexities involved in resolving the imbalance in land distribu-tion faced by the new South Africa – no easy task given the deeply subjective nature of the different people's relationship with the land.

A letter in the *Weekly Mail* newspaper a few years ago expressed the opinion of Dobs Mfeka, an African. He writes: 'The land is a gift from God to the people … all land. It is not like a house. A house is made of man's things. Land is not for sale. It is like air. The land is my blanket. I wear it like my ancestors … Land belongs to the black people who were living here long before the settlers came.'

Not All That Easy

For the early white farmers, it was not just a case of walking into the wilds and staking claim to a piece of farmland. The various governments at the Cape in the 18th and 19th centuries controlled the land, but immigrant farmers had easy access to it. Prior to 1813, farmers paid a small annual amount to the government for access to the land they farmed. But in 1813 the British effectively gave them tenure to it. By 1828, Coloured people were also allowed to own their own land under British rule. The same deal was extended to some African farmers later in the century. In Natal, under British rule, Africans could own land both in their specially designated reserves as well as in the rest of the province. These rights were continued into the 20th century and only came to and end with the promulgation of the 1913 Natives' Land Act.

However, prior to 1913, in the Afrikaner republics only whites were allowed to own land and black farmers were confined to the independent chiefdoms and scattered reserves – areas specifically set aside for them. African peasant farmers in the Transvaal and the Orange Free State had to enter into sharecropper arrangements with the white farmers.

The Horror Of The Natives' Land Act

The 1913 Natives' Land Act effectively prevented blacks from owning land outside of the reserves designated for them. It also forbad sharecropping and other forms of rent tenancy by black farmers on white land. Although it came into existence more than three decades ahead of the institutionalisation of apartheid, this Act was certainly the basis for their segregation policies.

This Act and some 86 other land laws, proclamations and regulations have been used to keep all but whites from owning a share of their birthright until the pillars of apartheid were scrapped in the 1990s. All those rulings had to be condemned to the scrap heap before land rights could become accessible to everyone again!

Blot on the Landscape

One of the greatest horrors in South Africa's recent land history is that of forced removals. To enforce its policy of segregation, the Nationalist government forced more than 3.5 million people to relocate to an area designated to them by the authorities. This applied to people living in the rural areas, towns and cities too.

Soweto was formed in the 1950s when the government decided to move all blacks who were living in and around Johannesburg, and especially in vibrant Sophiatown area, to their 'own' location or township, as these urban ghettos were called. The area of Soweto is an acronym for South Western Township.

The forced removals have caused abject misery and poverty, a dislocation and breakdown of family relations, and sheer degradation to some 10% of the entire population. Besides these, the cost in monetary terms for the implementation of the Group Areas Act is estimated at R4 000 million – money that if well spent could have made a major indent on the drastic housing shortage the country has faced for many decades.

Who Has What?

Under the apartheid system 13% of the country's land was set aside to make the homelands for the entire African population, which comprised 74% of the total population. To make matters worse, the homelands have only 16% of the arable land in the country, and the majority of the rural Africans have no other way of earning a living other than by farming. Thus there is little wonder that the homelands and so-called independent states have never been economically viable! Their population density is over 150 people per square km, and growing fast. In the rest of South Africa there are only about 20 people to a square km.

Varying Solutions

Many South Africans believe that without a solution to the land problems there can be no satisfactory solution to any of the other problems facing the country. Quite a daunting thought.

There are a selection of solutions on offer. I am not saying that all or any of them will necessarily be implemented under the new democratic government, as discussions on the land issue will rage for years to come. What is a certainty is that something will have to be done!

The most radical view comes from certain sectors of the PAC who believe that much of white-owned land must be returned to the Africans, without any compensation being paid for the expropriated land.

The ANC says its approach to land redistribution has to be pragmatic and realistic. There will not be a single model of land provision, or a simplistic approach to the seizing of land from whites and giving it to blacks. Wholesale nationalisation would not work either, it says, but it does offer one option: very simply put, there could be a ceiling on the amount of land an individual or company can own. That would free a fair amount of land for redistribution to those who have none. How this or any other approach would be implemented is a tricky issue and one that is going to take years to resolve.

The Nationalist Party is opposed to this ceiling idea, but at the same time concedes that most blacks do not have the financial muscle to enter the property market via the regular route of purchasing their own 'spot under the sun' – nor will they for a very long time to come. Hence there is agreement that some alternative must be sought.

According to a senior consultant in an accountancy firm, a land tax must surely be inevitable in the new South Africa, but he felt the ANC should introduce it for the right reasons of generating revenue and not for the wrong reasons of redistributing wealth. A land tax would be a good source of revenue creation without putting the brakes on the economy and could also promote productive use of land, he said.

With the scrapping of the apartheid laws, in theory, anyone can live anywhere in the country; but the vast majority of the population does not have the economic means to buy the land of their dreams.

AGRICULTURE

Agriculture in South Africa is practised on 84 million hectares of privately-owned farms, comprising 70% of the country's land which is in the hands of 60 000 white farmers. Farming activities take place on a further 16 million hectares of communally owned land – by black farmers.

Agriculture – which translates into food production for the nation and for export – is a major sector in the economy. But it is also subject to Africa's unpredictable weather conditions. The devastating drought of the early 1990s knocked some 2% off the country's already low growth rate, pushing it into negative figures. South Africa's food production is vital for the country's political stability and the survival of much of sub-Saharan Africa, most of which is not self-sufficient in food production.

PEOPLE OF THE SOIL

Never underestimate the powerful symbolic importance of the soil to both black and white rural people. They feel very strongly about the soil: the land they live on, work on and love. For many, farming is certainly not an easy way of life. Many barely scrape together a living, but for most of them the alternative of finding work in the towns and cities seems a fate worse than death. Of course, there have been times in the country's history when severe droughts or economic depressions, or a combination of both, have forced many rural people to seek work in the cities. Some have stayed and become urbanites, but many pine for the day they can return to their land.

The love of the land stretches to many a city slicker too. Those who can afford it, have bought smaller farms or small holdings where they can play at farming over weekends and holidays, returning to their city jobs during the week. Although this may have increased property prices, the negative side is that much of this land is not being used to its full agricultural potential.

BIG CITY LIFE

As farmers love their farms, so city dwellers love their urban homes, spending a lot of time and money on them. It is one of the things on which people stretch their finances to breaking point. The reason is perhaps that they tend to spend a lot of time at home and in their gardens. A lot of entertaining is done at home and children tend to spend a lot of time playing with friends at each other's homes, rather than playing in the few parks or shopping centres and streets.

The variety of homes is extensive, especially in the cities, ranging from huge mansions on a hectare of land with a swimming pool and tennis court, to more modest but still very exclusive homes with two to five bedrooms and beautiful gardens. Of course the majority of homes are slightly smaller, but of high quality.

Suburban houses have larger gardens and more tranquil settings than city homes.

Apartment living is not a top favourite among South Africans, probably because so much emphasis is placed on outdoor life, but

191

there certainly are a number of apartments for rent and sale, especially in the suburbs closer to the city centres.

Homes in smaller towns are usually more modest than in the cities, but can have larger grounds as costs are much lower and space is less of a premium. The townships, pushed to the outskirts of the towns by apartheid laws, are also modest and even poor in structure and design, but not quite so volatile as the big sprawling ghettoes around the cities.

RURAL LIFESTYLE

Rural farmhouses tend to be larger and more rambling than urban homes – probably because they tend to be built by the owners, and have bits added on as and when the need arises. There tends to be the main house and outbuildings called the farmstead or *werf* (pronounced 'verff') with the labourers' homes built some distance away. Labourers' homes are often made by the employees themselves. They are very simple mud-brick buildings, plastered with mud and roofed with thatching grass or corrugated iron sheeting. Floors can be made with a mixture of cowdung and earth – a much warmer and less expensive option to concrete. Some rural labourers build more traditional tribal homes.

The national electricity supply organisation, Eskom, has a policy to supply electricity to the rural areas as quickly as possible, but the vast majority of rural Africans do not have electrified homes, nor do some of the white farmers. Fuel-driven electricity generators are sometimes used but the most common light sources are candles and lamps.

TOWNSHIP STYLE

The townships, mostly situated on the outskirts of cities, are a far cry from the middle class, green suburbs. Most houses in these ghettos were built by the government with as little imagination as possible. Homes are as square and as small as matchboxes and many do not even have indoor sanitation. They are plastered to the land in straight rows with not much more than a hair's breadth of space between them. There are very few open spaces or parks in the townships and hardly a street is tarred.

Of course, there are affluent black South Africans who, until the demise of apartheid, were nevertheless forced to live in the townships and thus built large and beautiful homes there. When the Group Areas Act that segregated living areas was scrapped, some of the wealthier township dwellers moved into what were once exclusively white suburbs, but a number have chosen to stay in the townships among their friends and families.

PRACTICAL TIPS
Where Will You Live?

No doubt you've chosen the city or town you plan to live in, so your first move on arrival is to find a home. Generally this should pose no problem at all in the middle class suburbs of most towns and cities. South Africans tend to be very mobile, moving home fairly frequently which means that there are always loads of homes available on the rental and purchase markets.

Unless you know the suburb you wish to live in, or have friends and acquaintances who can help you choose, there is no better way than driving or walking around to see what appeals to you. If you have children, you need to find out where the schools they are likely to attend are, where the closest shopping centres are, and also how far the attractive suburbs are from your place of work. Distances in South Africa, even in the cities, are often greater than you may expect. Also, the cities and towns are generally served by good highways and road systems, but rush-hour traffic can be tedious and time consuming.

What To Choose?

There is ample rental accommodation in South Africa – both houses and apartments – and even more on the market to buy. The choice is yours. It may well be advisable to rent a home on a short-term lease if you are not certain of the city you've chosen or need to give yourself time to find out how things really tick. There is a limited amount of furnished accommodation which can be very useful if your possessions are in transit. But check exactly what 'furnished' means as I have heard of some folks who found out, after signing the short-term lease, that there was precious little in the apartment even though it was rented to them as 'fully furnished'.

An old Cape Dutch house that is beautiful to look at but could cost a bomb in upkeep.

You should be able to get short-term leases for three or six months at a time, while regular rental agreements usually run for a year or longer. After that time, either party has the right to give a month's notice to terminate the contract. Some people prefer three months' notice for termination, but most often you can negotiate your preference with the lessor.

If you do rent, be sure you have a well drawn-up lease from a good estate agent, and if possible get an attorney to give it the once-over before you sign up. There should be nothing complicated in a rental agreement, but be sure you understand your responsibilities. For example: you are responsible for the electricity and water bills, as well as the telephone bill (which usually arrive monthly), but you are not responsible for the rates and taxes which should be paid by the owner. Of course you can undertake to pay them, but ensure that this is then reflected in a much lower rental.

Once you are ensconced in your rented home, you may well be held responsible for drains that become blocked or other plumbing problems (this is quite legal), so be sure that you check that these are all in order before you sign the lease. Some of the older cities like Johannesburg or Cape Town have beautiful old homes built at the turn of the century and before – a sheer delight to look at and very wonderful to live in, as long as you ensure that as a renter you are not responsible for the quirks and foibles of an old house which can be quite costly – like very old electrical wiring or plumbing from the Dark Ages. Many of these homes have been modernised – just ensure this is the case with the one you rent.

Rent Or Buy? It's Your Choice

Your decision to rent or buy a home is based on so many factors, many of which are personal. But it will certainly help to have a local person highlight some of the pros and cons of the two options.

Once the initial rental period is over, you can usually move out of a home on a month's notice. Quite useful, if you are likely to be transferred in a hurry or if you find something you like better. It is also so much easier to rent if you are only going to be in the country on a short-term basis. But as a renter you are paying the mortgage for someone else, something you could be doing for yourself with the benefit of getting your foot on the first rung of the local property-market ladder.

The residential property market is quite volatile, but in the long-term it has generally gone steadily upward. If you intend to be in the country for a medium to long duration, it is quite wise to buy your home as it is a fairly sound investment, especially against inflation.

How To Pay For It

Almost all people buy their homes with a bank mortgage, also called a housing loan. Unless it is a very inexpensive property, you will need to put down a deposit, usually of about 10% and then borrow the rest from a bank or another financial institution. Mortgage rates are not fixed – they fluctuate with the bank base rate that is used by the government to manipulate the economy.

However the banks are fairly cautious about giving you a mortgage and they scrutinise your financial status thoroughly. Thus they are unlikely to lend you more money than they feel you can afford repayments on, which can be quite comforting if you feel a little unsure of your circumstances in a new land.

If you and your spouse both work, the bank will take your joint income into account when assessing the size of loan they will grant you. They also send evaluators to look at the home you plan to buy, then immediately tell you if it is an inflated price in relation to current market values.

Beware of The Pitfalls When Buying

Almost all homes are sold through an estate agent who takes a commission from the seller. You, as buyer, do not have to pay the estate agent a cent! Some estate agents are fairly competent but, from personal experience, I would advise that you be very tough with them from the start. Make it very clear exactly what you are looking for and let them know, in no uncertain terms, when they show you houses that do not fit your description. It can save you hours of wasted time.

When you do find a home that you think you like and can afford DO NOT let the estate agent push you into making a snap decision.

An offer to purchase a home is a legally binding contract. If you change your mind once you have signed it, it can cost you a great deal of money to nullify it. There is a horror story, doing the rounds here, of a foreigner who did not realise what the contract meant and had signed eight before he realised his expensive mistake. The duty should be on the estate agent to explain the finer points of the buying market to you, but they rarely do, so make sure you ask as many questions as you can.

Once you have actually made an offer to purchase a home that has been accepted by the seller, the whole process of ownership transfer clicks into action. In some cities this takes only a few weeks, but don't be surprised if it takes more than a month or two. There is nothing to stop you moving in as soon as a convenient date is agreed between you and the seller. You will pay them what is called 'occupational rent' until the property is legally transferred to your name. Once your name is on the title deeds to the property, it is legally yours and security of tenure is assured.

Almost without exception houses are sold *voetstoots* which means that any problems regarding the structure of the building are yours as soon as you take ownership of it. There are exceptions, but it usually means going to the law courts. The best way to avoid drama is to check for things like rising damp (not common in a dry country like this but it does occur), leaky roofs and gutters, rotting wood floors, and as I mentioned earlier, the electrical wiring and plumbing. If you discuss these issues with the seller, it is wise to note their answers and put them down in writing with their signatures and/or the estate agent's as proof of witness. This will ensure you a better chance if you do feel you have been misled and have to take the issue to court.

The North-Facing Syndrome

South Africa is fairly far south in the world, so the sun strikes the earth and your home at an angle from the north – more so in winter when it is way up in the northern hemisphere. Thus the saying 'a north facing home' means it is sited with the main living rooms facing north to make maximum use of sunlight and warmth. Although South Africa has a warm and sunny climate, homes that are not north-facing can be cold and dreary, especially in winter.

Another pointer to be aware of is: winters never get desperately cold, so homes here are very badly insulated and usually not centrally heated at all. People tend to huddle round electric or gas heaters in certain areas of the house while the rest remains rather chilly, especially at night. I have heard many a European immigrant say they feel colder in a Johannesburg home in winter than they ever did in London or Munich.

Freehold Rights

Most homeowners aspire to free-standing houses which almost always have freehold rights, or purchase rights that make you the sole owner. Cluster houses are also usually sold on freehold rights, but you are also bound to pay into a kitty for the maintenance of the communal gardens, exterior of the building and the like. However townhouses, which are generally a duplex home joined by communal walls but usually have their own private gardens, are sold by sectional title. This means that a corporate body, elected by the owners, governs or manages the entire complex and its surrounds. Owners normally pay a levy which finances the upkeep of communal areas. A sectional title means that you own the home and can do as you please with the interior, but may not alter the exterior without permission from the management. It is however, as secure a title deed as a freehold.

In decades past, apartment blocks were seen as one unit and mostly only available for rental. About 15 years ago, the laws were changed and apartments can now be purchased singly, although the legal structure is marginally different from a free-standing home. As with a townhouse, all apartment owners will also pay a levy for the general maintenance of the building. Of course, you are responsible for the interior of your home.

Currently, foreigners can buy property in South Africa and the status is not expected to change. However, if you have set your heart on buying your own home, it is wise to check with your nearest South African embassy or consulate at a date close to your departure as there will be many changes while on the road to a new democracy.

Sunday Cult

As I have said, South Africans are ever so keen to up and move home if they see something they like better. In more recent years this has led to a whole new Sunday occupation – house hunting. It starts on Saturday in the bigger cities. The major Saturday newspapers have hundreds of pages of 'Houses For Sale' listed in alphabetical order with a photograph of the home's best face, and a flowery (and often very inaccurate) description of the home. Most of the listed houses will be on show that Sunday from 10 a.m. to 5 p.m.

This means that an estate agent will sit in the home and anyone can walk in and have a thorough look at it, as the owners will not be there. The estate agent should be able to answer most of your questions and will know what sort of price the seller is hoping to realise. Often they have leaflets with the details of the house. These come in very handy when you have seen 10 or more homes in a day and the images of each start to merge with the other.

Prices quoted are almost always quite a bit higher than the buyer expects. This is why they will always ask you to make an offer. There is always room for bargaining, but if you really do want the home, remember that there are others who may have made an offer on the house too. It is the seller's right to choose the offer they prefer. If you have set your heart on a home, try and persuade the estate agent to let you know if there is someone else interested in it.

This form of Sunday entertainment – a jaunt to view homes on the market – not only by keen buyers but also by the curious, has become an urban way of life for many. For a newcomer, this ritual has two major benefits. Firstly you can get a very good idea of what South

African homes are like in the space of only a few Sundays, and secondly you can quickly discover the relative value-for-money in the different suburbs.

Any Shape or Size

Urban accommodation comes in almost any shape and size. Houses are built in almost any architectural style and also from a mixture of styles. Size depends very much on your bank balance and also your needs. In the past, the more affluent sought huge homes surrounded by huge luscious gardens on large properties. They employed a host of domestic and garden workers to help run the show. Today many are changing to compact, easy-to-run homes but the emphasis is still very firmly on outdoor living.

The Sad State Of Crime

Because of the increasing level of theft and violent crime, security is a major consideration when deciding the type of home and the suburb to live in. Many properties now have high walls around which may seem imposing and unfriendly, but it does help keep burglars out.

Burglar bars, electronically-operated gates or garage doors, and outside lights that are activated by movement are becoming more common as the crime rate rises. Most houses have burglar alarm systems and a fairly new trend is to have the alarm linked-up to an armed response company. This means that if the alarm is triggered while you are out, they will speed out to your home and investigate. If an intruder comes into the house while you are there, you can also hit a button to alert them and they will come to your assistance.

A number of people, particularly the elderly, are moving out of bigger homes into townhouses as this does afford more security, albeit less privacy.

Parts of certain towns and cities tend to have a heavier crime rate than others. Some of the reasons for higher crime rates are the proximity of affluent suburbs to poorer ones. This juxtaposition seems to cause increased burglary, as does easy access from a wealthy suburb to the maze of a nearby township. In some cities, the downtown areas tend to have a higher level of crime than the suburbs.

Ask your estate agent for advice on crime levels, but the most knowledgable will be the residents in an area you are considering buying a house in.

—Chapter Eleven—

THE ARTS

The image of South African culture being summed up in words like *braaivleis*, sport and beer drinking is not quite fair. There has always been a small but vibrant arts world encompassing both the performing and fine arts. In fact, one of the first records of western-style theatre in South Africa is found in a sailor's diary entry, in 1607. He was working on board one of the vessels calling at the refreshment station of the Cape at that time. The sailor mentions that they performed a play by Shakespeare on board the ship anchored in the harbour.

There is no doubt that a great deal of the earlier art forms was largely Eurocentric. Because of apartheid, however, artists in every discipline have played their role in commenting and condemning the ubiquity of that system. Hence, the arts has been one of the most successful mediums of bringing people of all races and cultures together in a spirit of mutual trust and understanding.

Generally sponsorship of the arts has not been vast, but the state and the private sector have made some funds available to further the creative spirit.

SO WHAT IS ART ANYWAY?

You certainly will still come across South Africans who are proud to announce things like: 'Who me? Go to the theatre/ballet? No ways mate – that's for sissies', or 'That's a painting? My dog could do better.' These are stereotyped responses and probably internationally similar. But there are nearly as many who have enjoyed the small, but varied productions and exhibitions available.

The variety of arts is widening now, thus there is more to choose from. There is the traditional Eurocentric theatre that a number of whites still feel most comfortable with. These range from Shakespearian plays to British-type comedy and farce, but then there are local interpretations of some of the great European works too. Traditional art forms are also expanding. More frequently these days, one can see very traditional tribal dance performed in less formal venues like open-air public places or at the weekend flea markets. Alternative theatre, rich in South Africa's cultural and political history, has also strongly developed especially over the last few decades.

The spectrum of painting and sculpture is equally varied, ranging from the internationally renowned and highly sophisticated pieces to works by amateurs that are sold in the flea markets and outdoor art markets.

AND WHO IS PAYING?

From the artists' point of view there is never enough state and private funding available. Their point is quite valid if it is seen in relation to the levels of arts sponsorship in the developed world. However, in a developing country where there are major and basic demands made on the state coffers for social services, education and housing, it seems unlikely there will be much left for overall arts development in the foreseeable future.

There has been some degree of state sponsorship, though. Most of the funding has been for the performing arts and, until recently, almost solely for the white community. Through the provincial administrations, performing arts councils were formed and they funded theatre, dance and music. Although these art forms were patronised by the mainly white community, at least it meant that theatre complexes were built in some of the major cities. It is now up to the new South Africa to vastly broaden the spectrum of these venues to service and represent the art of the different racial and cultural groups.

In some circles, there is a move to have the state-funded entities disbanded and to reconstitute them in a far less Eurocentric model. A more democratic representation of art is aimed for and involvement that is more community based.

There certainly are some wonderful alternative theatre complexes that grew up despite or because of apartheid. They are discussed a little later.

THE ROLE OF BIG BUSINESSES

The other major sponsors of the arts are the big corporations, particularly the large banks like Nedbank and Standard Bank. These organisations run arts competitions that assist artists in bringing their work to the attention of the broader public in a manner very few individuals, especially the up and coming young artists, would ever be able to afford.

For example, Standard Bank allocates a generous amount of sponsorship to fine arts in general and they recently added a large art gallery to its fairly new corporate headquarters. The bank also collects and promotes African art, and sponsors various exhibitions.

Nedbank on the other hand, tends to give a lot of sponsorship to the performing arts by funding top international performers, particularly jazz and classical musicians, and it also puts a lot of sponsorship into local music festivals, concerts and the dramatic arts.

HOW SERIOUSLY DO WE TAKE OUR ARTISTS?

Unfortunately, in the grand scheme of things, South African art in general is not accorded great importance by the nation. Perhaps some of the fault lies in the fact that our outdoor climate encourages more earthy, sporty pursuits. But there are groups and individuals who work hard to bring art to the public and the public to art.

A few art competitions are held, but these are financed by corporate sponsorships that have taken the place of government funding. In a country with such huge distances between major centres, this fairly generous funding enables the exhibitions to travel the country and people to see the work of artists who do not live in their area. This is also a very effective way of bringing artists to prominence and giving the public an overview of national works that wouldn't necessarily get into a commercial gallery because of their unusualness, quirkiness or because the artist is young and relatively unknown.

NOT TO BE MISSED

Standard Bank sponsors an annual arts festival in the university town of Grahamstown during the winter month of July. It covers all the arts and is certainly worth attending. The arts festival has become ever more popular, which I am sure has a lot to do with the very wide variety of performing, dramatic and visual art that is represented there. This variety includes a lively mix of imported and indigenous productions, both fringe and mainstream. Based in some measure on the Edinburgh festival, it offers everything from traditional theatre to the zaniest fringe productions, fine art and flea market-type craft. It is tremendous fun and certainly not to be missed by anyone who wants to have a tremendous amount of fun, has a love of the arts, or just wants to see a very broad spectrum of the country's artistic culture in one fell swoop!

The same bank also sponsors a Young Artist of the Year award which popularises the winner locally by taking their work round the country; and, to some degree, international acclaim is conjured up too. An exhibition of the artist's work is taken to the major cities where the winners are given the opportunity to interact with their peers, colleagues and students on an academic as well as a practical level. Buyers of these works include the major corporations like Anglo American, Rembrandt and the banks; private collectors; and state and private galleries. They can all view the works of the up-and-coming artist while it is on its tour.

There are other arts sponsorships, competitions and awards given across the arts spectrum, but per capita it is still only a drop in the ocean. Many deserving artists often have to eke out an existence or are forced to turn to other careers.

THEATRE
The Alternative Route

Theatre complexes like the Market Theatre (Johannesburg), the Playhouse (Durban), and the Baxter (near the University of Cape Town) have played important roles in offering an alternative vision of the performing arts instead of the traditional Eurocentric one.

With a new boost from the Johannesburg City Council, the Market Theatre complex is growing in leaps and bounds with the whole area being developed into a multi-cultural precinct. The first part of the theatre complex, developed some 15 years or more ago, was built in the original city produce market. The huge warehouse-type spaces of the old market and much of the original signage were kept in tact. Three theatres, a coffee bar, a pub, exhibition spaces and a book store were constructed within them. More recently, the Africana Museum has been housed in the complex as well as a wonderful jazz club.

Some of South Africa's most controversial and exciting theatre has been staged at this highly experimental venue, often to the extreme ire of the apartheid government. Some productions that were first seen at The Market – like *Master Harold and The Boys*, *Poppie Nongema*, or *Sarafina* – became world famous. The theatre complexes, in general, were some of the first multi-racial theatres in the country, defying apartheid laws.

Every Saturday, the theatre parking lot is transformed into one of the best flea markets in the country. For a small fee, anyone can rent the stall space and sell almost anything. Thus a huge range of South African and the other neighbouring countries' innovative craft, individualistic clothes, bric-a-brac, books, jewellery and almost anything else you can imagine is available.

The whole precinct has been revitalised over the years and has been one of the leading venues for multi-cultural social activities. As must be evident, it is one of my favourite spots and I highly recommend it to anyone who wants to get a great taste of how social life could, should and hopefully will be in the new South Africa.

Defiance In The Theatre World

As long ago as 1971, some of the theatres defied the apartheid laws and opened their doors to all races. By 1978, the government had bowed to pressure and 26 theatres were officially declared multi-racial. At this time, apartheid was still firmly entrenched and not even sport facilities, hotels or restaurants were open to people of all races. Fortunately, times have changed since then.

Energising the Jo'burg Theatre Scene

The city of Johannesburg has just spent what some consider to be a small fortune on renovating and improving its major theatre complex – the Civic Theatre. Many feel it is still an elephant: big, grey and somewhat imposing. But a huge dose of creative energy has recently been added when Janice Honeyman was appointed to lead it into a new era. She is one of the country's most highly regarded actors, producers and directors, particularly famous for her outstandingly innovative productions originally staged at the alternative theatres. I have no doubt she will bring the same degree of dynamism to her new role, resulting in enormous benefit for all of Egoli's citizens.

Academia Plays Its Role Too

The more liberal universities have also played an important role in developing local theatre by staging active, experimental productions. The focus is broad and a lot of indigenous productions have been staged, especially in recent years, as the universities have an increasing number of black students.

Very often the standard of the productions is excellent – and to prove it is not my own bias, I took a friend and long-time resident of Paris to a production at the local university. She was so impressed with the standard of the production and the ingenuity of the locally-written play that she trotted off to confirm from a stranger (in case I was having her on) that all the actors were undergraduate students. She felt some were of international calibre.

In spite of the talent available, funding was reduced for the dramatic arts departments because of the strain of increasing costs on limited education budgets. However, students always seem to manage something innovative enough to get their show on the road regardless of finances.

Some Actors Make It Big

Some South African actors and playwrights have been very successful overseas. It is always a dangerous thing to single out a few of the famous, for there will certainly be many more who will be left out. But I'll risk it and mention a few examples. Anthony Sher, famous on the London stages for Shakespearian drama, was born, trained and began his early career in South Africa as had the late Yvonne Bryceland. She was famous for, among many other things, her roles in the internationally acclaimed Athol Fugard plays. In the later part of her life, she split her acting career between South Africa and London. Janet Suzman, also well-known on the London stage, is another South African export.

In fact, Fugard's plays like *Master Harold and The Boys*, *Boesman and Lena,* and *The Island* have launched a number of careers. Yet another outstanding performer is John Kani who is famous for his deeply moving roles in Fugard's later plays. He is also highly regarded as a local Shakespearian actor. Now a well-known director, Kani plays an important creative role in the Market Theatre productions.

Actress Nomsa Nene really made her fame in the dramatised novel based on the tragic life story of a domestic worker, written by Elsa Joubert, an Afrikaans author. Both Elsa and Nomsa became household words abroad as this quasi-factual story hit the international arena. Nomsa travelled overseas playing the lead role and upon her return has made a great contribution to drama through her involvement with the once all-white Performing Arts Council of the Transvaal .

FINE ART

In terms of sponsorship, fine art has not been any where near as lucky as the dramatic arts have. Simply put, there just isn't any money coming from the government for the sponsorship of painting and sculpture as there are no equivalents of the performing arts councils.

It may sound very harsh, but one of the country's leading painters feels that the effects of not being subsidised has been positive. He said artists were forced to make their own way, to act independently. It may not have done great wonders for their bank balances, but it made them find a vocabulary and subject matter that was independent.

Very Anti-Apartheid

Like theatre, South African art reflected the urgent issues of the time and place – the socio-politics of the country. It too has played a major role in criticising the apartheid structures, especially over the last few decades. This work has been well supported by the major national museums and it's well worth a look at the exploratory and innovative ways artists have approached the subject.

A good example of such protest art is that of Paul Stopforth. One of his most famous projects is his documentation of the death of Steve Biko, the famous black consciousness leader, who was persecuted by the police. He acquired photographs of Biko's battered body and did a series of drawings based on his wounds, as well as the police interrogators. This work was banned by the government of the time, but it was recently legalised.

Some of the more common visual imagery of the time are landscape imagery showing destruction, burning, and fractured landscapes that depict the horrors wrought by apartheid and those that erupted in its overthrow.

A Great Diversity

There is a huge diversity of art production in this country that is the result of the cultural mix heightened by the urban, rural and indigenous ways of life. This means that in public museums you will be able to see traditional beadwork of extraordinary beauty and quality as well as avant garde artwork comparable to European or American productions. The diversity and quality of art available offers a wide selection to the wealthy or those who just can't resist the odd art purchase.

Although our local galleries have never been able to afford a huge number of works from the world-famous greats, like say the United States has, there are a sufficient number to still your longings until you tune into the local scene.

The mixing of traditions, or cultural osmosis as the experts call it, caused by the interaction between Eurocentric and Afrocentric traditions can often result in work of a unique calibre. A famous example is the work of African artist Tito Zungu that depicts skyscrapers,

A modern art gallery filled with contemporary South African work.

aeroplanes and other necessities of our 20th century culture in a mode that is very reminiscent of the African beadwork. You will certainly see some of his work in the major galleries.

Other names to look out for when you do make a trip to the Johannesburg Art Gallery, or the galleries in Durban or Cape Town, are painters Clive van den Berg, William Kentridge, Penny Siopis, Tommy Motswai, Willie Bester, Derrick Nxumalo and Bronwyn Findlay. You should also look out for sculptures by Cecil Skotnes, Andries Botha, Jackson Hlungwane, Bonny Ntshalintshali, Jochim Schonfeldt and David Brown. Again, this list is light years away from being exhaustive, but it will help direct your experience of South African art initially.

There are also some superb collections of African art from across the continent. One of the most splendid is that housed in the Gertrude Posel gallery at the University of the Witwatersrand in Johannesburg – an absolute must for anyone interested in African art!

CRAFT

There are still very active craft traditions in South Africa that have a functional role in indigenous rural societies. The people produce artefacts and objects of great beauty like beadwork and baskets, embroidery, ritual sculptures, food and drink serving vessels, and other containers.

More common to the urban dweller and more easily bought is contemporary craft. These are made with rural craft skills but with new materials and serving new functions in urban societies, particularly targeting the yuppies whose demands of art are different. It has become quite trendy to use these urbanised artefacts in urban homes as they serve a great visual and functional effect – I speak from personal experience! Examples of such works are very finely woven baskets made out of telephone cable wires, or candle sticks and picture frames fashioned out of flattened food and drink cans.

Traditional African curios.

Much of this craft can be bought in the outdoor markets that are springing up all over the major cities and towns across the country. The prices are good and the crafts are fun items. The museum shops and galleries sell good quality craft, but they are more pricey. Besides these, a variety of small shops and boutiques in the more avant garde suburbs also stock craft work.

MUSIC

If music is the food of love, there shouldn't be an unloved South African in the country! Because of our cultural diversity there is a plethora of different music styles and tastes.

Again because of past Eurocentricity, western classical music has played a prominent role and has received state sponsorship in a similar way as the performing arts have.

Our classical orchestras, and there are quite a few, are generally quite good. Now with the lifting of boycotts and sanctions, we are seeing, or rather hearing, some of the world's greats on our stages again.

Jazz has always had a prominent role in the country with greats like Hugh Masekela and Dollar Brand being our most well-known international players. But there is also an extensive array of excellent jazz musicians around.

Although jazz has always been popular, especially in the townships, more venues are springing up all over the major centres. Johannesburg's most famous is Kippies in the Market Theatre precinct. Apart from the regular artists, you may just see someone like Hugh Masekela pop in for a bit of a jam. What a treat! South Africa has developed its own brand of contemporary music that is a wonderful fusion of western and African sound. Johnny Clegg and his band, Savuka, have captured the soul of this amalgamation superbly. Paul Simon did the same when he came to South Africa to talent hunt for his "Graceland" album.

It is quite unfair to try and list the many great contemporary musicians and bands that play at clubs, gigs, in the open air –

So long have South Africans waited for international artists to perform that the performance of the London Philharmonic was completely sold out.

anywhere. But for those of you who really want to feel our rhythm, pick up a copy of the *Weekly Mail and Guardian* every Friday for a comprehensive list of the happenings on the music front. The opinions of their reviewers are reliable on most occasions.

Choral work has long been a favourite among many of the African communities and competitions are held from school level upwards. Much of their music is of a religious nature, though.

The mountainous region of Natal houses the world-famous Drakensberg Boys Choir. There, school boys with talent pursue their academic work as well as a hearty amount of singing. This choir has travelled around the world and hosted foreign visiting choirs too.

ARCHITECTURE

Although there is a South African-ness about some of our architecture, most urban buildings draw from both European and American styles. Each major region or centre does have a look of its own, partly because of the nature of the different settlers and also because of the climate and commercial differences.

Characteristics of the Major Cities
Cape Town

Cape Town has some of the oldest buildings in the country and in their rural simplicity lies some of the most beautiful structures. The old Cape Dutch farm houses, now most easily seen in the homesteads on many of the wine estates, were built mostly with readily available materials. They have high ceilings, very thick walls and timber was used for floors, doors, and window frames. The farm houses are usually painted white with thatched roofs and much of the woodwork is painted a traditional dark green. Many of the old homesteads are open for viewing as you take a trip through the wine country.

Cape Town also has majestic parliament buildings in the city centre, accentuated by an oak-tree-lined avenue leading up to it.

Durban

Durban has a more Victorian feel about its earlier architecture with some of the country's most beautiful civic buildings still operative in its city centre. The city hall, the old post office, Playhouse Theatre, the old railway station and the national museum are all in close proximity. It is quite wonderful to walk around this tree-lined area in the early evening or on a Sunday, studying the buildings unhindered by the weekday city rush.

The city's beach front is newly redeveloped into what many feel is a bit of a concrete jungle, but it has made this area accessible to many more people. In leisure hours it is a buzz of Durban's cross-cultural lifestyle as people run and cycle, walk or swim, or simply just stand and watch the sun rise over the sea or the surfers riding the pounding waves.

As the country's major port, Durban has a functional relationship with its harbour. I always get a great kick from being able to look down some of the city streets and, at the end of them, see major ocean-going vessels loading their cargo.

Johannesburg

Johannesburg is the new kid on the block. Although founded during the gold rush of 1886, architecturally it is a hard and modern city. There are some wonderful old buildings, but they are mostly in the downtown area. The original Rand Lords, the entrepreneurs who made their millions early in the city's history, built homes of magnificent opulence on the hills just north of the old city centre. Today many of these old mansions still exist mostly as corporate headquarters, company training centres and the like.

But Johannesburg is really a fast track, regenerating city. Old buildings frequently give way to newer ones with glass skyscrapers being very prominent on its skyline, reminiscent of modern American cities. This is not surprising since some of the most overt glass buildings were designed by the famous American Helmut Jahn. An example of one of his buildings is at No 11 Diagonal Street, next to the Stock Exchange in downtown Johannesburg.

A new monumental banking centre for First National Bank has just been completed in the city centre. It has an interesting concept with an innovative approach to street level culture. In addition to the spaces for hawkers and small shops, paths and walkways interconnect for easy access across its two-block mass. Hence, a people-friendly environment is the result.

A lot of the Johannesburg city life has spilled into the residential suburbs in more recent decades and many people never come into the downtown area these days. Areas like Sandton or Randburg (which actually have their own city councils now) are almost like satellite cities. They have their own office and shopping precincts surrounded by residential life. At least some of this decentralisation can be blamed on the white fear of the crime rate in the city centre as it becomes ever more Africanised. Personally, I don't avoid the city centre as I find life there to be a hub of the real South Africa; a melting pot of race, culture, creed and class. It does have a fairly high crime rate, but then so does New York!

Some Style – Or Lack of It

There is an array of architectural styles to choose from in South Africa. Most of them cribbed from various European countries and then somewhat adapted to suite our sunny climate. You can have a mock Tudor home if you so choose or a rustic, white Greek-style home. Spanish architecture, or more often a poor imitation of the coastal Spanish one, is quite a favourite urban-style home.

Some of the southern European-style homes make a lot of sense in our sunny climate, as do roofed verandas that allow outdoor relaxation without being too frazzled by the sun.

More recently, there has been a post-modern splurge as well as a move towards a type of neo-classical design, especially for townhouses and cluster home developments.

But it is unfair to brand all architecture with an imitative label. There are a number of architects coming up with domestic architecture that is appropriate to the climate, people, culture and available technology. The style of these homes is peculiar to the architect who designs them and are often a pleasure to live in.

Some Major Developments

If architecture is your area of interest, it is worth having a look at Bank City, the First National Bank complex in Johannesburg's city centre, the Victoria and Alfred waterfront developments in Cape Town harbour, and the redeveloped beach front in Durban.

In addition, Durban also has some beautiful and highly decorated Hindu temples.

THE CULTURAL BOYCOTT

Some 20 years ago the cultural boycott came into effect, resulting in South Africa becoming fairly self-sufficient in its cultural needs. Many artists felt it was not the right course of action to choose because it isolated the country even further and prevented the spread of internationally accepted norms and world-wide changes. Some artists got esoteric, saying there should have been a distinction between entertainment (which was forbidden by the boycott) and cultural productions. They felt that the latter should have been allowed because South Africa desperately needed to be exposed to the 'civilised norms of western society'.

An alternative view, by a performer, is that South Africa should have been bombarded with ideas instead. Professor Andre Brink, world-renowned author, echoed that performer's view when he said, 'Our society at all levels needs maximum exposure to ideas of authors, playwrights, poets and artists who have the ability to communicate their ideas to us and which can make us a more caring society as a whole.'

Nomsa Nene, a highly regarded actress who was the lead in the famous play *Poppie Nongema* believes that 'there is a need to send our works abroad especially indigenous plays which reflect the way we are, our hopes, our aspirations, our struggle and our potential as artists.'

A Raging Debate

Is there a role for artists in the political arena? Some answer with a hesitant 'yes'. Others radically agree, stating that culture is first and foremost an instrument of the struggle; it is the soul, an essential

219

aspect of the lives of the people both socially and politically. An even more radical opinion, and not very widely held, is that without organising ourselves culturally, achievement of the set political goals is impossible.

Pallo Jordan, of the ANC's cultural desk, urged artists to pursue excellence in their respective disciplines and to serve the struggle for liberation with excellent art. 'Let us remember also that the future imposes grave obligations on us all, artist and non-artist alike,' he once wrote.

He and many others in the arts world hope that the next stage in art development will be when artists cease to be conditioned by apartheid and emerge with works of universal appeal and relevance.

For too long most of our art, literature and music have thrived on apartheid for its recognition and relevance, say a number of academics. Artists must now outgrow their obsession with apartheid if they don't want to be forgotten in the future.

—*Chapter Twelve*—

ECONOMY

South Africa is still a land of great opportunity. It is a developing nation with an abundance of natural wealth, a large and youthful population, and different peoples that all contribute to its unique economic culture. That you can make an economic success in this volatile and changing land is a belief that holds true now as it ever did; but today it requires more effort, innovation, patience and dedication to make a go of it.

TALL POPPY SYNDROME? NO

Most South Africans believe that life is about earning a living, and preferably a good living. The wealth ethic here is very similar to that in America where people who are financially successful are looked up to. In fact, the nation's interest in the more prominent entrepreneurs and money magnates is seen in the dozens of magazine and newspaper articles written about them. There are often articles about their lifestyles, business deals and when it happens, not forgetting their fall from grace as well.

One of the most famous entrepreneurs is the leisure resort king, Sol Kerzner. His story is the classic rags to riches one that gives hope and inspiration to many who want to emulate his success. He started his business career by buying a flea pit of a hotel in Durban, upgrading it and moving on. His vision was as vast as the huge African skies and he moved up and on until he had developed an internationally recognised chain of resort hotels and casinos in the independent states within South Africa. His coup de grace is The Lost City, all R850 million worth of it. This top of the range ethno-Baroque hotel and entertainment centre is quite unrivalled for quality anywhere on the continent. Right now it is not doing as well as it should be, but the pundits say it will certainly make a profit once the country is on a more even political footing.

There are many more like Sol Kerzner across the land and its racial spectrum. They stretch far down into history when the mining magnates at the turn of the century made mega-millions and formed companies that have developed into the present-day corporations like Anglo American. This company was the brain-child of Sir Ernest Oppenheimer, whose son Harry recently developed it into one of the largest business entities in the world.

Something I find a little strange, perhaps from having lived and worked in many parts of the world, is that although most South Africans are greedy for money and the resulting quality of life that it can buy, this does not always lead to hard work. Perhaps part of the reason is ignorance born of sanctions-induced isolation. Some people are just not aware of how hard the high-flyers work in the rest of the world to afford their high standard of living.

The Lost City Hotel, part of a mega-entertainment complex – brainchild of self-made magnate Sol Kerzner. Photo courtesy of Sun International.

NOT A FAIR CHANCE FOR ALL

The general adulation of successful business people is tempered by the resentment of those who have not been able to get a foot on the economic-success ladder due to racial discrimination and the uneven playing fields prescribed by apartheid. The underprivileged tend to support socialist and communist organisations which is hardly surprising because their only view of capitalism has been that based on racial inequality.

There is the feeling among many of the underprivileged that white South Africans, in particular, owe them a living because they have been severely economically disadvantaged. This displacement of responsibility also emanates from their utter domination by the perpetrators of apartheid. Having been told where to live, where and at what to work and who to marry, there is little wonder that some people just gave up taking responsibility for themselves. But as more and more people realise that this land belongs to them and that they have a stake in their own future, they are beginning to take their lives into their own hands.

SELF-EMPLOYMENT

Opting for self-employment has not always been part of the South African business culture; but because of the poor economy and rising population growth rate, so more and more people have attempted to create their own income. Particularly over the last few years of economic recession, hundreds of thousands of high-school leavers have been unable to find jobs in the formal sector. As the recession bit ever harder, retrenchment became a daily occurrence.

Some of the reasons for the low levels of job creation lie in the country's recent economic policy of self-sufficiency, aimed at overcoming the apartheid-induced sanctions. Often this led to capital-intensive development rather than labour intensive projects. Meanwhile, discriminatory education has left millions of people ill-educated and totally untrained to fit into the economy. Unions then used their political might to gain better pay for their members – which were quite reasonable demands considering the paltry wages people were receiving in the 1960s and 1970s – but there was little attempt to link the increase in pay to an increase in productivity. Many organisations did not even try to embark on large-scale education and training programmes. Recently, this has been redressed to some extent with tax incentives being given for businesses that embark on worker-training programmes. But as it has often been the case in South Africa, this incentive for training has come too late and the incumbent government is now faced with the need for major national expenditure on education and training.

The changing or scrapping of petty trade laws has enabled a burgeoning of street hawkers, especially among the poorer socio-economic groups. Small business development is being encouraged with tax incentives and special loan schemes being the most notable of formal govenmental measures. But there is no doubt that more red tape needs to be removed to free business growth, hence stimulating job creation and the revival of the economy.

Rights For Hawkers

Not many years ago, Granny Harriet Moyo died at age of 101. She hawked fruit and vegetables for 58 years to earn an honest living. But for nearly all of that time it was illegal for her to do this: illegal to try and earn herself a meagre living. She was forced to pay fines and even spent time in jail simply because she wanted to hold her head up high by paying her own way through life. But she would not give up, she continued to work.

Until a few years ago, a long list of ludicrous and totally unnec-essary laws were used to either prevent hawking totally, or at least harass the hawkers so much that they could not earn a living. For example: hawkers had to wear white dust coats and move to a new spot every two hours. All hawkers wanted was to benefit from the free enterprise system championed by the government.

Hawkers selling traditional crafts and curios, a means of earning a meagre living. This privilege has only recently been legalised.

Now the liberalisation of trading laws has occurred and hawkers trade freely on almost every city and township street. They sell clothes and trinkets, cosmetics, small consumables, fruit, vegetables – anything that can be easily carried away by the shopper and quickly packed away at the end of the day by the seller. Reasonable prices are the great draw as they are frequently far less expensive than those in the huge stores.

THE LOGICAL PROGRESSION

A logical progression from the hawker stalls comes the 'spaza' shops. Almost solely found in the sprawling African townships, these small backyard businesses do a roaring trade. As capital is almost non-existent and unobtainable among the poor, it is left to the would-be

A spaza shop set up in a seafreight container donated by a local shipping line, Safmarine, to the Khayelitsha township community. Photo courtesy of Safmarine.

entrepreneur to buy a few goods with cash that is usually borrowed from mates or from a *stokvel* (see under 'Alternative Financing'). With the profit, a few more items are bought the next time around and, in a remarkably short time, a thriving business is on the go. A lot of the credit for the success of spaza shops must go to the township residents who support them. Spazas are usually open from about 6 a.m. to 9 p.m. every day of the week, while others are open as and when you need them.

There was a time when the state tried to stop even these entrepreneurs, but the desperate need to earn a living usually outstripped the authorities of their power in the end.

A quaint spaza shop story comes from South Africa's major shipping line, Safmarine. Faced with a number of old shipping containers that would normally have been sold for scrap metal, they decided to see if they could put them to better use among the poorer communities. After some research, they found the greatest need was for housing the spaza shops.

The interior of the spaza shop set-up in the seafreight container seen on the previous page. Photo courtesy of Safmarine.

ALTERNATIVE FINANCING

Economic impoverishment in much of the community has led to certain unique financial organisations being developed where the traditional western systems, like banks, are often not geared to help at all. *Stokvels* (pronounced 'stockfells') or *mohodisano* (pronounced 'moe-dis-sa-no'), which means 'we pay each other back', are township banking systems.

These informal banking systems are usually formed by a group of about 30 women, although men sometimes participate too. They all pool a sum of money each month with one person taking all the money once in rotation. This allows the family to have a lump sum of cash to buy their large purchases. Hire-purchases carry an extortionately high interest rate and a traditional bank loan requires interest, therefore the *stokvels* or *mohodisano* systems ultimately saves the individual some money.

Monthly meetings are held at a different member's home each time, these are also social occasions where food and drinks may be served and the participants can get together to discuss the problems of the day or their personal problems. Great emphasis is placed on moral and social support, a far cry from the standard attitude of a traditional bank manager!

Another way of beating the high cost of goods has developed in shops that serve the black community in particular. It's called a 'lay-buy' and means just what it says. If you cannot afford an expensive item, you pay a deposit and the shop will hold it for you. Every month, you pay a pre-arranged amount against the purchase price until you have paid the whole cost. Then the goods are yours to take home. Many people in the urban African community opt to buy high quality purchases, especially clothes, and this is one of the few ways that they can make them affordable. It is an arrangement between the shop owner and the purchaser alone.

The system of hire-purchase, also used by all communities to purchase expensive goods, is arranged by traditional finance organisations like banks and other lending institutions. But finance charges are very high which usually means you pay way over 100% more for the item than its original cost. Many people use this means of financing to purchase motor cars and big-ticket household items.

GATEWAY TO AFRICA

Now that South Africa is no longer a pariah state shunned by the rest of the world and most notably by our fellow Africans, we are again developing both diplomatic and trade links with almost every nation north of us. There are expectations that we will play a major role in the rest of southern Africa by being the new gateway to the north. We do have one of the best developed infrastructures on the continent and hence can be seen as a leader in the economic upliftment of sub-Saharan Africa. But in some ways this is a daunting prospect as there is a great deal of economic development needed in our own country.

Nevertheless, South Africa's infrastructure is already firmly in place and well on its way to being linked ideologically and physically with our northern neighbours. Our transport network is fairly efficient which includes road hauliers, freight forwarders, shipping and air transport companies. The country's recently privatised transport authority is Transnet which operates the ports, the railways and has a hand in road haulage too.

Web of Infrastructure

South Africa has a very well developed network of roads linking all major centres across the country. Many of the big centres are linked by high quality freeways, others by wide well-tarred roads. In recent times, some of the freeways and good trunk roads have had toll systems installed to cover the huge costs of road building. At present these tolls are not unreasonably high considering the comfort they provide when driving over long, long distances.

The deeper you travel into the rural areas, the less sophisticated the roads become; but even in the farming areas many of the smaller roads are tarred or high quality sand roads exist. Unfortunately the same cannot be said of the roads in the townships where very few are tarred, or in the homelands and independent states where cattle frequently wander across the roads at whim. Don't drive fast in these areas and be sure your brakes are good because hitting an animal will do severe damage to you and your vehicle.

The railway network in the country is also fairly extensive, with both passenger and goods trains offering fairly frequent services between major centres. If you are trying to send goods to the more outlying areas by train, you may well find the transport time very long. There are rail points to many of the outlying areas, but often vehicle transport is needed to get your goods from the end of the line to a destination deep in the rural regions.

Although South Africa has always had fairly good rail links with our northern neighbours, sanctions and anti-apartheid sentiment meant that co-operation between the various rail authorities was often strained. The changes in South Africa and the co-operative effort between all the sub-Saharan countries in transporting over 8 million tons of relief-food aid in 1992/3, has resulted in a successful transportation network being established that is now used successfully for cross-border transportation of commercial goods too.

South Africa's harbours and shipping industry are both well developed. Durban is the busiest port but Richards Bay, further up the Natal coast, moves the most cargo by volume as it is almost entirely a bulk port. Cape Town harbour is also a good natural port. The ports are run efficiently by the port authority, Portnet, which has a fairly large development budget. It is now exploring many privatisation options as a means of providing better services. This financial avenue is sought as the new government will have to use a large slice of the fiscal cake to help wipe out the social inequalities, leaving less for matters like infrastructure improvements.

HIGH-TECH COSTS

To some, the word 'Africa' conjures up images of tropical jungles or weird and wonderful wild animals. But South Africa also has large, modern, technically sophisticated cities – the concrete jungles of the twentieth century.

On the office front, computerisation, electronic data transmission, faxes (of course!) and all the other high-tech modern conveniences are as much a part of most businesses as they are in other developed nations in Europe, the United States or Asia. But because of the high protective import tariffs, high-tech equipment is very costly here. Even your standard desk-top personal computer costs an arm and a leg. So if you need high-tech equipment, try and bring it with you. Also make sure you don't have to pay duty on it by buying it well enough in advance of your departure. Information on the importation of office and work-related goods is best sought from your nearest embassy or consulate.

BANKING

Banking in South Africa is highly developed and closely regulated to protect the interests of the investors – namely you. The Registrar of Financial Institutions is the controlling authority and banks have to submit monthly and quarterly returns. The banking system consists of a central bank which is the Reserve Bank of South Africa. It sets rates, keeps a watchful eye on money supply, tries to control inflation in co-operation with the Ministry of Finance, and is ultimately responsible for all foreign exchange matters.

There are five or six financially strong high-street banks which have merchant bank divisions as well, and then there are a few banks that are solely merchant banks.

The South African high-street banking system is very sophisti-cated, particularly in terms of electronic banking. All the banks have ATMs (automatic teller machines) and the machines are linked to most banks, so you can do simple transactions like drawing or depositing money at almost any branch of any urban bank. If you should travel in the rural areas, do not expect to find ATMs on every corner – and remember, some small town banks close at lunch time!

Having said how good the banks are, many memories come flooding back to me of occasions when bank clerical errors, delays or personnel incompetence have driven me to levels of wild rage – such rage that I have threatened to move all my accounts to another bank, only to hear someone say, 'NO DON'T! I have just moved away from *that* bank.' These frustrations, though personal, stem from the lack of a service culture here. With fiercer competition born of the severe recession, a great deal of emphasis is now being placed on training personnel in customer service. We have a long way to go, though.

My strongest advice for a happier relationship with your bank is to get to know your bank manager personally. Don't tolerate bad service from day one. This way the counter staff get to know that you mean business. Also, make as much use of the electronic banking systems as possible.

TELECOMMUNICATIONS

Telkom is the semi-privatised parastatal that runs the only telephone network in the country at present. They are monopolistic despite their claims to the contrary. If you want a telephone, you have to get it through them. There is no alternative at present.

Until a few years ago the telephone system was run by the Department of Post and Telecommunications that, in typical bureaucratic manner, had very little concern for customer service. Telkom now has to spend a great deal of time and effort on bringing about an attitude and image change. But, unlike most subscribers who seem to have more negative than positive experiences with them, I can offer some praise for their attempts in changing their attitude to customers. The secret of success with Telkom (much like with the banks) is to be firm, clear and, above all, polite. Thanking them when they have gone out of their way to help you will pay good rewards the next time you need their service. Many South Africans still treat them with the contempt their quality of service deserved when they were a government department, but now this is to little avail on both sides.

Telkom supplies phone and fax lines (which are the same thing), telex lines, a host of electronic data transmission services, telephone instruments and switchboards. Most of the international telecommunication from South Africa is routed via a satellite, but some destinations still rely on the undersea cable. Either way, connections are usually fairly good.

A private enterprise public telephone shop in Khayelitsha, the African township outside Cape Town. It is also set-up in a donated seafreight container. Photo courtesy of Safmarine.

Public Phones: Don't Bank On Them

Although most of the affluent (usually white) South Africans have telephones in their homes, the bulk of the population does not. Public telephones are few and far between and do not always work. But in recent times, with the semi-privatisation of Telkom, sharp township entrepreneurs have set up businesses supplying public telephone services. They charge a bit more than a regular Telkom public phone, but they are guaranteed to work.

Mobile Phones

The mobile telephone industry has taken South Africa by storm and holding one close to your head has become one of the most popular fashion and business accessories in the last few years.

There are two service providers, MTN and Vodacom, with a third expected to be licensed soon. You can access the world of cellular communications either with a long-term contract with the service provider, which normally includes a free or very cheap telephone, or you can purchase your own phone at full market value and enter into a short-term, pay-as-you-go contract. Remember the South African system is GSM.

A familiar sight, particularly in Johannesburg, is artificial palm trees used to disguise the very high antennae used to provide mobile phone services, which cover most of the country except in some rural areas. Service is intermittent in the more mountainous areas, too.

CONTRIBUTORS TO THE GROSS DOMESTIC PRODUCT (GDP)

The corporate sector has not had everything its own way over the last decade and more. Four factors have influenced its growth pattern in the last five years or so: high interest rates, climbing inflation rates, a downward-spiralling economy zooming at a rate faster than the rest of the world, and the empowerment of trade unions resulting in higher wage demands.

THE MINING INDUSTRY

The mining industry has played a dominant role in the economic development of the country ever since the first solitary diamond was picked up near Hopetown in the Cape Colony, in 1867; and the first gold-bearing rock was discovered in 1886 near what is now Egoli, or Johannesburg – also called the City of Gold.

Contributing some R28 billion to the GDP, the mining sector is also one of the largest employers in the land. Mining is currently a private sector operation with mineral rights either purchased outright or leased from the state. There have been a few rumblings by some of the more militant political groups who want to nationalise the mining industry as a means of redistributing the wealth in the country. But generally this is not taken very seriously as the major political forces, such as the ANC, have shifted their economic stance away from strong socialism to an approach more in line with the social democracies of the western world.

There are six major mining enterprises and they are: Anglo American, De Beers, Genmin, Gold Fields of South Africa, Johannesburg Consolidated Investment, and the Anglo Vaal and Rand Mines. These enterprises have recently split into a few separate entities and a number of smaller, specialised ones that together operate some 900 mines and quarries.

For many years, the South African economy rode on the back of the nation's mineral wealth. In fact, because of it, the government was able to spend vast sums of money on the implementation of apartheid – the formation of the myriad governments for the separate homelands and so-called independent states, and the duplication of most government departments and services for the different groups and races. One can only dream about the economic well-being of the whole population that might have been, had those vast sums of wealth not been squandered!

AGRICULTURE

Agriculture now only accounts for some 7% of the country's economic activity or R11.6 million of the annual GDP, while only a century ago the country had an almost exclusively agrarian economy. Although the percentage of its role in the country's economy is dwindling, farming is still seen as one of the larger and more important sectors because it creates employment in the rural areas and is responsible for South Africa's self-sufficiency in food production. In fact, South Africa is usually a net exporter of food, particularly maize, to our northern neighbours. Very rarely do we need to import basic foodstuffs, as we did during the devastating drought that struck the entire sub-Saharan region in 1991/2.

The mining headgear at the top of an old mine shaft in Johannesburg. This is a constant reminder of the great strides taken in the sophistication of the mining industry.

Most farming is in the hands of white private ownership which was encouraged by generous tax concessions, loans and government aid during times of severe drought. Most often, the rural black farmers operate at a subsistence level and on a communal basis.

BENEFICIATION – THE WAY OF THE FUTURE

'Beneficiation' is the latest buzz word in South African economic circles. And it makes total sense. With a huge and largely unemployed population, what better way to create employment and that sorely needed commodity, foreign exchange, than to value-add to our raw materials at home before we sell them abroad. This is where the country's greatest industrial development potential lies.

Economists think that there can be very little significant economic growth in the entire southern African region unless South Africa maintains and strengthens a market oriented, export-driven economy.

The Industrial Development Corporation (IDC) is a financial organisation that has been developing projects that will enhance general industrial growth by placing particular emphasis on exports and employment potential. Some of the projects the IDC participates in may not create large-scale employment in themselves, but they do generate high levels of foreign exchange which in turn stimulates economic growth and job creation.

South Africa has recently embarked on some major beneficiation projects which are anticipated to move the economy upwards. The Alusaf Project is the building a new aluminium smelter at a cost of R7 200 million. By doing this they are hoping to boost the country's annual output by some 70%, with a commensurate increase in foreign exchange earnings. Another blockbuster undertaking is the Columbus Project, a R3 400 million expansion to the existent stainless steel producing facility in South Africa. The project will increase the country's production of stainless steel by 380 000 tons per annum, making it feasible for South Africa to be a major world producer of stainless steel containers.

EXPANDING LOCAL PRODUCTION

About R100 billion or one third of the GDP is produced by industry which includes manufacturing, construction, electricity and water supply. Although South Africa has seen a constant growth of the manufacturing sector since World War II, this is still the area most capable of future expansion. Although the will to change is there, the country is still an exporter of primary and intermediate goods, and an importer of capital goods. In an effort to become an exporter of manufactured goods, there are a number of concessions and business incentives to encourage businesses to move into the manufacturing sector.

The country has a small core of scientific, academic and business excellence; but this is balanced by the vast majority who have little or no education or skills, but are generally willing to acquire them. As a manufacturer, training will be your biggest tool and need. For your efforts, you are sure to reap a number of tax advantages on top of productivity improvements.

FOREIGN BUCKS ARE VERY WELCOME

South Africa welcomes foreign investors with open arms! Not surprising since both sanctions and the political turmoil of the last few decades has made us less appealing as a safe haven for your dough. Nevertheless this is a land of opportunity for the adventurous, and even the less adventurous. As the country moves towards democracy, hosts of business delegations from around the world have been coming to assess the investment potential to ensure they don't miss out on a good thing when it happens.

Although foreign investment in South Africa doubled in the 1970s, the 1980s saw a massive capital outflow. The was due to the disinvestment programme enforced by the United States, where almost all their major companies pulled out of South Africa either by just shutting up shop or by facilitating local management buy-outs.

239

The Johannesburg stock exchange is one of the barometers you can use for the level of foreign investment in the country. Right now the level of foreign holdings in listed companies is far less than it was in the 1970s and 1980s. However, the rate of decline has slowed down tremendously because of the falling away of sanctions. Linked to that is also the desire by many foreign businesses to use South Africa as a platform for investment and trade in the entire sub-Saharan Africa.

A POSITIVE APPROACH

A Taiwanese diplomat who spent a number of years with the embassy in South Africa, has since retired and stayed on as a businessman. With options wide open he could have gone to the United States, Taiwan or Hong Kong. But he chose South Africa because he feels the opportunities here are tremendous for people with a tenacious spirit. When I asked him why he had chosen to invest here, he gave me a point by point answer which follows:

- A debt swop organised through the Reserve Bank is another way of getting a good exchange rate on money brought into the country as working capital.
- The regional industrial development programme offers good incentives to companies willing to develop industries and businesses in designated under-developed areas, which also have a huge labour pool.
- There are currently a variety of export incentives available to manufacturers – it is essential to discuss this kind of thing with the Department of Trade and Industries.
- Currently there is freedom in equity participation, which means local companies can be totally foreign-owned, unlike many other developing nations.
- There is freedom in company incorporation which means private companies can have only one shareholder.
- There is freedom in marketing for foreign-owned companies which means they can sell in the local market, and are not forced

solely into the export market as is the case in certain of the developing countries.

- At present foreigners can buy property in South Africa.
- Immigration is not difficult. A foreigner is welcomed into the country as long as they have something to offer such as skills transferal or the ability to create employment.

THE PARIAH STATUS
It Came

Sanctions on South Africa first began as early as the 1960s in the General Assembly at the United Nations. But it was the mid-1980s' addition of financial sanctions to the existing trade sanctions that really caused the country severe economic problems. In the views of some individuals, this strain led to the capitulation of the apartheid regime.

Trade sanctions were gradually enforced and by the 1980s were quite firmly in place in most of the world. However, as is always the case with sanctions, it did not mean South Africa could not sell her goods abroad, but merely that it became progressively more expensive to do so. All the intermediaries had to do was hide the country of origin – such is the hypocrisy of trade. Sanctions hindered trade, but did not stop it. However, the ability of the country to maintain economic growth was affected because it had to be self-sufficient which strained its resources.

The Comprehensive Anti-Apartheid Act passed in the United States in the mid-1980s forbad trade relations with South Africa in an attempt to pressurise the country to abandon apartheid. All American companies in South Africa either pulled out or sold the businesses off to local management. Some feel that this move did not force the government's hand, but rather the reverse. It led to the perpetrators of apartheid drawing into their shells and pretending the rest of the world did not exist. Others, including me, feel that it at least gave the local non-voting majority the moral support they needed to force the hand of government.

There is little doubt that the effects of sanctions have been great. Money that should have been used for new business development was in some cases used to buy up existing businesses as the foreigners pulled out. Thus with very little new business development, there was very little job creation. This is one of the many causes of the country's major unemployment problem.

The financial sanctions imposed in the mid-1980s caused the country major problems. Medium and long term non-trade related credit to South Africa was closed off, resulting in a serious balance of payment problem and a debt standstill. This has all been resolved under the new democracy and South Africa now plays in the international markets alongside any other developing country.

In my view, one of the most severe effects of sanctions was the isolation of much of the business community from the international world at a time when business trends were changing and moving ahead at a great pace. Much of South Africa has been left behind, and it will take a number of years and a great deal of effort for many of our business people to catch up with the rest of the world. There are people in the business community here who aren't even aware of what they don't know. These people tend to be unaware of the approach to business and work in much of the world, and especially in the newly industrialising nations.

And Now It Is Going

The release of Nelson Mandela from prison on the 2 February 1990 and the legalisation of the ANC was the watershed that began the first wave of the lifting of sanctions. A year later, President F W de Klerk's announcement that the legal pillars of apartheid would be scrapped gave rise to an even greater wave of sanctions lifting. With the establishment of a transitional executive council en route to full democracy, the last vestiges of the pariah status fell away and the country now trades internationally under the same terms and conditions as anyone else.

FORMS OF BUSINESS ENTITIES

The laws governing commercial entities in South Africa stretch back to our early history and are based on Roman-Dutch law, like almost all of our law. But as a result of the British influence, particularly on commerce and industry, we have quite an English flavour to our mercantile, company and insolvency laws.

Current law provides for a number of business entities, most of which are universal in nature. Recently, as a way of encouraging small business development, an entity called the Close Corporation was formed. It affords the small business person the personal protection that a company would, without the major expenses of a full company structure such as full audit and registration costs.

For foreigners, the advantage of a branch against a corporation depends very much on the tax structure in your home country. However, figures show that the most common structure for foreign corporate investors is the private company.

Statutory Regulations For the Various Business Entities

Here follows a general description of the regulations for the various businesses. A good accountancy and auditing firm will advise you on which is most suitable for your needs.

- **Public companies** have limited liability and no restrictions on share holders exist. But very comprehensive reporting and disclosure rules are required including a mandatory full-scope audit.
- **Private (proprietary) companies** have limited liability and are not allowed more than 50 shareholders. Comprehensive reporting is necessary, but disclosure is limited and a mandatory full-scope audit is needed.
- ` **Close corporations** give you limited liability and you may not have more than 10 shareholders who must be 'natural persons', meaning people and not other entities. Limited reporting and

disclosure (to curtail costs) are needed, but mandatory auditing is not required.

- **Branches of foreign companies** have limited liability and do not need a local board. However they have the same reporting, disclosure and audit rules as for public companies.
- **General partnerships** may not have more than 20 partners. However no registration is necessary. No detailed reporting, disclosure or auditing is needed either and every partner is liable for ALL the debts.
- **Limited partnerships** may not have more than 20 partners. They must be registered with at least one partner being liable for all debts. Liability of anonymous partners is restricted and no detailed reporting, disclosure or audit is required.
- **Sole proprietorship** has no statutory regulations.

Chapter Thirteen

NEIGHBOURS

Until very recently South Africa's relations with her many neighbours and near-neighbours in sub-Saharan Africa have left a lot to be desired. Since the Nationalist government came to power in 1948, all these former colonies have gained independence. They opted for majority rule and, to varying degrees, have been supportive of the ANC in its struggle against apartheid and minority rule in South Africa.

In retaliation, the apartheid government conducted a destabilisation policy in the region. In effect, this meant South Africa attacked the ANC bases in various neighbouring countries, frequently killing large numbers of innocent civilians and damaging property, not to mention violating sovereign territory and enraging governments that were impotent in the face of South Africa's superior military might. South Africa also gave covert, and later quite open, support to anti-communist rebel guerrilla movements like Renamo in Mozambique (which was intent on overthrowing the Marxist Mozambique government) and Angola's Unita (which was fighting that country's left-wing government).

Now, with the move to a new era in South Africa, regional links are becoming well established, especially as South Africa with its good quality infrastructure is seen as the gateway for trade to and from the rest of the region.

A very potted history of each of these countries will be useful in understanding sensitive issues and sore points vis a vis past squabbles with South Africa, and particularly if you are going to do business with them.

BOTSWANA

The British declared Bechuanaland a Protectorate in 1885, but the local chiefs were allowed to rule their people with minimal colonial interference.

Later, having won their battle not to be incorporated into South Africa, their heir apparent, Seretse Khama married a white British woman, Ruth Williams, in 1948. The major row this caused, forced Khama to give up his right to rule. He lived as an ordinary citizen, but soon became active in party politics. In 1966, the Republic of Botswana was declared with Sir Seretse Khama (knighted at independence) as its first president. Khama kept the country on a stable, steady and politically moderate path until his death in 1980.

His successor, Dr Quett Masire, who had been vice president and minister of finance, maintained his intimate involvement in the country's economic development. His pivotal role in the country's economic success story led to an annual growth rate of some 8% in the

1980s, substantially higher than the population growth rate. By increasing government spending to improve the infrastructure, Botswana hopes to encourage a strong manufacturing sector and tourism industry to stimulate future growth.

South Africa's relationship with Botswana was probably the most strained during the 1980s when anti-apartheid resistance was at a high point. At that time, Botswana was not immune to South Africa's bully-boy de-stabilisation tactics such as threats to disrupt cross-border traffic which are so vital to landlocked Botswana's import-export trade with South Africa and the rest of the world. It was for this reason, too, that they could not impose sanctions on South Africa without severely harming their own people's wellbeing.

Having the upper hand enabled South Africa, in the mid-1980s, to force Botswana to expel the ANC bases despite Botswana being a non-aligned country that was only supportive of sanctions and the ANC as a means to end apartheid. However South Africa still launched cross-border air and land attacks on what were purported to be ANC bases, causing ever frostier diplomatic exchanges.

The new political climate in South Africa in the early 1990s has allowed relations between the two countries to greatly improve.

Botswana is a member of the Organisation of African Unity (OAU), the United Nations (UN), the Commonwealth and the Non-Alligned Nations. Its principled stand on issues like apartheid and its generally moderate approach have given it an effective voice in many international deliberations.

ZIMBABWE

The Republic of Zimbabwe, the internationally recognised successor to the British colony of Southern Rhodesia, arose in April 1980 from the ashes of a 14-year-long civil war between the ruling whites and the African majority. International sanctions and internal guerilla activity eventually led to the capitulation of the white minority regime, but not before the country was economically on its knees. Many thousands of white Rhodesians migrated to South Africa – at the time, the last bastion in Africa of white minority rule.

Zimbabwe, like Botswana and others, was affected by the instability South Africa wreaked on the region. And, being landlocked, the only route to the coast other than via South Africa was through the newly independent Mozambique. However, South Africa's support for the anti-government guerrilla rebels in that country meant they were constantly able to disrupt this vital rail link.

Zimbabwe's strong and vociferous support of sanctions against South Africa led to direct military attacks and harassment, especially on ANC bases in the late 1980s. However, with the release of Nelson Mandela in 1990, the legalisation of the ANC and the moves towards democracy, relations are far more cordial and will be normalised once a new government is installed.

NAMIBIA

By the early 1890s, the Germans had secured the boundaries of what is now called Namibia. They colonised it and called it South West Africa. The Germans began to set up their administration, but not without resistance from the indigenous people including the Hereros, Namas and other groups. They introduced systems of pass laws and vagrancy laws which severely curtailed the freedom of movement of local people. They confiscated large numbers of their cattle and, as a final onslaught, embarked on a massacre of the Hereros.

At the beginning of World War I South African forces, fighting on the side of Britain, ended the German occupation of Namibia. In 1920 Namibia came under the administration of South Africa as a League of Nations mandate territory. In theory, South Africa was supposed to promote the 'utmost material and moral well-being and social progress of the inhabitants of the territory', but in practice it was administered as though it was part of South Africa. Thus when South Africa began to enforce apartheid on her own soil, Namibia got a dose of it too.

The Swakomund railway station in Namibia was built by the early German colonialists. Many of the buildings of this period in Namibia have very steep roofs and snow-catchers as they do in Germany – rather a quaint sight in a desert land were rain rarely occurs and snow is unseen.

The United Nations tried for many years to coerce South Africa into ending racial discrimination and to transfer, progressively, full power to Namibians. But to no avail. Thus a UN resolution was passed in 1966, terminating South Africa's trusteeship of the territory.

At this time, the South West African People's Organisation (SWAPO), an indigenous liberation movement, which until then had agitated non-violently for change, launched an armed struggle against South African forces. The battle continued for many years both in the UN and on the ground with SWAPO.

As most of Namibia's resources are in alluvial diamonds and mining (controlled in large measure by South Africa's mega-conglomerates: Anglo American and De Beers), South Africa was obviously reluctant to part with this rich milk cow.

The saga is as intricate as a jigsaw puzzle: SWAPO had bases in Angola from which it attacked South Africans in Namibia. There was a civil war in Angola between the left-wing government forces, MPLA; and the guerrilla rebels, Unita. South Africa backed the rebels; and the Cubans helped the MPLA. The escalating cross-border raids led to South Africa invading Angola in 1983 and holding large areas in the south of the country for a prolonged period. Negotiations, five years later, brought to an end these years of conflict and led to Namibia's first general election. SWAPO leader Sam Nujoma became the independent nation's first president in 1990.

MOZAMBIQUE

The collapse of the dictatorship in Portugal to the left-wing in 1974, led to her pulling out of Africa with major implications for her colonies, especially Mozambique and Angola.

When Mozambique gained independence in 1975 under President Samora Machel, some 90% of the Portuguese population, who represented almost the entire skilled labour force, left the country. Some returned to the motherland, but the majority emigrated to South Africa. The new government formed by the Marxist liberation movement, Frelimo, strongly opposed apartheid and allowed ANC guerrillas to infiltrate and attack South Africa from bases within Mozambique.

In return, South Africa tried to overturn his government by backing the resistance movement, Renamo. This group sabotaged road and rail links, hydroelectric power stations and oil pipelines, as well as waging an out-and-out war and guerrilla atrocities on the pro-Frelimo civilians. In 1983, the South African airforce bombed a suburb of Maputo, the capital of Mozambique, attempting to hit ANC bases in retaliation for a major ANC bomb attack in Pretoria. If ANC guerrillas were killed, so were many innocent Mozambican civilians.

Over the years of de-stabilisation and civil war, millions of Mozambican refugees fled to South Africa, Zimbabwe and Malawi. By 1984, Mozambique, being politically and economically battered, signed the Nkomati Accord with South Africa. This was an agreement between the two countries that neither would allow 'enemy bases' on their territory. Two years later, President Samora Machel died in a

This is the recently restored Polana Hotel in Maputo, the capital city of Mozambique. During the civil war, the hotel fell into severe disrepair. With the coming of peace and the influx of aid workers, this excellent five-star hotel has been restored to its former glory and is run by a South African hotel chain.

plane crash and some sectors initially felt it could have been South Africa's doing. He was succeed by Joaquim Chissano.

Diplomatic relations between the two countries were strained to the limit, and Renamo's renewed impetus against the Frelimo government in 1986/7 did nothing to ease this. Many sources believed that Renamo was still being funded by elements in the South African Defence Force or at least the right-wing South African organisations with military connections.

At the end of the decade, the two countries again tried to re-establish relations. South Africa agreed to assist in the rebuilding of the country's infrastructure and re-establish roads, rail and sea links.

One of most serious affects of the civil war, conducted primarily in the bread basket region of the land, is its exacerbation of the severe famine which first threatened some 4.6 million people in 1989. In 1991/2 another severe drought and continued hostilities between the Renamo guerrillas and the Mozambican government again led to severe famine and the need for large-scale international relief aid.

In recent times, various ceasefires and peace initiatives between the two sides have been entered into, and broken – most recently, and ironically, brokered by South Africa. In 1992, the Portuguese added their weight to the peace effort and a very tenuous ceasefire began, and with it the rebuilding of the country.

With the assistance of foreign aid, some of the basic infrastructure is being refurbished and upgraded. The ports and some of the railways and roads are again operative. Consequently, trade within Mozambique as well as with the landlocked nations like Zimbabwe and Malawi is steadily increasing.

ANGOLA

Angola, also once a Portuguese territory, gained independence in 1975 after the change of government in Portugal. An internal guerrilla war caused most skilled people to flee the country and left the ruling Marxist-leaning MPLA government with a destroyed infrastructure.

The MPLA refused to share power with any other groups, forcing the opposition to disband or fight. Unita, led by Jonas Savimbi, decided on an armed struggle. Cuban forces entered Angola in a bid to help the ideologically compatible MPLA, while South African troops backed Unita. This war involved varying degrees of intensity, the most severe being in the 1980s when South Africa occupied large tracts of southern Angola for an extensive period.

In August 1988 South Africa announced a cease-fire agreement in Angola. Both South Africa and Cuba slowly withdrew their troops from Angola. Despite sporadic breakdowns due to violations of ceasefire, by 1990, peace in Angola was more than a pipe dream. Both the former USSR and the US are believed to have exerted pressure for a negotiated settlement.

The multi-party Angolan elections were held in September 1992 with the MPLA winning by a narrow margin. Unfortunately, Unita claimed the elections were unfair despite the opinions to the contrary by a battery of international observers. Sadly, only weeks after the elections a major civil war erupted again.

Peace was again brokered and held, on and off, until the end of 1998 when the government and Unita set upon each other again. The scale of the war has hotted up throughout the early part of 1999, displacing hundreds of thousands of rural people and exacerbating the already desperate levels of poverty and infrastructural decay.

LESOTHO

Formerly, a British protectorate called Basotholand, the independent Kingdom of Lesotho is entirely surrounded by South Africa. It developed as an impenetrable mountain stronghold in the time of the Mfequane, the great migration of southern African people in the early 1800s. In 1868 Britain annexed Lesotho and from 1930 it became a protectorate run by the local people, with minimal intervention.

In the 1950s and 1960s, Lesotho developed a political awareness and was granted independence in 1966. Chief Leabua Jonathan won the elections to become the first prime minister. Lesotho also has a king.

Although Lesotho became a member of the UN and the OAU, supporting their stance against apartheid, the harsh reality is that it is surrounded by South Africa and dependent on its economy. Many of its people are contract workers in South Africa. It also has to use South African transport and ports for all imports and exports, and is a member of the South African Customs Union Agreement.

Lesotho felt strongly that South Africa meddled in its internal politics during the 1970s and 1980s and that it was behind the attempted coup in 1974 against Chief Leabua Jonathan. Relations worsened in 1976 when Lesotho refused to recognise South Africa's puppet independent state of Transkei as a sovereign country.

In the early 1980s, a South African Defence Force raid on an ANC base near Maseru, the capital, killed some 30 ANC members and also 12 innocent civilians. The military coup in 1986 was also blamed on South African intervention as a means of attacking the ANC bases in Lesotho. Only a week after the coup, ANC members were deported to South Africa and the blockade of the country was lifted.

In 1992 King Moeshoeshoe who had fled into exile due to internal strife, returned to Lesotho from the United Kingdom.

THE KINGDOM OF SWAZILAND

Once a British Protectorate, the Kingdom of Swaziland nestles in a corner. It is a tiny independent country surrounded by South Africa on three sides with Mozambique on its eastern border. Like Lesotho, its national unity was formed at the time of the Mfecane. Around the turn of the century, South Africa tried to gain control of Swaziland from the British, but no sooner had they negotiated this then the Anglo-Boer War broke out and Swaziland was returned to British administration.

In 1967 Swaziland was granted self-government and the following year, independence. The tribal leader, King Sobhuza, became

The King of Swaziland is seen in traditional dress at a local trade show. He is walking with an employee of the Swaziland Sugar Association, a body representing the largest industry in the country.

head-of-state and in 1973, he abolished parliament taking all power into his own hands. A benevolent dictator, he ruled until his death in August 1982. After his death, various groups jockeying for power led to a degree of internal instability which was halted when one of his hundreds of children, King Mswati III, was crowned in 1986. Mswati's ability and political acumen have been tested ever since by those trying to gain power through close association with the young king.

Although neither for nor against the ANC, Swaziland was used as a conduit for ANC infiltration from Mozambique into South Africa. This led to South Africa attacking the ANC in Swaziland despite requests to respect its neutrality and sovereignty. Simultaneously, Swaziland was used as an 'address' for South African sanctions busting.

Swaziland has a relatively successful economy, dependent in large measure on its extremely viable sugar industry.

Chapter Fourteen

BUSINESS ETIQUETTE AND PRACTICE

South African business is like a rough diamond. Some facets may appear quite clear to you because they are quite western or international, like the workings of the banks and other financial institutions. Others will be strangely confusing, perhaps very parochial, such as the plethora of trade restrictions and tariffs, or the tax laws. Then there are matters like labour relations and the trade unions which have developed a very South African flavour cultivated by the issues particular to this country

South Africa is an exciting place to do business. You'll have a frustrating time and a confusing environment within which to run a business and turn a profit as it is no easy place to make an honest buck. But most people who try it seem never to get it out of their systems. It is indeed an inviting challenge.

THE SOUTH AFRICAN BUSINESS EXECUTIVE

Top South African executives tend to be in demand almost anywhere in the world as their high level of skills and quality training in the fast lane holds them in very good stead. Much of their experience is gained quickly and under less-than-easy circumstances. This is the result of the 'brain drain' of skilled people to more settled lands which has meant more hard work by those left behind, who tend to advance quickly.

Generally it is felt that South African businessmen tend to be more happy with a win-win state of affairs in a good business transaction, unlike their European counterparts who are far more likely to go for the throat and a win-lose situation.

In comparison to businessmen from the Far East, South Africans are generally not as shrewd or thorough in their perusals of a deal. A local businessman recently quipped, 'We're a young nation – a lot of our business is done on gut feel and like our rugby players need to learn to play in the international arena, so too do many of our businessmen.'

Some black businessmen tend to want to offer you the world, but may fail to produce the goods. Possibly this arises out of sheer lack of experience in the business world, thanks to forced exclusion from it in the past. But perhaps it also has to do with cultural mores and niceties of not wanting to say no even if you should.

The old-school Afrikaner businessman quite often has a dictatorial and know-all approach to doing business, rather like a civil servant, but is often sadly lacking in commercial maturity. It would, however, be unfair to say this of their younger counterparts who today run some of the most successful businesses and corporations in the country.

GRAFT – THAT DIRTY WORD

There tends to be a rather high acceptance of hand-outs or backhanders. One local businessman said he felt South Africans looked for a hand-out while their European counterparts would make it up by driving a hard deal. Graft is not a behaviour trend that is encouraged and arises from the belief in days past, especially among whites, that they are above the law. Now that the water-tight seals of apartheid have been broken, we discover that even the civil service has not set a good example because one major abuse of public funds has been uncovered after another.

In fact, in 1993 the serious fraud squad in South Africa investigated 22 800 cases of white-collar crime worth some R3.6 billion! And those are only the ones that have been caught. Recent research into the reasons for this type of crime puts some of the blame on a fear of an uncertain future because of the political changes taking place. Hence the mentality of 'let's take it all now in case there is nothing left in the future' exists. The long and stubborn recession is partly responsible for the crime too.

DOING BUSINESS

Consensus from a number of very active businessmen is that English-speaking South Africans are more open than their Afrikaans counterparts when doing business, possibly because they have been the community most involved in South African business for a longer time. Again, from lack of exposure and experience, you may find some African businessmen holding their cards very close to their chest in case they blow the chances of a good deal by giving too much away.

A word of advice for foreigners coming to South Africa to do business: you need to gain the confidence of the locals. Because South Africans have been out of the international business arena for some 20 years or more, upper most in their minds is that they are a little naive and could be exploited when doing business. Hence they may

259

often be more cautious and wary of outsiders and take their time in assessing your integrity and genuineness.

Certainly in a multi-cultural country there will be cultural differences in the approach to doing business, so don't expect uniformity. In the Indian community, the older businessmen are extremely shrewd, think long and hard about a deal, look for the last cent in a transaction and consider every alternative before they make a decision. They may well consult other family members, the bankers and auditors. Thus the top businessmen are highly unlikely to enter into a transaction unless it's an absolute winner. The result is that, despite apartheid barriers, a large number of them have built up extremely successful businesses. Some of the younger generation tend to be more flamboyant, less careful and sometimes less successful.

Financial institutions, accountancy firms and legal firms certainly follow a steel-door level of privacy here as they do anywhere in the developed world.

Do Words Hold Water?

Although by law and ethic your word is supposed to be your deed, in today's recessionary climate a deal that is not confirmed in writing holds very little water. With cut-throat competition for business, even some of the larger companies have been known to renege on verbal deals, after the fact, when faced with a better alternative. Verbal deals can be enforced by the courts but the cost, time loss and responsibility to prove that the deal was concluded is often not worth the effort.

Don't Be Too Pushy

How should you negotiate a deal? My best advice is to leave yourself a margin, but don't be too greedy. It is not really part of the business culture in South Africa, except perhaps in the Indian community, to bargain hard at all. If they feel your margins are too wide they are quite likely to walk away from the deal rather than drive a hard bargain.

In the current market there certainly are bargains to be had, but don't squeeze too hard. If you do, you may win this time, but as we say here, 'elephants have long memories' and when the business cycle comes full circle, as it usually does, you may well find the hands of friendship are not extended too far to you at a time of need.

Meddling Mummies

To know how much interference exists between the government (or public sector) and the business sector, I nonchalantly asked a gathering of business people for their views and there was one immediate answer: TREMENDOUS!

Of course, for a start, the Reserve Bank plays a major role in almost any international transaction and the general consensus is that, from its ivory tower, it quite often dots the 'i's and crosses the 't's a little too pedantically with not enough regard for the current state of play in the business world.

In the past, especially during the high secrecy of the sanctions era, the odd disastrous transaction had slipped through the net leaving some civil servants with a lot of egg on their faces, while some wiley crooks had a small fortune in the bank. Thus, too often the game plan is drawn in black and white with no room for grey and, more relevantly, with little or no commercial acumen.

Said one businessman who has had a number of deals scuppered in this way, 'The good guys are penalised for the deeds of the baddies because of the complexes of certain public servants. Complexes that have arisen from their own naivety, as well as the less-than-squeaky-clean reputation for corruption in both the public service and in commerce.'

But there is a brighter side. In recent times, the more senior public servants and politicians are fast realising the need for a more consultative and less autocratic approach to the business community. In the past, there were many government control boards meddling in the affairs of almost every sector in the country. Recently, many have fallen away, especially in the agricultural field. And many more are

261

expected to loose their teeth. It is quite strange that the governments of the past, while being maniacally anti-communist, had installed a bureaucracy of red tape and centralised control that could have given the old USSR a run for its money.

Generally it is felt that the new government will be well aware of the power of the business community and would like it on their side. After all, the success (or failure) of the promises made by the new politicians to the nation will be determined, in large measure, by the business community's efforts to lift the economy and the country out of the doldrums.

Exchange Control: Bane of the Developing World

Moving money out of South Africa is no snip. As in many developing countries, there is this little hitch called 'exchange control'. Introduced in 1961 to stem the outflow of capital from the country and to ensure a measure of stability in currency markets, exchange control limits the amount of money you can take out of the country. For a resident earning money in South Africa, the system is quite easy as there is an annual calendar-year limit per person for holiday expenses and a larger amount allowed for business travel. The ceilings for these amounts have been raised recently and are adjusted occasionally, so check with your local bank on both the amounts and the procedures.

Repatriation of capital that has been brought into the country is a far more complex procedure and if you have any plans to move your money back out of South Africa, you should investigate the whole matter thoroughly before you bring it in.

The new government is going to scrap exchange control, but it will be done slowly and in phases, hence it is likely to take a few years. Certain off-shore investments are already allowed.

To Establish a Joint-Venture or Not?

With the lifting of sanctions and trade boycotts, there is far more interest from the outside world in entering into joint ventures with

South African based companies. It can be a very successful way of operating in a country new to the foreign partner, as has been proved in many developing economies like Mexico, Indonesia or Thailand, for example.

If it's a route you may like to choose, take a look at some of the pros and cons:

- South Africans know the country, they know the culture and they understand the market.
- They have, most often, established beneficial contact with the financial institutions for raising finance and the like.
- It is advantageous to set up a joint-venture with a company that already has an established name and all the goodwill that goes with it.
- A local company, especially an established one, often has the advantage of having chosen and groomed good quality local staff – if you start out on your own you would have to start at the beginning by recruiting your own new staff.
- A local company should have a good, hands-on knowledge of local rules and regulations as well as the law, especially the complexities of commercial and tax law. A good grasp of the ever-changing vagaries of the import and export tariff structures is also a boon to a newcomer.

Advice from a senior business executive in Durban is to be sure you are aware of your legal status as a joint-venture partner. The South African law holds you 'jointly and severally responsible for your business' which means that both of you and/or either of you are responsible for the business and any debts it may incur. Certain liabilities can be limited by the formation of a limited liability company – but don't just bank on this – seek legal advice in advance.

As an added precaution, he says, 'Remember, marriages can go sour. Be sure you are geared to dissolve a joint-venture, if need be, in a manner beneficial to your business and your future in the country.'

But he is generally positive about the joint-venture route saying that using foreign expertise combined with local hands-on knowledge can be beneficial to the joint-venture partners as well as the country's economic future.

THE VEXATIONS OF TAXATION

Most taxes are levied by the central government, but local authorities charge assessment rates based on the value of properties situated in their areas. These are commonly called 'rates and taxes'. In addition, the fairly recently-formed regional services councils charge levies to businesses in their regions. There is also a Value Added Tax (VAT) on all but very basic foodstuffs and other necessities.

Currently, the tax system in the country is in a state of transition and is likely to remain so for some while yet. A major commission of inquiry into the tax structure completed its investigations in 1987. It made recommendations for some major changes like a broader-based, fairer system of taxation with a reduction in personal tax. Also a move towards a greater degree of indirect taxes and the adoption of individual taxation regardless of one's marital status was suggested. Certain recommendations were accepted by the government of the time and were in the process of being implemented (some have been) when the demise of the apartheid government began.

Obviously, the new government will have a new agenda. Already changes in taxation and tax structures are under consideration in an effort to find the most equitable way of resolving the country's major socio-economic problems.

TAXES SIMPLY PUT

Direct taxes are split into income taxes and capital taxes. Income taxes comprise individual income tax (an annual tax on partnerships and individuals) and company, or corporate, tax.

Individual Tax:

Individuals are taxed at progressive rates on their income from, or that is deemed to be from, South African sources. At the top end, these rates are as high as many of the developed nations, especially if you have investments that generate income in your home country that are not subject to the South African company tax. The individual's tax-year ends on the last day of February each year. A tax form will be sent to you which has to be filled out, by you, and returned to the Department of Inland Revenue. Temporary residents and immigrants who meet the income requirements for filling returns are obliged to register as taxpayers.

There are constant changes made to the individual tax laws and it is advisable to get professional help as ignorance is no excuse to the Receiver of Revenue, who has made it quite clear in recent times that tax offenders will be treated harshly.

Pay As You Earn – PAYE

If you are employed by a company, the onus is on the company to ensure you are registered as a tax payer. You will automatically have an amount deducted from your pay cheque each month – called PAYE – which should be calculated in accordance with the tax rates. It does no harm to check that you are being taxed sufficiently to prevent you from having to pay extra money to the Receiver of Revenue (the taxman) at the end of the tax year. If, once you have filled out your annual tax form, you find that you have been paying too much, you will be reimbursed by the tax department within a few months.

If your income is not too high, you may fall into the Standard Income Tax on Employees System, always referred to as SITES. If you fall into this system, your employer will still deduct the tax amount from your income, but you do not have to fill out the annual tax form. No tax system is as simple as it sounds, so it is advisable you discuss your tax responsibilities with your employer unless you are quite clear of what your responsibilities are.

Any income outside of your regular salary, such as interest on your bank savings account, is also taxable and there will be provision for you to declare this on your annual tax form.

However, if you are self-employed, the onus to register as a tax payer is on you – and my strong advice is that you do register as soon as you begin your business. Also, find out all you can about the tax system from a reputable firm of accountants and even employ someone in-the-know to assist you, at least at first. There is nothing worse than being a newcomer to a country and through ignorance (or indolence), becoming caught up in a sudden bureaucratic nightmare of communicating with an angered tax department. Staying on the right side of the Department of Inland Revenue is worth the effort!

Most self-employed people pay what is termed a 'provisional tax'. According to this system, you are liable to submit returns twice a year and your tax liability is assessed on what you are expected to earn in the next six months, based on your earning power in the previous six months. From personal experience in this category, I strongly advise some good professional help on this score, unless your income generation is very simple and stable. It is not impossible to follow the instructions on the tax forms sent to you, but the peace of mind from having an expert put it all together is mostly worth the cost.

Corporate Or Company Tax:

For some years company tax had been at a high 48%, greater than in many countries. But the 1993 budget set in place a two-tier system that reduced it to 40%, but added a 15% tax on distributable income such as share dividends. The aim of this, quite noble it seems, is to provide an incentive for re-investment that in turn would stimulate the much needed job creation.

Companies are subject to income tax only on their income from South African sources. No matter where the company is registered, income derived in South Africa is taxable, even when the source is outside the country.

The corporate tax system requires the filling in of an annual tax return. This should contain a computation of normal income tax and all the information necessary to compute the company's tax liability for the year. No payment is made with the return of the form as an assessment must be calculated by the local Receiver of Revenue.

Tardiness Costs You

The Receiver of Revenue is entitled to charge you penalties for late submission of tax forms of up to twice the amount of tax due. This charge is in addition to the normal tax due by you. In the statute books, there is also provision for a criminal conviction which carries a fine and a prison sentence. Although I can't say I know anyone personally who has gone to jail for filing their tax return form in File 13, it's not worth putting it to the test!

Read All About It

All the big accountancy firms produce booklets that explain the different tax structures. Be sure you get the most up-to-date information – South Africa is a land in transition in every aspect!

Those Other Taxes

Capital taxes include a donations tax. This tax is payable by South African residents and private companies on property that is donated and estate duties, a type of inheritance tax, payable on the value of property of a deceased person who was a South African resident at the time of death. Indirect taxes are imposed in three ways:

- Value Added Tax levied at the point of final sale
- excise and customs duties
- stamp duties charged on certain documentary instruments

Obviously once you are living and working in the country, you will be able to get a handle on the complexities of the taxes that affect you and your business. Those that don't, you can happily ignore.

THE POWER OF THE WORKERS

Labour relations and the power of organised labour are major factors in the South African business arena. Today the majority of the unions are well organised, generally well supported and tend to be skilled in their negotiations with management.

The first threshold of the labour movement in the 1920s and 1930s was slowly battered by waves of segregationist laws until much of the unions' influence was curtailed, if only temporarily. The racial divisions in the country were forcefully echoed in the unions as most unions had to be racially segregated. Today, of course, they are not, unless by the choice of the union itself.

The fight for recognition and the fact that most of the population had no political rights made it inevitable that the new surge of union activity, which burst upon the 1970s and continued into the 1980s, would be more militant and politically driven. As the only voice of the masses, strikes, work stoppages and the like were not only used to gain a living wage, but also to flex political muscles.

One of the most successful union leaders of the time, Cyril Ramaphosa, who headed the massive National Union of Mineworkers (NUM), learned his negotiating skills thoroughly in this field and has since become the ANC's chief negotiator in the determination of South Africa's democratic future. Ramaphosa, having spent a stint in government after the first general elections then entered the private sector and is now a very successful and high-powered businessman.

With more normalised channels for the nation's political energy, today's union leaders have focused their activities far more on the realities of the workplace. Demands have mostly been tempered by a good understanding of the current sluggish economic situation and the need for a joint management-union solution to benefit all. There is also far more emphasis on the improvement of the quality of labour with many of the negotiations centering around skills upgrading, rather than merely a cash package. However, never lose sight of the extremely low quality of life experienced by most workers (who are predominantly black), especially when compared to their management staff (who are predominantly white).

Currently, management generally does not accord labour the status it has acquired in most developed countries. Moves to redress this are underway. If successful, it is hoped that the resulting development of skilled black senior management will balance the scales.

The largest umbrella body for trade unions is the Congress of South African Trade Unions, COSATU, which is an extremely powerful organisation. When it lends its muscle to issues like the major work stay-away protests and rolling mass action of 1992, it can enlist the support of millions of workers.

THE OLD BOYS' NETWORK

There certainly is an old boys' network, also called the 'old school tie' syndrome, in South African business. Mostly links and friendships are established at high school, and very specific high schools too – the private, elite boys schools of Michaelhouse, Hilton, Bishops, St Johns and a few others. In later life, these links are used in the business community to pass business tin the direction of friends. But unlike countries such as the United Kingdom, where the barriers are almost impenetrable, South Africa's old boys' network can be overcome with a fair amount of determination and effort.

When a large portion of the economy was in the hands of the English-speaking whites, these ties paid off well, and were quite successful in keeping many lesser mortals waiting in the wings. However, the upsurge of Afrikaner businessmen over the last decades and the new political movements in the country over the last years have dampened the sway of the old boy's network. It would be fair to say today that if you have good skills or products to offer, no one is going to ask where your old school tie is.

SMALL IS BEAUTIFUL

Since South Africa is faced with massive levels of under-employment and unemployment, together estimated to be 40%, every avenue to create employment is being explored. One of the most successful attempts seems to be the encouragement of small business, particularly ethnic arts and crafts' development, as this is seen as one of the most attractive and sought after products.

Current economic trends indicate that neither the conglomerates nor the public sector are likely to be able to make a dent of any marked size in the unemployment figures – hence South Africa (and the rest of the world) is looking to small business development to create the bulk of employment opportunities.

In 1981, the Small Business Development Corporation was established to encourage small entrepreneurs. Today it operates in four areas:

- financing of loans from as little as R50 to the million rand scale
- developing industrial hives where small manufacturers can operate in a group situation and keep overhead costs to a bare minimum
- providing support services including a library service, a mentor programme where retired business people give freely of their time to help new businesses get off the ground, and an educational institute offering courses from the most basic of how to operate a calculator to courses in labour relations and management studies
- lobbying to promote the interests of small businesses and create awareness of small entrepreneurs.

Loans are granted on business viability and are generally open to South Africans, but if foreign direct investors set up a fully-fledged company in the country, the SBDC will consider financing the project. It does not operate in the homelands or the marginally independent states within South Africa, however.

THE CURSE OF STUBBORN INFLATION

South Africa has been dogged by inflation that has stubbornly kept to double figures for many years despite various attempts to reduce it. From spiralling quite out of control in the eighties to unofficial estimates of nearly 30% (and official ones 10 or so points lower), it now hovers just off single figures and there are hopes to reduce it further.

MONOPOLIES: A 'NO-NO'

The Monopolistic Conditions Act gives the government the power to curb monopolistic practice which is termed as an 'undesirable trade practice'. The Act aims at preventing agreements or actions by any person that would restrict the output or disposal of any commodity, or limit the facilities for its production or distribution. Companies may not enhance or maintain prices, nor prevent or restrict the entry into the market of newcomers. In addition to these, there are a host of other 'may nots'.

But in practice, this Act is rarely practised. Over the years, especially in the sanctions era, more emphasis was put on South Africa's self-sufficiency and a lot of cartel-type behaviour seemed to go unchallenged. There have certainly been occasions when a major corporation saw an entrepreneur as a threat and bought them out for many millions of rand more than they were really worth. This was done to just move them out of the market. Not all the blame can be laid at the feet of large organisations as small businesses were only too pleased to be paid over the top for their efforts.

However, rumblings in the ANC camp indicate that they would be less tolerant of any action that is likely to increase prices to the detriment of the consumer. Already in the 1990s there have been more complaints than any other decade that were brought before the Board of Trade, the body that investigates undesirable trade practices.

—Chapter Fifteen—

FAST FACTS

The easiest way to begin to fit into a new society is to be able to hold your own in social conversation. Every nation has its pet subjects of conversation and, in South Africa, some of these are hung around the current volatile and changing political situation that is easiest gleaned from the daily press. But there are other facts that the locals grow up learning at school and at play which become part of their sub-conscious.

To help you get through some of those tricky moments when you simply don't understand the flow of the conversation, here are some names and numbers. This is not an exhaustive list as important facts covered in the previous chapters will be left out. But it should help you out until you get to know the ropes.

THE RIGHT TERMINOLOGY FOR THE REGION

South Africa, more correctly called the Republic of South Africa, is the country at the southernmost tip of Africa. However southern Africa (with a small 's') is the southern region of the continent and includes the countries of Angola, Zambia, Malawi, Mozambique, Namibia, Botswana, Zimbabwe, South Africa, Swaziland and Lesotho. When this region is called sub-Saharan Africa, it may also include Kenya, Tanzania and Zaire.

POPULATION

Population estimates are never easy in developing countries, and South Africa is no exception. The most recent population census carried out by the new government in 1996 indicated that there were some 40.6 million South Africans. The population density is about 31 people per square km. Obviously this is much higher in the cities and very much lower in some of the rural areas.

CAPITAL CITIES

South Africa has three capitals: Pretoria is the administrative capital, Cape Town is the legislative capital, and Bloemfontein is the judicial capital. There is currently a long drawn out debate as to whether government should be located in one capital city and if so, which city. There is no easy answer in sight!

TIME ZONES

Although the country is wide from east to west, there is only one time zone – two hours ahead of Greenwich Mean Time. This means that life tends to start earlier in Durban than Cape Town since many South Africans tend to rise with the sun, or just after it. Also, there are long enjoyable summer evenings in Cape Town when darkness falls way after 8 p.m., while in Johannesburg there is not much summer twilight after 7 p.m.

CURRENCY

The South African Rand, which came into existence with the formation of the Republic in 1961, is a metric currency with 100 cents to the Rand. Coins range from the silver-coloured R5 to a minute copper 1 cent piece. The notes come in R10, R20, R50, R100 and R200. There is rumour of a higher denomination note coming into circulation to keep up with the devaluation of the currency, but it is just a rumour at present.

THE COMPLEXITY OF NATIONAL SYMBOLS

With the changes in South Africa, the national symbol has changed, too – in a complex way. The protea has replaced the springbok as the national emblem for all sports, except rugby, where the springbok emblem, as well as the term "the springboks" to refer to the national team players, is still supreme.

One of the first tasks of the nation after the fall of apartheid was the design of the new flag, which is brightly coloured and favoured by most South Africans. It is very much in evidence at all international sporting matches both at home and abroad, as is the habit of painting one's face to look like the flag.

The national anthem was also changed in 1994 to accomodate the new-look South Africa and now combines some verses of the much favoured liberation song, *Nkosi Sikeleli i'Afrika,* with verses from the old national anthem.

NKOSI SIKELELI' IAFRIKA

For almost all black South Africans, and a fair many whites too, *Nkosi Sikeleli' iAfrika* has become the stand-in for a national song. In the apartheid days, it was often branded as the ANC national anthem, but in reality it is a beautiful hymn of peace and blessing that is sung across southern Africa. It was composed by Enoch Sontonga in 1897. You may find yourself in a situation where you will enjoy joining the crowds in this uplifting tune so here follows the English version:

Lord bless Africa
Let her horn be raised
Listen to our prayers
Lord bless we, her children
Come spirit, come holy spirit
Lord bless we, her children

God bless our nation
Do away with wars and trouble
God bless our nation
Do away with wars and trouble
Bless it, bless it, Lord
Our nation, our nation.

These are the words most Africans will use:

Nkosi sikelel' iAfrika
Maluphakanyisw' uphondo lwayo
Yizwa imithandazo yethu
Nkosi sikelela
Thina lusapho iwayo

Morena boloka
Sechaba sa heso
O feditse dintwa
Le matswenyeho
Morena boloka
Sechaba sa heso
O feditse dintwa
Le matswenyecho
O se boloke – o se boloke
O se boloke morena sechaba sa heso
Sechaba sa heso

PUBLIC HOLIDAYS

As with some national symbols, some of the public holidays are sure to change to reflect historical happenings of importance across the covered in the previous chapters will be left out. But it should help you out until you get to know the ropes.

THE RIGHT TERMINOLOGY FOR THE REGION

South Africa, more correctly called the Republic of South Africa, is the country at the southernmost tip of Africa. However southern Africa (with a small 's') is the southern region of the continent and includes the countries of Angola, Zambia, Malawi, Mozambique, Namibia, Botswana, Zimbabwe, South Africa, Swaziland and Lesotho. When this region is called sub-Saharan Africa, it may also include Kenya, Tanzania and Zaire.

POPULATION

Population estimates are never easy in developing countries, and South Africa is no exception. The last census put the population at 40.5 million with 77% being African, 11% white, 9% coloured and 2.5% Asian. Nearly 22 million people live in the urban areas. Life expectancy is 65 years, while the infant mortality rate is 66 per 1000 babies born.

CAPITAL CITIES

South Africa has three capitals: Pretoria is the administrative capital, Cape Town is the legislative capital, and Bloemfontein is the judicial capital.

TIME ZONES

Although the country is wide from east to west, there is only one time zone – two hours ahead of Greenwich Mean Time. This means that life tends to start earlier in Durban than Cape Town since many South Africans tend to rise with the sun, or just after it. Also, there are long enjoyable summer evenings in Cape Town when darkness falls way after 8 p.m., while in Johannesburg there is not much summer twilight after 7 p.m.

STEPS THROUGH HISTORY

Human existence in South Africa dates to the Stone Age man who lived two to three million years ago. Much later, the Europeans arrived after they got over their fear of falling off a flat earth. Soon they realised that there was a great land mass down in the south, so thus began the recorded history of South Africa.

1488 Portuguese sailor Bartholomeu Dias is thought to be the first European to round the Cape and land on what is now South African soil. Inadvertently missing Cape Town due to storms, he first sighted land on the eastern seaboard, and put in at Delagoa Bay, now called Durban.

1652 Dutchman Jan van Riebeeckset up a refreshment station at what is now Cape Town as the halfway mark between Europe and the Far East.

1688 French Huguenot refugees arrived and settled at the Cape.

1785 The first British occupation of the Cape.
Shaka, the great Zulu chief and warrior was born this year too.

1806 Second British occupation of the Cape.

1807 Only a year later, the British abolished slavery.

1820 The British settlers arrived.

1835 The Great Trek began.

1856 The famous Xhosa mass cattle slaughter that was predicted by the young orphan girl, Nongquasi, occurred.

1867 The Hope Town diamond was found and the diamond rush was on.

1886 Gold was discovered and Egoli, or Johannesburg, was born.

1893 Mohandas (Mahatma) Gandhi arrives in the country to defend an Indian client.
The first ever South African world champion, cyclist Lourens Meintjies, is crowned.

1896 A highly contagious disease swept through cattle and game, killing thousands across the land. It was called the Rinderpest, and this word is sometimes used colloquially to mean someone of great age, as in 'He is as old as the Rinderpest.'

1897 The first motor car arrives in South Africa.

1899 The traditional liberation hymn of the masses, *Nkosi Sikeleli iAfrika* or God Bless Africa, was written.
The Boer War starts.
The famous colonial hotel in Cape Town, the Mount Nelson, opens its doors for the first time.

1902 The *Rand Daily Mail*, was started on its way to becoming one of the first liberal newspapers in the country.

1905 The Cullinan diamond, one of the largest in the world was found. It is now in the British crown jewels.

1906 The first Springbok rugby team goes to play in England.

1908 South Africa goes to the Olympics and sprinter Reggie Walker wins a gold medal.

1910 Union of South Africa is formed with General Louis Botha as the first Prime Minister.
The South African Native National Congress, the forerunner of the ANC, was formed.

1913 Gandhi begins the Passive Resistance Movement against racial discrimination.
The Native Land Act was passed, preventing Africans from owning land where they chose.

1914 South African troops invade German West Africa – now Namibia. (My grandfather was one of them.)

1916 In the Battle of Delville Wood in the First World War, thousands of South African troops were killed. Altogether some 12 000 South Africans were killed fighting in the First World War.

1918 A great flu epidemic killed many people.

1920 Van Ryneveld and Brand made the first air flight to England.

1922 The Rand Revolt occurred and 214 people were killed when a major miners' strike was put down by the government of the day.

1924 Radio broadcasting begins.

1927 The first tourists visit the now famous game reserve, the Kruger National Park.

1928 The South African flag is flown with the Union Jack for the first time.

1930 White women are given the vote.

1931 South Africa follows Britain in coming off the gold standard.

1932 *The Bantu World*, a daily newspaper aimed at blacks was started. It was the forerunner of today's *Sowetan*, the large Johannesburg black-oriented daily.

1938 Professor J L B Smith identifies the coelacanth fish, presumed to be extinct until then, and considered one of the greatest ichthyological finds in the world.

1948 The National Party wins the 'white's only' elections for the first time. This is seen as the beginning of formalised apartheid.

1953 Bertha Solomon steers the Matrimonial Affairs Act through Parliament.

1955 Dr Hendrik Verwoerd becomes Prime Minister and the harsh realities of apartheid are enforced.

1960 The Sharpville shootings occur, killing 67 people.
Whites vote on a referendum for republican status of the country.
Great African leader and member of the ANC, Albert Luthuli, wins the Nobel Peace Prize.

1961 South Africa becomes a republic and adopts decimal coinage.

1964 The Rivonia Treason Trial of eight ANC members including Nelson Mandela takes place. They are sentenced to life imprisonment.

1967 Chris Barnard performs the first heart transplant in the world at the Grooteschuur Hospital in Cape Town.

1976 Soweto student riots begin.
Television begins in South Africa!

1984 The last sitting of the Westminster-style parliament in South Africa. The new constitution comes into force allowing three separate houses – for whites, Coloureds and Indians.
The National Union of Mine Workers, to become one of the most powerful unions, is formed.

1985-6 A state of emergency is declared in 36 magisterial districts around the country, particularly in the big urban areas.
The major trade union umbrella body, the Congress of South African Trade Unions (COSATU) is formed.

1987 The United States steps up its sanctions campaign against South Africa.
The ultra-conservative Conservative Party becomes the official opposition in the 'whites-only' government.

1990 Nelson Mandela and the other Treason Trialists are released from jail after being imprisoned for trying to end apartheid. The ANC, the South African Communist Party and many other banned political organisations are legalised.

1991 President F W de Klerk makes a watershed speech declaring the removal of the major legal pillars of apartheid. The Convention for a Democratic South Africa (CODESA) is created and empowered to draw up a declaration of intent to move South Africa from apartheid to democracy.

1992 The whites vote 'Yes, for change' in a referendum seeking a mandate for the government of the day to continue towards democracy for all.
The wheels fall off CODESA and it comes to a standstill. Along with it, the economy spirals even further downward.

1993 The new CODESA, called the Multi-party Negotiating Council, comes into operation.

1994 First ever democratic election held in South Africa in April and Nelson Mandela takes his seat as president of the country in May of the same year.

1996 Consitution of South Africa adopted on May 8 and amended in November.

1997 President Mandela hands over the reins as president of the ANC to Thabo Mbeki, who was then vice president of the country.

1999 South Africa votes in its second democratic election on June 2 and Thabo Mbeki takes over as president of the country, as Mandela steps down.

RECENT LEADERS
Political Leaders

Initially the leaders of the government were prime ministers, but when the Westminster system of government was swapped for the tricameral parliament, the state president became the leader of the country. Here follows a list state leaders starting from the most recent:

Thabo Mbeki - current President
Nelson Mandela - first ever President of a democratic South Africa
F W de Klerk - President
P W Botha - Prime Minister, then President
B J Vorster - Prime Minister
H F Verwoerd - Prime Minister
J G Strydom - Prime Minister
D F Malan - Prime Minister
J C Smuts - Prime Minister
L Botha - Prime Minister

Liberation Leaders and Other Political High-flyers

Albert Luthuli   One of the earliest members of the ANC and recipient of the Nobel Peace Prize.

Oliver Tambo   Leader of the ANC in exile for many years. He became its head in South Africa once it was legalised but later retired due to ill health and died recently. Nelson Mandela then took over.

Walter and Albertina Sisulu   This husband and wife team are members of the ANC. Walter went to jail with Mandela and was released at the same time too. Albertina devoted her whole life to the fight against apartheid and was very prominent in the women's movements.

'Pik' Botha   South Africa's minister of foreign affairs and currently the world's longest-serving foreign minister has since retired from politics.

Bishop Desmond Tutu   The Anglican bishop who spoke out for the oppressed when most other leaders where in exile or in jail. Winner of the Nobel Peace Prize.

CULTURAL QUIZ

Do you think you know enough about South Africans to appear to be one of us? Try this quiz to see how much you know and understand us.

SITUATION ONE

You and many other rugby fans have been in a pub or someone's home watching the last match in a rugby test series on TV. The South Africans have just lost to the Australian Wallabies in a 1-2 match. Do you:

A. Cheer loudly because you are really a Wallaby supporter having just come from that side of the world?
B. Commiserate with your hosts or pub mates, but give reasons for why you feel the Aussies deserve to win?
C. Keep your feelings to yourself and just discuss the merits and de-merits of the play?

Comments:

Perhaps not the most honest approach, but certainly the most likely to keep your nose in its rightful place on your face is Option C. Besides, discussing the game can keep you drinking with the 'boys' for a number of hours.

Option A is the worst response you could have. Rugby is as close as you can get to a religion without a god to many white South Africans in particular. Insulting their national team is as bad as insulting them personally. Beware of even taking sides in the national league until you know your ground a little better.

Option B will most likely not get you into trouble, but it may exclude you from the general conversation as the locals will think you are just not part of them.

SITUATION TWO

You are negotiating a deal with a South African supplier of, let's say, perspex sheeting (or 'plexiglass') – a material that you wish to make into bathroom fittings in your factory. You have set up the preliminary discussions via fax or telephone. You then arrive at the corporate head office to discuss the final deal with the national sales and marketing manager. He puts forward an offer of a given price for the commodity. Do you:

A. Jump at the offer, sign on the dotted line and hope you can make enough mark-up on the product to keep in business?

B. Throw up your hands in horror and propose a 50% reduction, expressing your disbelief at the outrageous price and mentioning the fact you could get it elsewhere at a better price?

C. Quietly and knowledgably discuss the offer making it clear that the price is too high, but that for a better deal you could perhaps guarantee quicker payment, or a larger quantity of purchase among other alternatives.

Comments:

If you follow option A you will probably not have got a good deal as South Africans may do business in 'European' style, but that does not preclude them from trying to get as much for their product as possible.

Option B is most likely to antagonise and perhaps even intimidate your supplier – and a South African with their back against the wall can be quite unreasonable. There is a chance they will just say, 'Well get it elsewhere, then.' This situation may not be so easy as many markets are protected from imported materials with high import tariffs and your local supplier could be part of an informal/unofficial cartel. By this I mean that you may not be able to get the product cheaper anywhere else.

This leaves you with option C which is the most common way business is conducted here. Give a little, take a little. The most favoured catch phrase at present is to try for a win-win situation. It is probably the most appropriate way to go, unless you are VERY sure of your options.

SITUATION THREE

You are invited to a dinner party by your boss at their home. Do you:

A. Accept quietly and verbally ensuring you know the correct time, address and date, also asking what the dress code should be and if there is anything you could bring to add to the meal?

B. Say 'yes' and whoop around the office telling everyone, including those who may well have not been invited, that you are off to eat with the boss?

C. Nonchalantly say you guess it would be fine but you need to check to see that you are not otherwise engaged and will get back to them nearer the time?

Comment:

Option B will ensure that you are not ever invited again, and may well even get you a terse note that the dinner is off or postponed. It is not a done thing to discuss overtly with your colleagues matters such as a dinner invitation from the boss.

Option A is the most usual way a South African employee would respond to the invitation. Express the pleasure at being invited without being obsequious about it, get the correct information about the nature of the function so as not to be too casually or formally dressed. The offer of a little assistance will most likely be turned down in a boss-employee situation, although it would be wise to bring a small gift of chocolates or flowers to the function.

Option C is not a wise option as it is too casual an approach for a boss-employee invitation. It is more likely the approach you would use if a good friend made you a casual invitation for supper with them.

SITUATION FOUR

You and your spouse are invited to a provincial level rugby/soccer/cricket match to be played in the big sports stadium in the city where you live. Mention is made of going out to dinner after the game. Do you:

A. Dress for dinner in smart casual clothes: women in evening make-up and high-heel shoes, and men in tie and sports jacket?

B. Wear jeans or shorts (depending on the weather and if you are in a covered stadium or not), T-shirt and sneakers, hats and sun-glasses and a lot of sun-screen on your exposed skin?

C. Do you decline because you know it will be shown on TV and you just don't know how to act at a South African sports match?

287

Comments:

Option C is certainly not the way to make friends nor get to know the local way of life. South Africans will make an effort to encourage shrinking violets into the group, but only for a limited time. If you are invited to a game and its the kind of recreation you like, go even if you do feel a little ill at ease. It is the best way to learn how it's done.

Option B is the way to dress for sport matches, unless you are invited to a boxed seat. In that case, it may be a bit more formal and it would then be quite in order to ask what dress code is best. Casual is the code word at sports matches, especially as behaviour and team support gets quite rowdy and boisterous. If you know where you going for the meal after the match, you could bring a change of clothes with you but chances are that you will go somewhere casual or have sufficient time to go home to shower and change.

Option A would make you stand out like a sore thumb at the match and perhaps make your hosts feel a little ill at ease for not explaining the causal nature of the event to you. You would not be ostracised, but you would feel a little left out.

SITUATION FIVE

You are at a cocktail or dinner party with a group of acquaintances and the subject of South African politics arises. The locals start a heated debate defending whichever party they support and slagging all the others they do not. Do you:

A. Join in, taking sides and expressing strong views on which you think is correct and why, adding for good measure just what is wrong with the way the country is, or was, run?

B. Listen politely and keep mum. Or make as innocuous a comment as you can when asked for your view?

C. Switch the conversation to the politics of your home country?

Comments:

Option C may well work if the rest of the group knows of your country's politics and it could be a great way to diffuse what so often becomes an unpleasant slanging match. But if your land is too distant for them to know much about, it will probably not draw their swords from each other's necks.

Option A could be quite exhilarating as long as you are well-informed on matters, and as long as you are prepared for the knocks you may get for 'being a foreigner meddling in our affairs'. You may lose friends if they become too upset at your views.

Option B is the easiest way out, rather boring but safe. Politics and religion tend to bring some of the most rational and sane people to flash point in a matter of moments. Stay out of the fray until you are sure of the sensitivities of your friends.

DO'S AND DON'TS APPENDIX

DO

* Stay a while to greet others. The norm is to exchange a few pleasantries rather than rush off with a quick "Good day!" This practice builds strong working relationships. Your South African counterpart would also expect a good handshake.

* Make every effort to socialise and meet new people. It is not difficult to start a conversation with a South African. Listen and observe, and you will learn quite a bit about living and working in the country.

* Use politically correct language. There is a growing awareness of the need to refer to the "challenged" rather than the blind or deaf and to steer clear of offensive terms like "garden boy" (when the person concerned is an adult) and *kaffir*.

* Tip your waiter. Tipping constitutes the bulk of a waiter's income. Only a few places charge a service fee, and that usually applies to tables for more than ten. So leave a tip (10% or more) if you have been served reasonably well.

* Ask those seated around you if they would mind you smoking, before you light your cigarette.

DON'T

* Smoke in public places. Stringent anti-smoking laws allow smoking only in designated areas or outdoors. Several restaurants, bars and offices have chosen to maintain non-

smoking environments. There are usually signs at the entrances indicating the policy that prevails in a particular building.

- Give your Muslim host alcohol as a gift. A box of chocolates, rather than a bottle of wine, would make an appropriate gift.

- Eat with your left hand in an Indian home. This is an insult to the host. Eat with your right hand only.

- Serve your Muslim or Jewish guest pork. Muslims, Jews and a majority of the black cultures do not eat pork (or any of its derivatives). Some Jews do not eat shellfish, depending on how strictly they follow their religious practices.

- Swear. Swearing is generally unacceptable, but this is changing as the country continues to modernise and open up to the international community.

- Touch a wild animal in a nature reserve. The penalties for touching a protected animal are huge. It is also an offence to capture or keep certain wild animals.

- Let your estate agent push you into making a hasty decision. Clarify from the start what you are looking for, and consider carefully before deciding to purchase a property. And you are not required to pay the agent a cent.

RESOURCE GUIDE

EMERGENCIES AND HEALTH
Emergency Numbers
Ambulance **10177**
Emergency police unit **10111**
Look in any telephone directory for a list of police stations. City telephone directories list all emergency numbers (fire brigade, electricity and water supply, weather, rescue, etc.). If you have trouble with an emergency call for the ambulance, fire brigade or police, call **1022**. Mobile phone users can call **112** (same number for both MTN and Vodacom network subscribers). The operator will contact the police or ambulance, depending on the emergency.

Hospitals
The Medicross Healthcare Group (national toll-free number **08 0011 1010**) has a variety of day-care and outpatient medical facilities, such as doctors, dentists and radiologists. The major private hospital groups are Netcare, Afrox Healthcare and Medi-Clinic Services.

Cape Town:
Groote Schuur Hospital (Observatory) Tel: 404 9111
Red Cross Children's Hospital Klipfontein Road Rondebosch; Tel: 658 5111
Tygerberg Hospital Franzie Zyl Avenue, Tygerberg; Tel: 938 4911
Cape Town Medi-Clinic 21 Hof Street, Oranjezicht; Tel: 464 5500
Durbanville Private Hospital 45 Wellington Road, Durbanville; Tel: 980 2100

Durban:

Addington Hospital Erskine Terrace South Beach; Tel: 327 2000
RK Khan Hospital Road 336 Chatsworth Circle; Tel: 403 3223
Crompton Hospital 102 Crompton Street Pinetown; Tel: 702 0777
Entabeni Hospital 148 South Ridge Road Berea; Tel: 204 1300

Johannesburg:

Johannesburg Hospital Jubilee Road Parktown; Tel: 488 4911
JG Strijdom Hospital (now **Helen Joseph Hospital**) Perth Road
Auckland Park; Tel: 489 1911
Sandton Hospital Medi-Clinic HF Verwoerd Drive Bryanston; Tel:
709 2000
Morningside Hospital Medi-Clinic Rivonia Road Morningside;
Tel: 282 5000
Milpark Hospital, Guild Road Parktown; Tel 480 5600
Linksfield Park Clinic 12th Avenue Linksfield West; Tel: 640 7555

Lost and Found Services

Look in the classified section of local newspapers. Advertising a find
carries no charge; advertising a loss costs.

Sports and Fitness Facilities

Besides the major health club group Health & Racquet (recently
bought out by Richard Branson and the Virgin group), there are tennis
clubs, golf courses, shooting ranges and bowling clubs in the major
metropolitan areas. Clubs are advertised in the local knock-and-drop
newspapers and the *Yellow Pages* for each city.

Facilities for the Disabled

Facilities for the disabled are slowly being built into restaurants,
hotels, shopping malls, government buildings and on the streets. But

standards vary widely from place to place. Anyone with a disability should call in advance to check the hotel or restaurant's accessibility.

HOME & FAMILY
Estate agents
Acutts Tel: 201 6489 (Durban); Web: www.acutts.co.za

MaxProp Countrywide Tel: 674 1093 (Cape Town), 789 4448 (Johannesburg); Web: www.maxprop.co.za

Pam Golding Tel: 851 2633 (Cape Town), 312 8300 (Durban), 380 0000 (Johannesburg); Web: www.pamgolding.co.za

Realty 1 Elk Tel: 465 8736 (Cape Town), 561 1391 (Durban); 882 2800 (Johannesburg)

Seeff Tel: 557 1115 (Cape Town), 765 4655 (Durban), 444 6663 (Johannesburg); Web: www.seeff.co.za

Childcare and Education
Estate agents in the areas in which you are considering living can tell you about the local schools and facilities.

Housekeeping Services
Organised maid services are limited and not highly competent. Domestic workers and full- or part-time gardeners are usually employed through word-of-mouth.

MANAGING YOUR MONEY
Tax and Legal Advice
Arthur Andersen (Cape Town) Shell House 9 Riebeeck Street; Tel: 408 1200; (Durban) Clifton Place 19 Hurst Grove Berea; Tel 202 8388; (Johannesburg) 5 Summit Road Dunkeld West; Tel: 328 3000; Web: www.arthurandersen.com

Deloitte & Touche (Cape Town) Sanclare Building 21 Dreyer Street Claremont; Tel: 670 1500; (Durban) 2 Pencarrow Crescent Pencarrow

Park La Lucia; Tel: 560 7000; (Johannesburg) 20 Woodlands Drive Woodmead; Tel: 806 5000; Web: www.deloitte.com

Ernst & Young (Cape Town) Ernst & Young House 35 Lower Long Street; Tel: 410 5500; (Durban) 20th Floor 320 West Street; Tel: 304 4456; (Johannesburg) 4 Pritchard Street; Tel: 498 1000; Web: www.ey.com

KPMG (Cape Town) Westbank House 21 Riebeeck Street; Tel: 419 4040; (Durban) 20 Kingsmead Boulevard Kingsmead Office Park; Tel: 327 6200; (Johannesburg) 85 Empire Road Parktown; Tel: 647 7111; Web: www. kpmg.com

PriceWaterhouseCoopers (Cape Town) The Terrace 34 Bree Street; Tel: 418 3900; (Durban) 102 Essenwood Road Berea; Tel: 250 3700; (Johannesburg) 2 Eglin Road Sunninghill; Tel: 797 4000; Web: www.pricewaterhousecoopers.com

Banks
Standard Bank www.standard.co.za
First National Bank (FNB) www.fnb.co.za
Nedcor www.nedcor .co.za; **Absa** www.absa.co.za

Insurance Agencies
Old Mutual Tel: 08 6060 6060; Web: www.greenline.co.za, www.oldmutual.co.za
Auto & General Tel: 08 0001 5777
Fedsure Life Assurance Tel: 086 0086 0086; Web: www. fedsurelife.co.za
Sanlam Tel: 021 916 5000; Web: www.sanlam.co.za
Liberty Life Tel: 086 045 6789; Web: www.libertylife.co.za

ENTERTAINMENT AND LEISURE
Restaurants and Cafés
See the annual *Wine Magazine* booklet, *Top 100 Restaurants in South*

Africa, found in bookstores across the country. John Platter's *South African Wine Guide,* also found in bookstores and updated annually, walks you through the many, often very good, South African wines. Restaurants in Cape Town include:

Aubergine 39 Barnet Street Gardens; Tel: 465 4909; Web: www. aubergine.co.za

Rhebokskloof Estate Agter-Paarl; Tel: 863 8386

Savoy Cabbage 101 Hout Street; Tel: 424 2626

Durban: **Harvey's** 77 Goble Road Morningside; Tel: 312 9064

Jaipur Palace Riverside Hotel 10 Northway Durban North; Tel: 563 0287

Le Troquet 860 Old Main Road Cowies Hill; Tel: 266 5388

In Johannesburg, bistros and pavement cafés line favoured streets, particularly in mixed-zone business / residential areas like Sandton, Melville and Greenside. Restaurants seeking star ratings tend to be safely ensconced in shopping malls with secure parking.

Chaplin's 85 4th Street, Melville; Tel: 482 4657

First Avenue Café The Codfather Centre, 1st Avenue Rivonia; Tel: 803 1939

Sam's Café 11B 7th Street, Melville; Tel: 726 8142

Ugo & Mama Teresa's 102 Corlett Drive, Birnam; Tel: 440 4655

Shopping

Major shopping areas: **Cape Town** Victoria & Alfred Waterfront, Century City shopping centre, Green Market Square (open-air market for artisans and hawkers); **Durban** Pavilion shopping centre, the Stables craft market (Wed and Fri evenings, Sundays and public holidays), Musgrave shopping centre, the Mall La Lucia shopping centre; **Johannesburg** Sandton City shopping centre, Rosebank Mall shopping centre and its rooftop flea market (Sundays), Eastgate and Westgate shopping centres.

Nightspots

Aside from the Waterfront, the area around Loop and Long between Strand and Riebeeck streets in the city centre is the best place to get a feel for what is happening on the dance scene in Cape Town. Many of the mainstream jazz clubs double as restaurants and the Captour *Jazz in the Cape* brochure highlights current venues.

In Durban Sand Pebbles is a beachfront favourite. In Morningside Bonkers is the club of choice among younger South Africans.

In Johannesburg Rosebank has emerged the hot spot with clubs, bars and coffee shops scattered throughout the neighbourhood. Rockey Street in Yeoville also has a lively nightlife scene with clubs and bars offering everything from jazz to grunge (but a warning: the street attracts drug dealers and addicts). The Randburg Waterfront is a gimmicky mall-like development of about 100 restaurants, bars and clubs clustered around an artificial lake.

Cinemas and Theatres

The dominant movie houses are Ster-Kinekor and Nu Metro, but there are less established groups like Avalon taking on the major players. Supper theatres have also taken off with new venues opening regularly and not-so-popular ones closing down every few months or so. Tourist information bureaus for each city publish guides on what is happening every month. Tickets for shows, movies, concerts and other events can be purchased at the door or booked at Computicket outlets across the country or by telephone.

Bookstores and Libraries

There are public libraries in most municipalities, and membership is free to people living or working in the neighbourhood. Many libraries have interconnected computer systems allowing borrowers to utilise the facilities across a broad spectrum of libraries. National bookstore chains include Exclusive Books, CNA and Adams. They have outlets in shopping centres and central business districts across the country.

Museums and Art Galleries

Cape Town:

Castle of Good Hope Buitenkant Street; Tel: 408 7911

South African Cultural Museum Corner of Adderley and Wale streets; Tel: 461 8280

South African National Gallery Government Avenue Gardens, Rhodes Memorial, off Rhodes Drive Rondebosch; Tel: 689 9151

District Six Museum 25a Buitenkant Street; Tel: 461 8745

Durban: **Durban Art Gallery** City Hall Smith Street; Tel: 300 6234

Local History Museum Corner of Smith and Aliwal streets; Tel: 300 6241

Sea World South Beach; Tel: 337 4079

Natal Museum of Military History Corner of Snell Parade and Old Fort Road; Tel: 332 6302

Natal Sharks Board M12 Umhlanga; Tel: 561 1001

Johannesburg: **South African National Museum of Military History** 20 Erlswold Way; Tel: 646 5513

Gold Reef City Northern Parkway off N1 Ormonde; Tel: 496 1600

Lippizaner Centre Dahlia Road Kyalami; Tel: 702 2103

See also each city's *What's On* guide, local tourist offices, and books like the *Readers' Digest Illustrated Guide to Southern Africa*.

Alternative Lifestyles

The South African constitution specifically includes a sexual orientation clause that guarantees full and equal rights for gays, lesbians, bisexuals and transgender people. The website www.q.co.za is a comprehensive introduction to gay and lesbian activities and lifestyles in this country, offering information on news, entertainment, equality and travel.

TRANSPORT & COMMUNICATIONS

Telephone Codes

The international dialling code for South Africa is **27**, followed by the area code (minus the zero) and the subscriber's number.

Area dialing codes are: Cape Town **021**; Durban **031**; Johannesburg **011**. Area codes for the rest of the country can be found in the introductory pages of the telephone directories.

Telephone Service Numbers

National and International enquiries **0903**
Local enquiries **1023**
National collect calls **0020**
International collect calls **0900**

Post Offices

The Post Office operates more than 1,500 depots in the suburbs and central business districts. There are also private postal agencies. In the urban areas, South Africans can choose street deliveries for their mail or post box numbers at the local post office. Street deliveries are free-of-charge. Post boxes carry an annual rental charge, when there is a street delivery option. Otherwise the post box address is free.

Buses, Taxis and Trains

The public transport system in South Africa is not as developed as in other parts of the world. Besides the ubiquitious mini-bus taxis, each city has more subdued, Western-style taxis. But these do not always cater sufficiently to individual needs, and most business people and visitors prefer to hire cars or purchase their own vehicle. Bus and train routes and schedules can be obtained from tourist information outlets.

South Africans drive on the left. The country has a superb network of multi-lane roads and highways, some of which charge a toll. The speed limit is 120khp (75mph) on major highways and 60kph (37mph) on city streets, but drivers are notorious for breaking these. Seat belts are compulsory.

MEDIA
Newspapers and Magazines
There are about 30 major publications, four of which are in Afrikaans and the other 26 in English. This includes newspapers aimed at black readers, such as *The Sowetan* and *City Press*. Except for the weekly independent *Mail & Guardian*, the best-known newspapers are owned by a handful of commercial groups, namely Independent Group, Times Media Newspapers and Caxton Group.

A wide selection of local magazines covers interests from health and cooking to cars and travel. The satirical *Noseweek*, one of few investigative magazines, is developing a reputation for uncovering corruption in high places.

Television and Radio Channels
The South African Broadcasting Corporation's *Channel Africa* offers the continent entertainment, while *SABC Africa* provides a news and information service from an African perspective. Channel One is for young viewers; Channel Two has a public focus and caters for the 11 language groups; and Channel Three is the revenue-earning entertainment channel. SABC competes directly with the powerful and lucrative pay-TV M-Net and the free-to-air e-TV station for some 11 million viewers daily.

Once a state monopoly, South African airwaves have been opened up to more than 100 radio stations licensed by the **Independent Communications Authority of South Africa** (tel: 011 722 0000). Most are local community radio stations, but there are commercial stations broadcasting talk shows, sports programmes and music on both AM and FM channels.

LANGUAGE

Although English is widely spoken, South Africa actually has 11 official languages: Zulu, Xhosa, Afrikaans (South-African Dutch), Pedi, English, Tswana, Sotho, Tsonga, Swati, Venda and Ndebele. Language classes for a range of languages, including English, French, German and Zulu, are listed in the *Yellow Pages* (directory of services) for each city under 'language tuition.'

RELIGION AND SOCIAL WORK
Religious and Volunteer Organisations

South Africa is 78% Christian, with small percentages of Hindus, Muslims and Jews. The Constitution guarantees freedom of religion, but nearly 20% of the population profess no religious affiliation. Each religion has a presence. Meeting groups and times and places of worship are advertised in local newspapers.

The South African National Non-Government Organisation Coalition (Sangoco) is the umbrella body for about 4,000 of the country's volunteer and non-government organisations (NGOs). Sangoco consists of provincial and sectoral affiliates working in various areas of development, such as land and health.

The national office is in Johannesburg (tel: 011 403 7746; fax: 011 403 8703; web: www.sangoco.org.za); the contact person is Penny Dlamini. The Cape Town regional office is headed by Jessica Fortuin (tel: 021 706 2050; fax: 021 706 0765). The Durban regional office is headed by Hlengiwe Gasa (tel: 031 307 1061; fax: 031 306 2261).

GENERAL COUNTRY INFORMATION
Weights and Measures

South Africa uses the metric system.

Appliances and Utilities

Appliances must be 220V or adaptable to this voltage. Water and electricity supply come under one account, opened through the local municipality. Bring identification documents, a copy of your property lease or purchase agreement and a cash deposit to the municipality's customer centre to open the account. The connection can be made in 24 hours. The relevant phone numbers are 400 4910 (Cape Town), 300 1911 (Durban) and 490 7000 (Johannesburg).

Telkom landline applications can be made by phone at 10219 or in person at branches in the city of residence. Applications take 10 to 14 working days to process. Mobile telephones, contracts and prepaid user packages can be acquired through a host of service providers.

Necessities and Documents to Bring

South Africa has a sound infrastructure, and almost all goods and medications can be acquired in the country. Bring your birth and marriage certificates (including birth certificates for accompanying children), qualifications, medical certificates, police clearance certificate, passport and identity documents. Full details on what is required to apply for a work permit should be acquired from South African embassies and consulates. The requirements differ according to the terms under which you will be staying in the country.

Pre-Entry Vaccinations

Pre-entry vaccinations are not required, except for people travelling from areas affected by yellow fever. Nevertheless the British Airways Travel Clinic recommends people be vaccinated against Hepatitis A and B, typhoid, tetanus, polio and rabies. Certain parts of South Africa are malaria high-risk areas, and travellers should seek medical advice from a local pharmacy or British Airways Travel Clinic before visiting these areas. Further information ahead of arrival can be obtained from British Airways Travel Clinics around the world.

Government Internet Search Engines

Local search engines include Ananzi and Alta Vista. Government websites end in org.za or gov.za. The official website for the government's communication and information services is www.gcis.org.za. Other sites: www.polity.org.za, www. gov.za, www.sars.gov.za and www.saqa.org.za

General and Tourist Advice Bureaus and Websites

South African Tourism (Satour) Tel: 011 778 8000 (head office in Johannesburg); Web: www.satour.co.za

Cape Town:
Cape Metropolitan Tourism Web: www.gocapetown.co.za
Cape Town Tourism Pinnacle Building, corner of Burg and Castle Streets, City Centre; Tel: 4264260

Durban:
KwaZulu-Natal Tourism Authority 303 Tourist Junction, 160 Pine Street; Tel: 304 7144; Web: www.tourism-kzn.org

Johannesburg:
Gauteng Tourism Upper Level Rosebank Mall, Rosebank; Tel: 327 2000; Web: www.gauteng.net

Immigration, Residency and Nationality Issues

Deal with these through the South African embassy / consulate in your country before leaving. The officials will advise on documentation, permits and visas to produce.

Country Statistics

South Africa extends from the Tropic of Capricorn to Cape Agulhas at 35 degrees south. It lies in the southern temperate zone, mostly on plateaus above 1,200m (4,000 feet). The coastline covers 2,954km between the Atlantic and Indian Oceans; the shore, lined by sandy beaches, is fringed by forests in the east and desert in the west. The country covers an area of 1,219,090km, making it larger than Germany, France and Italy combined.

Though rich in grasslands, savannah and forest, the country is mostly dry thornveld and semi-desert. Average rainfall is 464mm per annum, a little more than the world's average. 'Sunny South Africa' boasts from 7.5 to 9.5 hours of sunshine daily, compared with 3.8 in London and 6.9 in New York.

Occupying only 4% of the landmass of Africa, South Africa has more than half the cars, telephones, autobanks and industrial facilities of the continent. Most of these are in Gauteng, the nation's industrial heartland, although its smallest province geographically. Gauteng consists mainly of the metropolitan areas of Johannesburg and Pretoria and the industrial area around Vereeniging. Gauteng produces more than half the country's gross domestic product (GDP), which is by far the largest in Africa and greater than that of Egypt, Nigeria and Kenya combined. The gross national product per capita is $3,400, and the country was ranked number 45 in the latest World Development Report.

BUSINESS INFORMATION
Business Organisations
Afrikaanse Handelsinstituut (AHI) Tel: 945 3593 (Cape Town), 904 3197 (Durban), 012 348 5440 (Praetoria); Web: www.ahi.co.za
Business South Africa Tel: 784 8000 (Johannesburg)
Cape Chamber of Commerce and Industry Tel: 418 4300 (Cape Town); Web www.capechamber.co.za
Chamber of Mines of South Africa Tel: 498 7100 (Johannesburg)
Durban Chamber of Commerce and Industry Tel: 335 1000; Web: www.durbanchamber.co.za

Foundation for African Business and Consumer Services (Fabcos) Tel: 385 1203, 425 6647 (Cape Town), 4684231 (Durban), 3333701 (Johannesburg)

Johannesburg Chamber of Commerce and Industry (JCCI) Tel: 726 5300; Web: www.jcci.co.za

KwaZulu-Natal Marketing Initiative Tel: 907 8600 (Durban); Web: www.kmi.co.za

National African Federated Chamber of Commerce (Nafcoc) Tel: 336 0321 (Johannesburg)

South African Chamber of Business (Sacob) Tel: 358 9700 (Johannesburg); Web: www.sacob .co.za

Legal Aid Agencies

The Legal Aid Board can be contacted by phone at 021 461 5531 (Cape Town), 031 304 3162 (Durban) and 011 836 0421 (Johannesburg). The website www.legalaid.co.za is currently under construction.

FURTHER READING

History, Cultural History And Current Affairs

Reader's Digest Illustrated History of South Africa: The Real Story.
History of Southern Africa by J D Omer-Cooper.
History of Southern Africa by G Parker & P Pfukani.
A New Illustrated History of South Africa by Trewhella Cameron.
A History of South Africa by Martin Roberts.
The Mind of South Africa by Allister Sparks.
Foreign Relations with Neighbouring States since 1948 by Jean
    Hayward.
Uprooting Poverty: The South African Challenge by Francis Wilson
    and Mamphela Ramphele.
Washing of the Spears by Donald R Morris.
Shaka Zulu by E A Ritter.
Indaba My Children by Vusamazulu Credo Mutwa.
Beating Apartheid and Building the future by the South African
    Institute of Race Relations.
Culture in Another South Africa by W Campschreur and J Divendal.
The South African Chinese: Their Way of Life by Melanie Yap.

Women In South Africa

The Story of An African Farm by Olive Schreiner. This is a novel by
    a dedicated feminist who was many decades ahead of her time.
Breaking the Silence. A century of South African Women's Poetry
    edited by Cecily Locket.
Raising the Blinds. A century of South African women's stories.
Women and Resistance in South Africa by Cherryl Walker.
Putting Women on the Agenda edited by Susan Bazilli.
Women and Gender in Southern Africa to 1945 edited by Cherryl
    Walker.

Dictionaries And The Like

Dictionary of South African English, Oxford University Press.
Ah Beg Yaws by Rawbone Malan. A humorous look at South African pronunciation.

Novels by South Africans About South Africa

Any of the many novels and collections of short stories written by Nadine Gordimer, Nobel Prize Winner for literature such as the novels *Burger's Daughter, July's People* and *The Conservationist*, or the collections of short stories like *Why Haven't You Written?*

Jock of the Bushveld by Sir Percy Fitzpatrick.

Confession of an Albino Terrorist by Breyten Breytenbach, and any of the other South African novels he has written.

Mittee by Daphne Rooke.

Good Looking Corpse by Mike Nicol.

White Tribe Dreaming by Marq de Villiers.

Anything written by Herman Charles Bosman such as *Jurie Steyn's Post Office, A Bekkersdal Marathon* or the collection called *Bosman at His Best.*

Anything by Andre Brink including *A Dry White Season* and *Looking on Darkness.*

Circles in the Forest by Dalene Matthee.

Anything by Alan Paton, the most famous of which is *Cry the Beloved Country*. He has also written excellent non-fiction.

The Great Outdoors and Conservation Issues

Guide to Southern African Game and Nature Reserves by Chris and Tilde Stuart.

The Guide To Backpacking and Wilderness Trails by Willie and Sandra Olivier.

Guide to Trail of Southern Africa Jaynee Levy.
Best Hike in South Africa by David Bristow.
Adventure Holiday in Southern Africa compiled by Tracey Hawthorne.
Going Green edited by Jacklyn Cock and Eddie Koch. On people,
    politics and the environment in South Africa.
A Four-Wheel Drive in Southern Africa by Andrew St Pierre White.
The Green Pages is a directory of green organisations in South Africa.
    Contact the *Weekly Mail & Guardian* newspaper for a copy of this.
Reader's Digest Illustrated Guide to Southern Africa.

On the Humorous Front

Arthur Goldstuck's *The Rabbit in the Thorn Tree* and *The Leopard in
    the Luggage* are delightful accounts of urban legends, some true
    and some questionable.

Gus Silber, well-known here for his cynical humorous look at life, has
    written two books on life in the new South Africa called *It Takes
    Two to Toyi-Toyi* and *Braaivleis of the Vanities*.

The Arts Debate

Culture in Another South Africa by W Campschreur and J Divendal.
The Arts in South Africa: A Force For Social Change by Julius
    Eichbaum.

THE AUTHOR

 Dee Rissik is of a typically mixed background common to many in South Africa. Her father's family is from generations-old Cape Dutch origins, while her mother's side is of British ancestry. A journalist by profession, she finds in it an ideal career as it coexists with her penchant for travelling. Her home base is Johannesburg but believes she will live anywhere in the world for a period of time to gain cultural experience on a multi-dimensional level. Having lived and worked in many parts of Europe including London and Southeast Asia, she has first hand experiences of being a newcomer to a country.

A published writer many times over, she has written for a wide range of newspapers and magazines on topics ranging from politics to travel and health. Dee is also the author of the book, *Women In Society, South Africa* published by Times Books International.

INDEX